LIMITED ACCESS

LIMITED ACCESS

TRANSPORT METAPHORS AND REALISM
IN THE BRITISH NOVEL, 1740–1860

Kyoko Takanashi

UNIVERSITY OF VIRGINIA PRESS
Charlottesville and London

University of Virginia Press
© 2022 by the Rector and Visitors of the University of Virginia
All rights reserved

First published 2022

1 3 5 7 9 8 6 4 2

Library of Congress Cataloging-in-Publication Data

Names: Takanashi, Kyoko, author.
Title: Limited access : transport metaphors and realism in
the British novel, 1740–1860 / Kyoko Takanashi.
Description: Charlottesville : University of Virginia Press,
2022. | Includes bibliographical references and index.
Identifiers: LCCN 2022010690 (print) | LCCN 2022010691
(ebook) | ISBN 9780813947570 (hardcover) | ISBN 9780813947587
(paperback) | ISBN 9780813947594 (ebook)
Subjects: LCSH: Metaphor in literature. | Travel in literature. |
Realism in literature. | English fiction—18th century—
History and criticism—Handbooks, manuals, etc. | English fiction—
19th century—History and criticism—Handbooks, manuals, etc.
Classification: LCC PR858.M475 T35 2022 (print) |
LCC PR858.M475 (ebook) | DDC 823/.009—dc23/eng/20220711
LC record available at https://lccn.loc.gov/2022010690
LC ebook record available at https://lccn.loc.gov/2022010691

Cover art: "Views of London no 3, Entrance of Tottenham Court
Road Turnpike, with a view of St James's Chapel," Heinrich
Joseph Schütz, 1813. (© The British Library Board)

For my parents, who generously gave me access to so many opportunities

CONTENTS

Acknowledgments   ix

Introduction: The Transports of Reading   1

1 · Delivering Narrative to Consumer-Readers:
Staging Inclusion in Fielding's *Tom Jones*   27

2 · Noisy Vehicles and Oversensitive Readers:
Miscommunicating Feeling in Sterne's *A Sentimental
Journey* and Smollett's *Humphry Clinker*   55

3 · Local History for Distant Readers:
Narrative Transmission in Scott's *The Tales of My Landlord*   82

4 · Information Overload in Industrial Print Culture:
Shortcuts to Knowledge in Dickens's *The Pickwick Papers*   112

5 · The "Prae-railroadite" and the Railway Generation:
Sharing Memories in Thackeray's *Vanity Fair*   139

Conclusion: George Eliot and Contingent
Access to Literary History   167

Notes   181

Bibliography   207

Index   221

ACKNOWLEDGMENTS

I am pleased to finally be able to express my gratitude in print and to acknowledge the numerous people who made this book possible during its long and meandering journey towards publication. This book would not exist without Deidre Lynch. Without her encouragement, I would not have had the confidence to pursue a PhD, or the courage to develop a project spanning multiple literary periods. I am deeply grateful for her mentorship and support. At Indiana University Bloomington, I had the privilege of working with Richard Nash, Mary Favret, Lee Sterrenburg, Ivan Kreilkamp, and Janet Sorensen, who helped to shape the original project in exciting ways. The Center for Eighteenth-Century Studies at Bloomington taught me what academic knowledge-making looks like in action. I have learned—and continue to learn—from numerous graduate school colleagues at the State University of New York at Buffalo and at Indiana University Bloomington, including Celia Barnes, Timothy Campbell, Siobhan Carroll, Evan Gottlieb, Greg Kinzer, Ioana Patuleanu, Adam Sills, the late Adrianne Wadewitz, and Paul Westover.

Indiana University South Bend provided me with institutional support and a place that I am delighted to call my academic and professional home. My colleagues Bobby Meyer-Lee, Karen Gindele, Matt Shockey, Kelcey Ervick, Benjamin Balthaser, Jake Mattox, Josh Wells, Elaine Roth, Chu He, and Rebecca Brittenham have graciously listened to my ruminations at different stages as I worked through this project. The Women's and Gender Studies Governing Board invited me to present a portion of my work, which helped keep it alive. I thank the many, many students at IUSB I have had the privilege of teaching over the years. Their engagements with novels—especially when they were most honest about their dislike of a novel—prompted me to think with urgency about how various readers might access narratives differently. Outside of teaching, my service work has taught me to think deeply about student access to education in ways that influenced this project, and I am grateful to colleagues and campus leaders who have given me opportunities to engage these broader issues. This project was partially supported by Indiana University's New Frontiers in Arts and Humanities program, which enabled me to carve out time to begin turning this project into a publishable manuscript. I am also grateful to Brenda Phillips, dean of the College of Liberal Arts and Sciences at IUSB, for funding to help with the final stages of this project.

Numerous colleagues I met at conferences have provided various contributions, from source references to thought-provoking conversations in ways they may not even be aware of: Sarah Allison, Geoff Baker, Danielle Bobker, Nick Bujak, Miranda Burgess, Kevis Goodman, Yohei Igarashi, Jake Jewusiak, Beth Lau, Casie LeGette, Ruth Livesey, Richard Menke, Cara Murray, Mark Parker, Kate Singer, Peggy Thompson, and Maria Su Wang. End-of-the-semester lunches with Sara Maurer and Yasmin Solomonescu have been invaluable in reminding me that I belong to a scholarly community. Annika Mann helped me navigate the publication process, and I greatly benefited from her moral support as well as her expertise in media theory and medical humanities. Mary Mullen was my cheerleader extraordinaire; she kept me accountable, taught me to be a better Victorianist, and helped me cross the finish line when my spirits were flagging.

Portions of this book draw upon previously published material. An earlier version of chapter 2 appeared as "Mediation, Reading, and Yorick's Sentimental Vehicle." An earlier version of chapter 3 appeared as "Circulation, Monuments, and the Politics of Transmission in Sir Walter Scott's *The Tales of My Landlord.*" I am grateful to Duke University Press and Johns Hopkins University Press, respectively, for permission to reuse this material.

It has been a great pleasure working with the University of Virginia Press. Angie Hogan, my editor, has been a patient, able, and reassuring guide throughout, despite the unexpected challenges caused by the pandemic. I also thank the University of Virginia Press editors and staff—including but not limited to Clayton Butler, J. Andrew Edwards, and Ellen Satrom— for their professionalism and efficiency. Many thanks to Toni Mortimer for the thorough and much-needed copyediting. The three anonymous readers for the press were all incredibly generous, constructive, and insightful and challenged my thinking in the best of ways. This book would not be what it is now without their feedback, though any shortcomings in this book remain my own.

Lee Kahan read more versions of this manuscript than I can count and has corrected so many of my numerous ESL errors along the way. He taught me how to write a thesis, how to teach, how to play tennis, the joys of mid-century modern design, and the pleasure of living with cats. I don't know how I can possibly repay him for his partnership and support that have allowed me to grow into who I am today; I look forward with pleasure to spending the rest of my life trying my very best.

LIMITED ACCESS

INTRODUCTION

The Transports of Reading

A recurrent trope in eighteenth- and nineteenth-century British fiction compares reading to traveling: numerous novels assert that the pleasures of novel reading are similar to the joys of a carriage journey. Henry Fielding's *The History of Tom Jones, A Foundling* (1749) claims that reading the novel is like taking a stagecoach journey with the chatty narrator as a fellow inside passenger.[1] Sir Walter Scott's *Waverley; or, 'Tis Sixty Years Since* (1814) compares the experience of novel reading to a post-chaise journey in search of picturesque scenery.[2] George Eliot's *Felix Holt, the Radical* (1866) implies that the outside passenger of a stagecoach has the privileged perspective of a reader who gains access not only to a view of the landscape but also to the stories of modern life that unfold there.[3] Each of these texts defines the pleasures of reading and of traveling by variously emphasizing the communal contexts of storytelling, the delights of seeking picturesque scenery, and the joys of occupying a seat that comes with a good view. But in all of these texts, the analogy underscores the immersive pleasures of realist narratives that transport readers into fictional worlds even as they sit quietly in their armchairs.

At the same time, these fictional texts also draw attention to the limits of access that travel often entails and in so doing unsettle the comparison between reading and traveling to reveal additional conceptual and political layers that are at stake in the analogy. Fielding's vision of his novel as a communal stagecoach journey appears much less inclusive when we consider the numerous characters in eighteenth-century fiction—like the eponymous hero of Fielding's *Joseph Andrews* (1742)—who are denied

I

passage in a stagecoach because of their appearance or class status.[4] Scott uses the post-chaise journey not only to promise the rewards of continuing to read his novel, but also to excuse the tedious historical detail that he must present to readers before he can move on to the more amusing parts of his narrative. To reach "picturesque and romantic country," Scott asserts, readers and travelers must also expect impediments like "heavy roads, steep hills, sloughs, and other terrestrial retardations."[5] And while Eliot's outside passengers glean stories of English life from the landscapes they see, the coach that carries such passengers rattles quickly past the shepherd who remains oblivious to the goings-on of the nation at large, thus excluding him from the pleasures of narrative.[6] Such examples suggest that the social and physical barriers to travel also inhere in realist narrative. Just as some people have limited access to transportation as a means of pursuing their journeys, there are those who have limited access to the pleasures of being transported into fictional worlds. Just as transportation provides limited access to places off the beaten track, realist narratives may provide limited access to representations of distant times and places. Transport enables authors to imagine and to describe the pleasures of immersion in realist texts, but it also helps to reveal barriers that prevent this pleasure from being truly inclusive.

Throughout the eighteenth and nineteenth centuries, writers and readers compared the mental transports of novel reading with modes of physical transportation that enabled increasing numbers of people and texts to circulate throughout Britain. Rather than affirming the immediate, immersive, and joyous experience of reading realist fiction, however, such comparisons prompted writers to recognize barriers to access that prevent some people from experiencing the pleasures of stagecoach rides and novel reading alike. The writers featured in this study use transportation as a metaphor to conceptualize how novels are implicated in a network of mediation that prevents some readers from experiencing the transports of reading. Such awareness that limits of access inhere in novels—just as they do in transportation systems—may seem to undermine the promises and potential of novelistic realism. On the contrary, I argue, this very awareness helped writers to continually reimagine and reshape realism—and confirm the generic identity and history of the realist novel in the process—as they strive to make their novels more inclusive by affirming alternative models of reading, knowing, and engaging.

Limited Access thus explores the tension between the ideal of readerly absorption and the limits of realism that threaten to exclude some readers from the world of fiction. It does so by focusing on what I refer to collectively as "transport metaphors": the use of transport as a figure and material object that helps novelists explain how their narratives work and how they can or cannot help readers access the fictional worlds they represent. When Yorick imagines his book as a "new kind of vehicle" in Laurence Sterne's *A Sentimental Journey* (1768) or when the narrator of William Makepeace Thackeray's *Vanity Fair* (1848) laments the loss of stagecoaches and the stories that came with them, they use one medium (transportation) to imagine the capabilities and limits of another (novels).[7] These transportation-obsessed authors often take the adage "reading is like traveling" quite literally; they use stagecoaches, mail coaches, railways, and other means of transportation as analogies or formal principles that shed light on how their own texts function as vehicles that can carry readers into the world of fiction—or prevent them from doing so. As literary figures that point both inward and outward, transport metaphors draw on the similarities between reading and technologies of mobility. By drawing on the objective characteristics of transportation, such metaphors conceptualize the historical and material conditions of mediation in the attempt to explain how texts can transport readers. But by subordinating the vehicle (transport) to the tenor (novel reading), transport metaphors risk downplaying their own historical and conceptual complexity. I seek to shed light on the complex work of transport metaphors by refusing to take them as straightforward commentary on how realist novels work. Transport metaphors do more than assert that reading is like traveling; they help writers theorize the mediating work of novels in relationship to the processes of mediation in the world at large to explore shifting concerns about readerly access. In response to these transport metaphors and the boarder challenges they surface, writers featured in this study continually negotiate realist form in their attempts to expand the possibilities of access for readers.

Transport metaphors draw attention to how the pleasures of reading realist fiction are rooted in formal questions as well as assumptions about how inclusive the novel as a genre truly is. This book thus weighs in on long-standing debates about inclusivity and the novel. It is possible to understand the history of the novel in eighteenth- and nineteenth-century Britain—or the trajectory of the realist novel's "rise" as Ian Watt famously called it—as a history of increasing inclusivity and diversity that made novel reading pleasurable to a broader audience.[8] Scholars such as Michael McKeon, George Levine, and Catherine Gallagher have built on and revised Watt's account to demonstrate how the novel innovates throughout the period of Britain's modernization to broaden its scope of representation so as to include people of different classes, genders, and regional cultures, adopting an increasingly secular, empirical worldview.[9] Scholars continue to identify new ways in which realist fiction performs epistemological work to alternately engage readers in doubting and believing, presenting an ever-wider world for readers by drawing on empirical procedures like scientific experimentation, anthropological observation, or cultural semiotics.[10] This epistemological work of the novel, however, exists in tension with ideological ones, as prominent postcolonial and Marxist critics such as Edward Said and Terry Eagleton have shown.[11] Thus, critics continue to find new ways in which realism commits ideological violence so as to hegemonize, oppress, and marginalize. Not only are people, cultures, and alternative ideologies under-represented, stereotyped, or omitted altogether, entire literary traditions can be relegated to the sidelines in a discourse that privileges realism.[12] But these critiques often lead not to a rejection of novelistic realism but to a call to broaden our definition of realism to include hitherto neglected national literatures or subgenres.[13] Through repeated experiments in both form and subject matter, according to these literary histories, realist novels become more inclusive and more "realistic" in ways that make the pleasures of novel reading available to an ever-wider variety of readers.

While building on this critical tradition, *Limited Access* scrutinizes the metaphor of reading as traveling to question the extent to which diverse readers have access to the transports of reading. While scholars have keenly debated the problems of inclusivity in realist fiction (such as who does or does not get represented and which works do or do not count as realist), few have questioned how inclusive the novel-reading experience is for diverse readers. Studies of the realist novel tend to assume that specific formal and representational characteristics of the novel trigger anticipated responses in readers so that the inclusivity of readers has been largely assumed. Thus, we assume that a reader ultimately experiences understanding, belief, and pleasure when encountering the text, rather than misunderstanding, boredom, or alienation. The epistemological project of the novel, in other words, is grounded on a tenuous assumption that readers do indeed have access to the text, its meaning, and its pleasures, and ideological critique has hitherto been limited in its ability to challenge this assumption. Such an approach to the novel, however, does not account for the differential access of readers to the texts they read, not only in terms of access to the physical text but also to comprehension and pleasure. Despite interventions such as those by Leah Price and Elaine Auyoung that advocate for a more nuanced understanding of different kinds of reading or the complexity of the reading process itself, novel studies have largely overlooked the relationship between the formal and representational strategies of the novel and readers' capability of access, leaving reader-response criticism and the field of the history of books and reading to puzzle over this question.[14] The lack of attention to differential access of readers is further underscored by the increasing prominence of disability studies—a field that challenges fundamental normative assumptions, often by foregrounding problems of access.[15] The lack of discussion about the limited access of readers, I suspect, reflects the degree to which we—literary critics, including myself—take pleasure in realist fiction.[16] It is thus a product of our own critical fantasy; we project onto the novel's history our own ideals of cultural democracy, thus envisioning the novel as a genre that anyone can "get into" as long as it is realistic enough.[17]

Limited Access challenges the assumption that techniques of realism make fictional worlds accessible to all readers by reframing the history of the realist novel as a history motivated by questions of readerly access. I argue that transport metaphors helped novelists continually reflect upon and negotiate their own narrative practices by seriously pondering the possibilities of limited access for readers. From Henry Fielding and Laurence Sterne to William Makepeace Thackeray and George Eliot, the authors featured in this study imagine how physical spaces of travel compared to the space of the printed page that presumably brought readers, authors, and characters together. But, for these authors, the experience of travel—and the transport metaphors that came with it—continued to change over generations as stagecoaches, mail coaches, and railways rapidly succeeded one another. Far from expressing a simple and universal truth about the nature of reading, transport metaphors compete with one another and change over time along with the shifting cultural, historical, and material environments in which novel writing and novel reading took place. Stagecoaches alone, for example, can variously signify physical mobility, communal or exclusive spaces, the regularity of clocked time, a national network, the speed of delivery, and the conventions of picaresque narrative. As the following chapters will detail, the communal interior of the stagecoach gains significance in the context of the expanding public sphere of eighteenth-century print culture, while it diminishes in relevance for later generations of writers as other concerns—such as national belonging or generational change—take precedence. Transport metaphors highlight varying concerns about limited access over time because they are not just literary tropes but conceptual tools that connect the mediating work of novelistic texts to the historical, material, and social realities inhabited by both authors and readers. Through transport metaphors, authors constantly reassess what readers can and cannot access, what counts as relevant and realistic, and what barriers interpose themselves between readers and the messages that their narratives seek to convey. Through this process, writers continued to revise, reject, or reconfirm formal practices of realist narrative by imagining and reimagining reader engagement.

Transport works as a metaphor for reading because it helps to elucidate the phenomenology of reading; it explains how texts can move readers, even as they remain physically stationary. Alison Byerly, for instance, argues that "a defining feature of the nineteenth-century realist novel is its effort to generate an almost physical sense of presence within the fictional world," and shows how an archive of "virtual travel narratives" modeled narrative strategies for realist fiction.[18] Byerly associates the novel's effort to generate a sense of immersion with travel rather than with transport, suggesting that transport is fundamentally more "mechanical" and "utilitarian."[19] But even a limited focus on land transport shows how this utilitarian means of getting from one place to another can lay the epistemological foundation for creating a sense of belief necessary for readerly immersion. James Chandler considers wheeled transportation as a key figure for narrative probability and Miranda Burgess identifies how mobilities enabled by transportation technologies are intertwined with affective movement—including that generated through reading—in literary and philosophical texts of the Romantic period. As Chandler and Burgess both remind us, transport is a figure intricately tied to a long history of mediation in which writers and thinkers have theorized how affect operates across distance through intervening bodies and technologies including print media.[20]

As a mediating agent that moves bodies and things from one place to another, transport also addresses questions of inclusivity by showing how some people and things move within a network while others fall outside of it. Jonathan Grossman lays the groundwork for understanding transport as an infrastructure that mediates a networked society. Just as Richard Menke claims that realist novels order and make sense of information circulation through new media, Grossman suggests that realist novels order and make sense of the circulation of bodies through public transport.[21] While Grossman argues that public transport was central to how Dickens and his readers imagined the workings of a networked community where individuals crisscrossed one another in unexpected ways, Ruth Livesey and Charlotte Mathieson build on and complicate Grossman's argument by drawing attention to how transport shapes ideas of nationhood in fiction by modeling complex engagement with place, both local and global, past and present.[22] Both Livesey and Mathieson usefully highlight the uneven access that technologies of mobility create by drawing attention to the differential experiences of mobility by various classes of people as well as the various localities that fall outside of the network. These studies affirm the importance of attending to public transportation that Celeste Langan advocates for in today's context; they draw attention to the "social construction of mobility" and suggest that we are not all equally mobile.[23]

By turning to transport metaphors as figures where questions about mediation, reader engagement, and inclusivity intersect, *Limited Access* explores how authors imagined and theorized reader engagement within a complex network of mediation. If the various "figurations" of reading represented within the text, to use Garrett Stewart's term, offer insight into the diverse array of readers that authors envisioned in the process of writing, transport metaphors draw further attention to how these readers invoked by narrators are embedded in a network of mediation.[24] When Sterne worries that vehicles—both physical and textual—might interfere with affective communication or when Scott imagines how readers might access obscure local narratives by juxtaposing a national mail-coach network with immobile monuments in a local cemetery, they imagine the accessibility of their narratives not just in terms of narrative strategies but also by taking into account the technologies as well as the numerous narratives, genres, objects, and bodies that surround themselves and their readers. Mediation is a process through which ideas and things travel across distance, whether spatial or temporal; by imagining readers within such a framework, these novels emphasize the distance between author and reader in order to conceptualize the complex and convoluted processes necessary to overcome such distance.

INTRODUCTION · 7

Throughout the book, I frequently collapse the distinction between transportation and communication—as opposed to Grossman who draws a clear distinction between the two—to reflect how these authors theorize mediation as a messy, wayward process.[25] Transport can stand in as a metaphor for reading precisely because these authors did not always distinguish between the movement of physical bodies and of information, ideas, and affect. By assuming that "mediation does not reduce to media," these novels practice a nascent version of what Régis Debray calls "mediology," which he characterizes as a study dedicated to "medium and median bodies, to everything that acts as milieu or middle ground in the black box of meaning's production, between an input and an output."[26] In his manifesto, Debray calls for a study of how ideas such as Christianity and Marxism (an example more pertinent to this study would be the novelistic canon) become institutionalized in our cultures through a process of mediation that is both social and material, encompassing the conditions of production, distribution, organization, reproduction, as well as reception.[27] Taking into account everything from literary techniques and transportation infrastructures to social milieu and technological change, the novels examined in this study refuse to simply ask how novels function as media to engage readers; they also ask how novels can continue to communicate with and engage readers amidst a sea of *communiqués* that compete with them for survival.

In attempting to better communicate with their readers, these novels unknowingly participate in a collective effort to consolidate the genre of realist fiction and to make the transports of novel reading accessible to future generations of readers, despite implicitly characterizing past novels as inaccessible. Novels open up new models of reading and knowing to generate and renew reader engagement, often by scrutinizing their readers' limited access to the works of their predecessors. Dickens, for example, undermines the models of knowing promoted by eighteenth-century stagecoach novels by describing the comical misapprehensions of the Pickwickians throughout their rambling coach journey. By doing so, he calls his predecessors' bluff when they equate experience of the world with wisdom. In the character of Sam Weller, Dickens provides an alternative model of knowing that does not depend on having the time and money to travel. While limited access was just as much a concern for eighteenth-century novels as it was for nineteenth-century ones, authors writing after the consolidation of the genre in the early nineteenth century—when Scott, Anna Laetitia Barbauld, and others anthologized and institutionalized the novel—tend to reflect more frequently on the works of their predecessors.[28] This is yet another way in which the mediological imagination is at work in the history of the novel. The "institution" of the novel, to echo Homer Obed Brown's phrase, depends on the continual revisiting and revising of previous novels and their formal attributes by successive authors and readers.[29] Rather than simply dismissing past novels as obsolete, the gesture these authors make in updating the genre for present and future readers contributes, counterintuitively, to the genre's institutional coherence and continuation.

Transport Metaphors

The etymological origins of the word "metaphor" indicate how closely metaphor and transport are intertwined—indeed, physical transport lies at the heart of metaphor.[30] It is hardly surprising, therefore, that transport metaphors by no means appear exclusively in prose fiction. James Boswell records a conversation with Samuel Johnson, for example, in which they compare the rhythm and style of two poets, suggesting that Alexander Pope's poetry is like a "coach and six" that goes at "a steady even trot."[31] Like Fielding's *Tom Jones,* George Farquhar's farce *The Stagecoach* (1704) compares theatrical space with the inside of a stagecoach.[32] Transport metaphors often appear implicitly when lovers of literature describe acts of mental transport, as Leigh Hunt does when he describes "the world of books" to which a reader may be transported at any time.[33] But it is in realist novels that transport metaphors recur repeatedly through the course of the long history of the genre, whose capacious and lengthy narrative form required a metaphor that can simultaneously capture a sense of spatial expansiveness and temporal duration.

As a literary and historical figure that recurs throughout the eighteenth and nineteenth centuries, transport metaphors draw attention to the continuous and cumulative history of realist novels across centuries in ways that exceed conventional periodization.[34] Both Byerly and Livesey note how representations of transport recur in eighteenth-century novels, only to dismiss their continuity with the specific work of transport in nineteenth-century fiction. While Livesey acknowledges the importance of the stagecoach in eighteenth-century fiction as "an ever-ready analogy for the collective experience of being transported into a world of fiction which travels through a locally specific, but generally recognizable landscape," she asserts that there is a disjunction with nineteenth-century novels where "these mobile communities of speech become much less apparent in the novel."[35] In contrast, Byerly sees continuity in the way the reader "is often invited to accompany the narrator as he or she moves through the various physical settings described," but eighteenth-century novels like *Tom Jones* are distinct because of their limited focus on the journey of the picaresque hero.[36] As Chris Ewers illustrates, however, eighteenth-century improvements in infrastructure helped writers to pattern novels of the period to register the nuanced effects of increasing linearity and speed, among other changes.[37] This book explores the continuity between eighteenth- and nineteenth-century fictions' use of transport that these scholars gesture towards but skim over. It traces a long history of the realist novel by identifying how transport metaphors perform a specific conceptual task: they make visible how writers theorize the shifting conditions of mediation and of reader engagement.

My decision to characterize authors' use of transport as "transport metaphors" is informed by Neil Postman's argument that a medium performs more than its technological function; it also works as a "media metaphor," that is, a means through which we imagine how the world works. For Postman, the "printing press, the computer, and television are not . . . simply machines which convey information. They are metaphors through which we conceptualize reality in one way or another. They will classify the world for us, sequence it, frame it, enlarge it, argue a case for what it is like."[38] Postman considers media as occupying dual ontological roles, as technologies that have objective existence and as metaphors that function as figurative vehicles for conceptualizing "reality" at large. As a technology that connects people, bridges distances, and delivers messages, transport works as a media metaphor in numerous novels, and this is precisely what critics have located in nineteenth-century fiction. When Grossman argues that transport helped Dickens conceptualize and represent a networked society where individuals move through time together even as they pursue their own paths, or when Livesey posits that stagecoaches and mail coaches helped novelists envision a modernizing and mobile nation that is nevertheless anchored in local affect, they identify how authors use transport to make sense of the world around them and to represent that understanding in fictional form.

Because transport, as media metaphor, plays a key role in conceptualizing reality, it helps authors imagine what kind of reality readers inhabit and how the novel can become a more inclusive space for these readers. When Sterne imagines his own text as a figurative vehicle that communicates sentiment, he envisions how transportation vehicles can jolt a passenger out of good humor as well as how his very text might impede the affective communication it strives to accomplish. Chapter 2 argues that physical experiences of transport affirm Sterne's understanding of how affect travels promiscuously between subjects and objects; this theory of affect, in turn, informs the way Sterne imagines how his own text might engage or disengage his readers. This example indicates that transport metaphors shed light on how transport as media metaphor prompts authors to conceptualize how mediation works, and it is in this context that authors imagine reader engagement. Christina Lupton, for whom Sterne's *A Sentimental Journey* promotes a particular kind of entertainment where readers delight in their own powerlessness in the face of media, urges us to ask "the phenomenological questions of what happens when mediation registers in discourse."[39] Lupton turns to mid-eighteenth-century texts—many of them quite obscure and forgotten—that flaunt themselves as media to answer this question, arguing that histories of the novel fail to attend to the way mediation appears thematically within representations by casting generic self-consciousness as a mere impetus for literary innovation and by subordinating the work of self-reflexivity to a broader narrative outlining the teleological development of the genre.[40] Turning to transport metaphors in canonical fiction as a site where we can locate how "mediation registers in discourse," I foreground the continuous work of reader engagement in the long history of the novel, in which formal change is incidental to, rather than the end goal of, the novel's self-reflexivity.

While this study draws on the history of transport, it focuses less on the historical and technical nuances of transport than what conventions of new historicism would lead one to expect. Instead, it focuses on a history of transport mediated through metaphors to trace a literary history shaped through the constitutive force of metaphors. As a nexus that connects the act of novel reading to the processes of mediation surrounding it, transport metaphors are simultaneously literary and historical. They gesture towards historically specific material and technological conditions by drawing attention to changes in transportation technologies and the effects they produce. But they also appear as a literary figure that shapes and reshapes how we understand mediation and how narratives work to generate such an understanding. In order to trace the changing nuances of a specific transport metaphor in relationship to the long history of the novel, *Limited Access* focuses exclusively on the metaphor of land transportation rather than ranging widely to cover alternative methods of transportation or the unique expressions of reading as traveling that emerged in the course of global exploration and imperial expansion.[41]

The broader history of transport with which this study is concerned can be summarized very briefly: it begins when stagecoaches—the first publicly available long-distance passenger carriage—had become a fact of life in the 1740s, and it ends in the mid-nineteenth century, just when it seemed inevitable that railways will annihilate stagecoach routes throughout the nation. This period witnessed the early stages of what Philip Bagwell calls "transport revolutions," when horse-drawn carriages gradually became lighter and speedier through improvements in suspension systems, framing, and better roads, only to be replaced later by steam engines and railways.[42] The period also witnessed continuous advances in road transport from legislative efforts involving road maintenance and toll roads to systemic and infrastructural improvements such as Robert Palmer's mail-coach system and John McAdam's innovation in road construction.[43] Even as road transport continued to improve, the railway boom of the first half of the nineteenth century dramatically changed the nation's landscapes by building bridges and boring tunnels, making industrial modernity a felt reality and bringing people and places closer together.[44] The history of transport is a history of increasing speed and access that decreased the temporal and spatial barriers to mobility. But, Livesey reminds us, "for all the easy allure of thinking of the mail and stagecoach as a coherent national system—then and now—it was . . . patently limited in the extent of its actual network," especially in Scotland and Ireland.[45] Regional reach was not the only way in which passengers experienced limited access; cost and even social codes precluded many from using public transport.[46] Gendered codes of conduct, for instance, restrained genteel young women from traveling alone, making women's experience of travel a distinctly gendered one.[47] While innovations in transport technologies certainly helped to make travel more affordable and widespread, it by no means made all Britons mobile in the same way or to the same degree.

Transport metaphors, while informed by this history, provide less insight into technological innovations than they do into the conceptual work involved in theorizing mediation. As the material manifestation of both individual mobility and print's mediating potential, transport affords insight into both the promises and pitfalls of mediation. Transportation connects characters and readers into a network but also leaves gaps where people may fall outside the network; it brings men and women together into a shared space but also excludes or marginalizes others; and it manifests the passing of time, even as some (like Eliot's shepherd) remain oblivious to all but the rising and the setting of the sun.[48] The numerous affordances of transport as an object and metaphor provide rich grounds for authors to conceptualize mediation. In considering the conceptual possibilities opened up through metaphor, I follow scholars who convincingly argue for metaphors as highly generative epistemological tools. Laura Otis, for instance, outlines the scientific and popular discourse of the nineteenth century that likened telegraph wires to an organic nervous system and argues that such a metaphor was not just a way for scientists to explain concepts to laypeople but also a site of cross-pollination between the organic sciences and communication engineering.[49] Devin Griffiths, while focusing on analogies rather than metaphors, makes a similar point about the generative potential of comparison in scientific discourse and emphasizes how analogies originate in historical fiction as a "tool that brings the relation between the previous ages and the present into focus."[50] Especially in the discourses of science and mediation, where the investigator's task often requires theoretical investigation of phenomena that escape or exceed direct observation, "we learn how to think" by associating one thing with another.[51] In addition, for both Otis and Griffiths, metaphors also render such conceptualizations portable so that ideas can travel between persons and across disciplines. Metaphors are especially central to the history of what John Guillory calls the "media concept," as Otis demonstrates in the nineteenth-century context. Tracing a prehistory of media when "the concept of a medium of communication was absent but wanted for the several centuries prior to its appearance," Guillory shows philosophers relying frequently on metaphors to theorize mediation in the absence of media as a defined concept.[52] The practice of using one thing to think about another is evident throughout the history (and prehistory) of media theory from the numerous historical figures featured in Clifford Siskin and William Warner's *This Is Enlightenment* to Marshall McLuhan, whose extensive use of metaphors has itself become an object of study for media theory.[53]

But metaphors can also be reductive, and transport metaphors are not exempt from this problem. Metaphors create possibilities for new ways of thinking by bringing things and ideas from different domains into a contingent relationship with each other, but attempting to fix that relationship can limit the potential of metaphor, as Paul Ricoeur reminds us.[54] The metaphorical affordances of transport can flatten out the historical and technological nuances of transport so that objects "become metaphorical (and meaningful) through a loss of many of their specific qualities," as Elaine Freedgood puts it.[55] Freedgood advocates for a "strong metonymic reading" that recuperates the object's history in all its richness and thus rejects metaphor (and its cousin allegory) as a rhetorical device that forecloses the possibility of generating meaning outside the framework of the text. Her rejection of metaphor assumes the critical tradition grounded in I. A. Richards's seminal work that creates a clear hierarchy between vehicle and tenor, subordinating the vehicle to the role of "symbolic servitude" and stripping it of its historical, material, and social qualities.[56] By stripping the vehicle of its unique qualities, metaphor has a tendency to universalize and hence to dehistoricize meaning. When we refer to Fielding's extensive use of stagecoaches as a metaphor of reading, for example, the impulse is to simply understand the gist—a hypothetical reader might think to themselves, "oh, the chapter breaks are places of rest, like stopping at inns"—and to move on without paying heed to the stagecoach as a historical object. Such a reading can and has led critics to dismiss eighteenth-century novels' use of stagecoaches as "just" a metaphor or analogy or allegory—as something less nuanced, complex, and historically specific than the metaphors that appear in the nineteenth century.

This book attempts to rescue transport metaphors from the trammels of metaphoricity and to restore historical specificity to the models of reading that these authors envisioned through them. In using transport metaphors to theorize reader engagement, authors look not only inward towards the text to imagine the experience of novel reading but also outward towards the social and material reality they and their readers inhabit. Transport metaphors bridge the act of reading with larger processes of mediation so that novels are not just reflections or representations of an external world; they model mediation to performatively engage readers in that process.[57] Thus, while chapter 2 situates Sterne's textual vehicle in relationship to a contemporary medical discourse that puzzled over the relationship between the human soul and its vehicle, the physical body, chapter 5 relies on close readings of fictional and non-fictional texts to locate Thackeray's reminiscences of the stagecoach era and the stagecoach novel in the context of larger questions about history and personal memory. As chapters 4 and 5 in particular suggest, transport metaphors travel not only across contemporaneous discourse but also across time so as to render necessary conceptual negotiations between past and present models of thinking; the eighteenth-century stagecoach novel, in which stagecoaches stand not only for a transportation network but also as a particular model of empirical, epistemological, and literary experience, appears in nineteenth-century novels as a conceptual framework that must be engaged and overcome rather than simply a generic precedent. As the vehicle changes, so too does the tenor; as the tenor changes, so too does the vehicle. Far from maintaining a stable, hierarchical relationship across time, the vehicle and tenor that constitute transport metaphors continue their reciprocal negotiations and thus testify to the human ability to imaginatively engage pressures wrought by history and technology.

Engaging Readers

The definition of the word "transport" helps to highlight why transport lends itself to metaphor—especially a metaphor that attempts to capture not only the dynamics of mediation but also the mechanics of reader engagement. Samuel Johnson, for instance, lists contending definitions of the word "transport" in *A Dictionary of the English Language* (1755). His definition consists of "1. Transportation; carriage; conveyance," "2. A vessel of carriage; particularly a vessel in which soldiers are conveyed," and "3. Rapture; Ecstasy."[58] The first two definitions focus respectively on physical conveyance and prison transport to draw attention to the means of moving something from point A to point B. Both definitions highlight how moving people, things, and texts requires some kind of medium: ships carry soldiers and convicts to distant lands; railway carriages transport people to different cities; coaches and wagons transport commodities from one part of Great Britain to another; and mail coaches deliver newspapers and books to readers across the nation. Transport in this sense reminds us that time and space separate us from one another, and that the history of modern technology is, in part, a history of how we have tried to minimize these barriers to more easily access people, places, and things. However, the third definition of "transport" signifies emotional transport and sweeps away such barriers to suggest that the laws of physics need not bind us to the time and space we inhabit. Sudden and strong emotions may carry people outside of themselves and away from the here and now. One can be carried away without the need for tedious carriages. These definitions of "transport," then, express the need for technological means to overcome time and space as well as the ultimate desire to do away with such mediation altogether.[59] The word "transport" thus captures the contradictory impulse that Jay Bolter and Richard Grusin locate at the heart of media culture, which "wants both to multiply its media and to erase all traces of mediation: ideally, it wants to erase its media in the very act of multiplying them."[60]

This paradoxical principle not only underpins transport but is also a defining feature of novelistic realism: realist novels strive for immediacy while they proliferate representational techniques. Instead of exploring the diversity of representational strategies associated with realism, focusing on transport metaphors helps to highlight the various motives that lead to numerous experimentations on the part of writers. Scholars today tend to understand the realist novel as a highly self-reflexive genre that is fully aware of its own problems and possibilities that shift alongside changing social, historical, and epistemological concerns.[61] This self-reflexivity suggests that realism is not a defined set of formal characteristics but an "effort" to engage readers and a "striving" for representing objective reality that prompts writers to continually invent and appropriate new strategies.[62] Transport metaphors underscore the "effort" of realist fiction to engage readers by highlighting not a particular formal characteristic of novels but the logic that underpins authors' decisions to adopt, adjust, or discard different narrative strategies. Thus, this book does not focus on a defined set of formal characteristics of the novel like omniscience, simultaneity, or thick description. Rather, each chapter begins with a transport metaphor specific to the author and to the time period that draws attention to unique problems of access that authors envisioned for their readers; each example of transport metaphor, in turn, leads to different formal negotiations and conceptual solutions that take a different shape for each author. Chapter 1, for example, shows how Fielding's metaphor of novel reading as a communal stagecoach ride appears in the context of Fielding's worries about how to engage readers who voraciously and uncritically consume texts proliferated by the periodical press. Newspapers and magazines deliver a particular quantity of information of dubious quality to readers with the regularity of a stagecoach, predetermined by the publication schedule and the space of the printed page. Fielding's metaphor of novel reading as a communal stagecoach ride, then, works as a countermetaphor that responds to the problems of a rapidly expanding print culture. In contrast, chapter 5 explores how Thackeray's metaphor of "prae-railroadites" gestures towards the gap between those who are familiar with narratives and the world before the railway and those who are familiar only with the railway present. Thackeray builds on the workings of memory to accommodate readers who may be unfamiliar with the stagecoach past and the stagecoach novels associated with that past. Each chapter thus explores how the diverse array of narrative experiments in the novel are rooted in how novels think—that is, how they theorize reader engagement.

As the examples in the previous paragraph indicate, the "readers" with whom this book is concerned are not actual readers but those imagined, textually inscribed readers whose attributes, characteristics, and models of reading and thinking surface within the texts themselves. While this study occasionally relies on studies of the history of books and reading as well as reception studies to associate textually invoked readers with actual historical readers, it is primarily interested in those readers who emerge within the pages of the novel because they provide the best insight into how authors metaphorically imagined the workings of reader engagement in terms of access. In locating readers within the text, I respond to Garrett Stewart's call to attend to the figure of readers—and their possible responses—that are textually inscribed in the form of direct addresses to the reader and metafictional moments showing characters in the act of reading. Critiquing Wolfgang Iser's concept of the "implied reader" as insufficient for fully exploring reader engagement within realist fiction, Stewart argues that rather than "closing the text off from its context, a rhetoric of figured reading . . . offers the only *textual* (hence the only *readable*) registration of that context (the social world of reception) as it impinges most closely upon—by being invoked by—the novelistic utterance."[63] Stewart is thus interested in locating readers within the text rather than outside of it (as Iser does) and claims that it is by coordinating the two figurations of readers within the text (the directly addressed "you" and the figure of readers embedded in characters) that novel readers are able to position themselves in relation to the narrative.

While various figurations of readers appear in the pages of novels, critical tradition has favored readers who properly experience the pleasures of realist narrative. Indeed, Stewart provides numerous examples of how the novel figures diverse kinds of readers, but he ultimately subordinates these various readers to a single arch-reader who is the main subject of his study—the "conscripted reader." The readers invoked by the text might be naïve or skeptical, attentive or inattentive, sagacious or ignorant, but the kind that matters most for Stewart is the "conscripted" reader who submits to "voluntary conscription" and implicitly subscribes to the program set forth by the text.[64] And it is by such willing submission, according to Stewart, that readers are transported into fictional worlds. It is important to note that, for Stewart, readers are not passive entities, since "conscripted reading is often a function of the scripted difficulties thrown in the path of a reading"[65] That is, readers are actively engaged as the text makes various demands upon the reader—to comprehend, to evaluate, to interpret. Hence, Stewart's argument informs that of Byerly, who builds on current studies of virtual reality to argue that interactivity is crucial to a sense of virtual presence.[66] In both analyses, reader engagement is thus pre-staged within the linguistic, rhetorical, and formal functions of the novel; as readers overcome obstacles to reading, they find themselves participating further in the texts' own agenda. But because Stewart is, first and foremost, interested in the immersive pleasures of reading realist fiction, he overlooks those readers who fail the conscription test; such readers only serve as foils for the conscripted reader.

In contrast to Stewart and others who focus on how readers buy into the pleasures of realist narrative, this book mobilizes what Stephen Best and Sharon Marcus have called "surface reading" to take the figures of marginalized readers figured within the text at face value. Questioning the critical imperative to delve into a text to discover hidden meaning, Best and Marcus present an alternative model of reading that pays attention to what lies on the surface of texts.[67] While appearing on the surface of the text, the numerous readers represented in texts who misread, misunderstand, disapprove, forget, or simply get bored by the text have nevertheless been passed over. They are victims of a symptomatic reading that sees texts as coercing (or nudging, to use a gentler term) readers to read in a certain way in order to promote their own ideological or aesthetic agendas. As critics, we have been trained to see through these readers in order to identify them as examples of how not to read. There are obvious examples of textually inscribed readers who are indeed presented as examples of how not to read; Catherine Moreland from Jane Austen's *Northanger Abbey* comes to mind as a character who is explicitly judged by the narrator as being at fault for reading Gothic fiction too literally. But not all "bad" readers are necessarily judged by narrators. As chapter 1 details, Fielding's narrator constantly assumes that his readers are ignorant, forgetful, and prone to make hasty assumptions, and while he certainly attempts to scold them into submission on many occasions, he frequently lends a hand to help these readers navigate the intricacies of his narrative. Chapter 3 demonstrates how Scott's

18 · LIMITED ACCESS

narrator equally consults readers of historical and legal documents who are familiar with genuine local history as well as the female reader whose authority stems from having avidly consumed the contents of three circulating libraries. Novels do not always privilege certain kinds of readers over others but instead fold "bad" readers into texts in an effort to engage them.

To fully appreciate the work of these textually inscribed "bad" readers requires us to question our assumptions about how we read by reading into and through those transport metaphors that seem to provide easy answers about how realist narratives should be experienced. Such a model of reading requires us, for example, to pause before taking the narrator of *Felix Holt* at face value when she associates the outside passenger of a stagecoach with a reader who has ready access to stories of English life; it forces us, instead, to attend to the predicament of the shepherd whom the coach passes rapidly by and who seems equally excluded from the pleasures of reading and of traveling.[68] Taking for granted the metaphor of "reading as traveling"—innocuous as it seems—contributes to the marginalization of textually inscribed readers who experience the text otherwise. To subscribe to this metaphor is to emphasize the desire for immediacy at the cost of ignoring the plodding materiality of transport; to buy into this metaphor is to downplay the possibility of limited access that realist texts consciously display to give precedence to the fantasy of access that these texts tantalizingly pose.[69] Critics like Lupton and Deidre Lynch have cautioned us against "our investment in the history of mimesis," since it can prevent us from seeing "reading and writing practices as local accomplishments— as social technologies that depend on certain verbal forms, practical exercises, codes of deportment, and capacities for pleasure and that permit their users to engage in particular sets of activities."[70] These textually inscribed readers are hidden from our view because of our willingness and desire to uphold the idea that "reading is like traveling." Readers who don't read the "right" way have always been there, on the surface of the text, but critical tradition has accorded little value to these readers.

Instead of showing how novels nudge readers into a particular model of reading where the transports of novel reading can only be experienced through immersion in a virtual reality, the following chapters suggest that these novels concerned with reader engagement work to affirm alternative models of reading and knowing. Like Stewart, I see these texts as communicating with their readers by anticipating their responses, addressing them directly, nudging and even reprimanding them as occasion calls. But they

INTRODUCTION · 19

also imagine the limits of readers' abilities to comprehend, to buy into the illusion of the text, to take its truth claims at face value. Rather than coercing readers into understanding, many of these texts express a kind of resignation that what they present will not be fully accessible to readers. In doing so, they also negotiate and experiment with narrative strategies that take into account the limited access of readers while validating and accommodating alternative models of reading. They validate readers who read for a sense of belonging rather than trying to understand the intricate nuances of the text (chapter 1); they validate readers whose imagination roams outside of the text to material objects rather than focusing on the affective messages of the text itself (chapter 2); they validate readers who consume popular fiction rather than genuine historical narratives (chapter 3); they validate readers who read scenes from novels out of context rather than within it (chapter 4); they validate readers who want to skip over descriptions that fail to appeal to them rather than seek meaning in historically accurate descriptions (chapter 5). In so doing, these novels teach us that there can be many different ways to "get into" a text that pose alternatives to a single, normative model of reading. It is not that these novels give up on the attempt to engage in coherent meaning-making for diverse readers, but that these novels might be kinder and gentler, more forgiving and more accommodating towards "bad" readers than they have been heretofore characterized.

The Mediological Imagination

By foregrounding the work of transport metaphors in realist fiction and by taking seriously how narrators attempt to engage readers by opening up alternative models of reading, this book seeks to grasp what Guillory refers to as "the nature of mediation" which, in his view, depends on "affirming the communicative function in social relations, that is, the possibility of communication."[71] For Guillory, studying literary genres, like other cultural and artistic forms that now appear institutionalized in our current culture, requires attention to a process of mediation that is both social and technological; scrutinizing the process of mediation is critical for understanding, for instance, "the problem of literary canon formation"—to invoke his own prior work—that involves both media technologies (such as print and, increasingly, digital media) as well as social processes (including, but not limited to, the publishing industry as well as educational institutions).[72] While

Guillory claims that cultural critics tend to avoid tackling the question of mediation by collapsing "the mediations performed by the media back into representations," I suggest that it is possible to locate within novelistic representation a communicative impulse that leads to a "recognition of the inherent difficulty of communication and the diversity of its strategies and modes."[73] Kevis Goodman provides us with a model for doing so when she examines how long poems of the eighteenth-century and Romantic period "[confront] the *failure* of mediation" to produce pleasure by pondering the way "their verses compete and clash with rival media, or pathways of perception and communication."[74] When Sterne complains that vehicles get in the way of sentimental communication, or when Thackeray worries about communicating the pleasant memories of a stagecoach journey to young readers of the railroad era, they both surface possible barriers to communication and negotiate strategies for overcoming them. These novels' efforts to engage and include readers are thus an effort not only to represent but also to communicate with readers; hence this project assumes that representation, like media, is a means to an end, and that end is to engage readers, to get the message across to its destination, to communicate. Thus, while I draw upon studies and theories of media, I subordinate concerns about media proper to attend, instead, to the concerns that novels express about communication and mediation.

Communication is an act fraught with anxiety—as though there might be serious future consequences—for the novelists I study, and Debray helps us understand why. Like Guillory, Debray is interested in the larger processes of mediation rather than media in and of themselves and advances the need for what he calls "mediology"—a study of the complex processes of mediation to trace how some ideas become institutionalized in our cultures while others fade away into obscurity. While communications—like the act of novel reading—can possess an "immediate, direct, and joyously transitive nature,"[75] they are not just one-time acts that deliver clear messages for Debray. As immediate as communications may seem, he argues, they are always accompanied by two shadowy companions—the "noise" that comes with every act of communication and the prospect of transmission that looms in the future. Debray asserts that neither companion to communications is merely a matter of technology; each is also shaped by social conflict and the attempt to establish shared meaning within a community.[76] Transmission is a process that happens over time—a series of communications that, through repetition and endurance, create a culture's legacies and inheritances.

There are many messages, many communications, but not all of them survive to create a sense of culture that unites a body of people. For communications to survive and to become transmitted legacies, it is not sufficient for them to be recorded in print or in digital form, since "the machine is a necessary but not sufficient interface."[77] One must also account for how human agents and institutions intervene in this process to determine which pieces of recorded information are worth transmitting, and which pieces of data should be neutralized and regarded as mere background noise.

Transport metaphors underscore the extent to which novels imagined and theorized this complex and multilayered nature of mediation as a process that is both material and social, individual and collective, spatial and temporal. In doing so, they exhibit a mediological imagination, one that seeks to understand how we establish shared meaning amidst a cacophony of communications using both technological and social processes. The communications that these novels imagine are messy and convoluted; far from assuming that a clear message is conveyed by the medium from the addressor to the addressee, novels actively imagine how communications can misdeliver and prevent readers from accessing textual meaning, understanding, and pleasure. In attempting to communicate not just information but also affect, these novels imagine how the medium might deliver or distort the message; how intervening bodies can register, block, or reroute feeling; how competing genres are capable of helping or hindering their cause; how novelistic conventions may work as a shorthand for or an obstacle to communicating with readers; and how readers themselves are likely to bring various degrees and kinds of literacy, experiences, and cultural capital to bear on their reading. Refusing to conceptualize communication with readers as an act that takes place within the framework of a single, defined ontological register (i.e., through textual representation), these novels blur the boundaries set by modern disciplinarity that Bruno Latour has so insistently critiqued; they insist that communications are simultaneously discursive, material, and social.[78]

By paying close attention to how transport metaphors highlight particular communicative concerns of novels across the period, it is also possible to trace the process of consolidation and institutionalization of the realist novel as a genre. While the novels featured in this study persistently stray imaginatively beyond the boundaries of textual representations by conceptualizing communication and mediation across disciplinary domains, they become increasingly genre conscious after the turn of the nineteenth century when, as scholars such as Clifford Siskin, William St. Clair, and Homer Obed Brown have demonstrated, novels became a recognized and recognizable genre. As each of these scholars' arguments testify, the history of the book—including the quantitative study of literary publishing as well as studies of para-literary activities like reviewing and anthologizing—has provided the most reliable means of understanding the institutionalization of the novel.[79] Building on these studies, I identify how novels increasingly work to confirm their generic identity in the course of their history. While the narrators in the novels of Fielding, Sterne, and Smollett certainly refer to their literary predecessors as well as contemporaries, they are primarily concerned about how to communicate with readers within the context of an expanding print culture, where fiction was just one among many print and commercial products that vied for consumers' attentions. Their nineteenth-century counterparts, represented in this study by Scott, Dickens, and Thackeray, continue to be preoccupied with reader engagement and imagine how the rapidity of print circulation and the changing technologies of transport facilitate or impede communications with readers. At the same time, they also increasingly imagine that their readers assume certain generic conventions associated with the novel. For Scott, circulating libraries and mass-produced novels create generic expectations in his readers that he must account for to facilitate readers' access to his historical novels, and Dickens and Thackeray indicate the need to contend with the generic pattern of eighteenth-century stagecoach novels that they imagined was familiar to readers. Novelistic representation itself, for these writers, takes on the function of new media that Lisa Gitelman describes to emerge as "socially embedded sites for the ongoing negotiation of meaning as such."[80] Thus, they demonstrate the need to revisit novels written by their predecessors, asking which narrative strategies they should adopt, negotiate, or discard to better communicate with their readers in a changing context of mediation. In doing so, they also unconsciously confirm the generic identity of their texts; the very need to revisit and to revise generic precedents set by their novelistic forebears ironically reinforces the novel's institutional status.[81]

Thus, the history of realism I envision is not a history of formal innovations that led to the achievement of realism. Rather, it is a long history of realist fiction's ongoing endeavor to better communicate with and engage readers historically. Transport metaphors did not just help writers theorize the uneven access of people, places, and things in a given historical moment.

They also worked as sites for considering how narratives and histories from the past remain accessible in a print public sphere, and how writers' own works communicate with readers in the context of a cumulative literary history. Novels may strive to become accessible to diverse readers, but they must do so while contending with legacies from the past as well as the threat of future obsolescence.

Each of the following chapters traces how authors conceptualize mediation through transport metaphors in order to address different concerns about readerly access. The shifting nuances and competing conceptual framework of the transport metaphor that each author focuses on leads him or her to experiment and negotiate with realist form to open up different models of reading and knowing so as to hopefully overcome the pitfalls of limited access for readers. Chapter 1 focuses on the stagecoach as a transport metaphor to explain and critique the artificial culture of reading that the increasing number of periodical publications seemed to impose. In the pages of *Tom Jones,* Fielding uses the stagecoach—a media metaphor often associated with the regular delivery of news—to reimagine novel reading as a communal experience that diverse classes of readers can access. Chapter 2 turns to the mid-eighteenth-century discourse of sensibility in which writers frequently used the figure of the vehicle as a transport metaphor to interrogate the idea of selfhood, affective communication, and the distinction between textual form and content. Sterne's *A Sentimental Journey* and Smollett's *The Expedition of Humphry Clinker* work both with and against the vehicle metaphor to highlight limited access to unadulterated sentiment and to envision an alternative model of reading that engages readers in a feedback loop between textual representation and material reality. Chapters 1 and 2 lay the foundation for the remaining chapters by highlighting novels' preoccupation with reader engagement and the tenuous process of communication upon which it is grounded.

The remaining chapters continue to explore how transport metaphors conceptualize mediation and reader engagement while drawing further attention to the increasing need for authors to negotiate precedents set by their novelistic predecessors after the novel became a recognized and institutionalized genre at the turn of the nineteenth century. Chapter 3 focuses on Scott's use of the mail coach as a transport metaphor that highlights the systemic limit of circulation that marginalizes authentic local history while proliferating common narratives. He suggests that the national circulation network exemplified by the mail coach gives readers limited access to authentic local history and negotiates this problem by using frame narratives to outline a process of transmission that makes historical narratives accessible to readers of popular literature. Chapter 4 highlights how, for Dickens's *The Pickwick Papers,* the stagecoach is not just a transport technology; its ontological status is complicated by the fact that the stagecoach simultaneously stands for a robust network of national circulation and a generic trait of eighteenth-century novels. The dual ontological status of transport leads Dickens to expose how such a network limits access to knowledge and to propose an analogical model of reading and knowing. Chapter 5 explores Thackeray's *Vanity Fair* alongside other texts that further complicate transport metaphors by contrasting competing technologies of transport: the coaching network and the railway. The dueling media metaphors prompt authors like Thackeray to muddle the ontological status of stagecoaches so that they stand simultaneously for a technologically deterministic past and an outmoded narrative. Emphasizing how young readers have limited access to cultural memories of a stagecoaching past, Thackeray relies on readers to access their personal memories to engage with the text on their own terms.

The conclusion turns to George Eliot to ruminate how transport metaphors shed light on the problems of apprehending literary history itself. Eliot's own transport metaphor seems to straightforwardly compare a stagecoach ride and realist narrative, only to unsettle that comparison by drawing attention to the tenuousness of the present moment. Imagining narrative transmission within a temporal continuum extending from a forgotten past to an unknown future, Eliot suggests that how we understand reality is itself contingent on our limited perspective.

1

Delivering Narrative to Consumer-Readers
Staging Inclusion in Fielding's *Tom Jones*

Henry Fielding's use of stagecoaches as a transport metaphor makes him a key figure in the history of realist fiction; his stagecoach metaphors assert that readers share the experience of reading, following protagonists as they pursue their journeys throughout the narrative. While Fielding variously refers to *Tom Jones* as a "Heroic, Historical, Prosaic Poem" or "prosai-comi-epic writing" to draw attention to his own experimentation with genre,[1] scholars have often taken his transport metaphor at face value to explain how Fielding contributes to the emergence of formal realism. This chapter takes a step back from the seeming transparency of Fielding's transport metaphor to explore, instead, how it emerges in response to Fielding's anxieties about diverse readers in an expanding print culture. Fielding—like his contemporaries Shaftsbury and Hume—tackles the philosophical problem of how members of society with diverse opinions, backgrounds, and ways of thinking can come together to form a community that is nevertheless held together by the shared understanding of its members. Instead of assuming the existence of a unified society or public in an expanding print culture, however, Fielding theorizes how readers may experience barriers to participating in a print-based community, especially since existing communities fail to successfully generate shared understandings that create a unified society because of the faulty processes of mediation. On the one hand, the printed periodicals that contribute to the expanding public sphere can provide useless information because of their need to deliver news with the regularity of a stagecoach. On the other hand, local communities held together by traditional ties generate public opinion that is regarded as truth based on faulty assumptions of a gossip network. Instead of assuming a shared understanding with readers, Fielding engages diverse readers by associating his novel—especially his introductory chapters to each book—with stagecoaches and other temporary places of gathering where people can share, if not the same understanding, at least the same experience.

Thus, rather than taking Fielding's transport metaphor as a firm guiding principle that he uses to confidently shape his realism, I argue that it is a reactionary countermetaphor that Fielding presents in response to numerous other competing transport metaphors within an emerging print culture. In the final book of Henry Fielding's *Tom Jones,* the narrator famously bids farewell to his readers, whom he considers as fellow travelers in a stagecoach, heading towards the last stage of their journeys (*TJ,* 808–9). He characterizes the prefatory chapters to each book of *The History of Tom Jones, A Foundling* as resting places like inns where passengers may alight and take rest, eat food, or socialize. He considers his readers as travelers, who may alight at these virtual stages to rest their eyes, go off to dinner, doze off, or bicker with the narrator. Instead of taking a journey on the road, the readers of *Tom Jones* thus virtually travel through the pages of the novel in company with the protagonists and the narrator—even as they sit quietly in their armchairs. This oft-revisited metaphor puts Fielding at the center of intersecting debates about the rise of the novel in the eighteenth century, focusing on the extent to which Fielding's narrative succeeded in creating an objective representation that could create consensus among readers. While some scholars emphasize the objectivity presented in Fielding's novels as a crucial component of realism that enables readers to share a consensus about the fictional world he presents, others doubt readers' ability to apprehend Fielding's objectivity as such, especially given the complexity of his novels and the unstable characterization of narrative authority throughout his novels.[2] In addition, *Tom Jones* is famously central to Wolfgang Iser's conception of the "implied reader," but scholars have since pointed out that the readers implied by Fielding are multiple rather than singular in their backgrounds as well as their possible responses.[3] And finally, while two grand narratives of eighteenth-century print culture—the ideas of imagined communities and the public sphere—both locate the origins or ideals of a print-based community in the emerging print culture of the period, scholars have increasingly drawn attention to how such communities were more ideal than real.[4]

Many of the critical disagreements about Fielding's contribution to realism stem from the degree of confidence that scholars attribute to the fictional narrator and hence to Fielding's own fictional representations; I explicitly consider Fielding as a writer who is anxious about the objectivity of his narrative and the degree of consensus—and hence communal understanding—that his fictional representation can generate. I do so not so much in the context of large-scale ideological and epistemic shifts as scholars like Michael McKeon have done but in the context of a particular culture of mediation that Fielding implicitly conceptualizes within his novel.[5] The culture and period in which Fielding wrote witnessed new temporal and spatial forms—such as periodical publications and other diurnal forms—that failed to establish a communal sense of shared time and space, filling readers' minds instead with miscellaneous content. At the same time, habits of mind nurtured by a traditional communal life underpinned by its own dynamics of mediation also persisted in ways that disrupt participation in a print-based community. Fielding's representations throughout the novel attempt to establish a coherent narrative in spite of modern commercial forms on the one hand and persistent attachment to local communities on the other. Thus, Fielding's narrator must labor to establish the textual space as a realm in which the author and reader share the same conditions and experiences of mediation by spending time together in the same space.

Rather than consider objectivity as Fielding's end goal, then, this chapter argues that the formal realism of *Tom Jones* is the by-product of Fielding's attempt to theorize access to the virtual community of print and how his own novel might mediate such access by mobilizing existing physical, cultural, and social forms. Taking Partridge as an example of a "bad" reader whom Fielding uses as a test-case to consider the effects of faulty mediation, I explore how Fielding imagines various readers as conditioned by existing practices of mediation to either indiscriminately take in information without fully weighing its merits or coming too hastily to a general consensus. Fielding suggests that such readers could not reliably establish consensus based on what Benedict Anderson calls "homogeneous empty time"—the modern sense of time as a neutral medium that coordinates everyone's lives and events.[6] Instead, Fielding likens his text to scenes of commerce that create temporary communities in which people gather with a common object—such as the theater, the ordinary, and the stagecoach. It is in such places, then, that Fielding's narrator is able to imagine the possibility of shared experience that will give readers access to a virtual community, despite misunderstandings along the way.

Staging Fullness

Fielding's metaphor of the stagecoach as a communal space of narrative appears in response to cultural anxieties about how to communicate with diverse readers in an expanding commercial print culture that drove readers to consume miscellaneous texts instead of coming together to form a virtual community. This is evident in the preliminary chapter to Book II, when the narrator of *Tom Jones* explains "what kind of a history this is; what it is like, and what it is not like." The narrator is intent on associating his history writing with "the method of those writers who profess to disclose the revolution of countries," rather than newspapers, which is a form of "history" that "preserves the regularity of [its] series," very much like "a stagecoach, which performs constantly the same course, empty as well as full" (*TJ,* 67). The similarity between the stagecoach and the newspaper holds true for the narrator because they both possess a form, a container, that needs to be filled and delivered regularly. The coming and going of stagecoaches not only gave Britons access to printed texts but also gave them a new way to measure time that became more and more pervasive. Stagecoaches—along with other technologies like chronometers, diaries, and other "diurnal forms" that Stewart Sherman argues were central to the early eighteenth-century conception of temporality[7]—enforced upon eighteenth-century men and women an increasing sense of the regularity of time, since the improvements in roads and carriages made such regularity increasingly possible.[8] Hence, the newspaper "consists of just the same number of words, whether there be any news in it or not" (*TJ,* 67). As circulating people, objects, and print increased in number, writers and readers started to think of circulation in terms of the most accessible vehicle that was available to them. Thus, writers including Fielding drew analogies between newspapers and stagecoaches because they both perform the same stages according to their scheduled routines and do so whether the vehicle is empty or full. In other words, newspapers were not just print media but also temporal ones; the form of the newspaper and its regular and timely distribution enforced the idea that time was full of events, just as newspapers were filled with words.

The stagecoach metaphor that Fielding works against underscores not only the need for newspapers to keep pace with time, but also a sense that time was measured by the need to fill space with miscellaneous content. As Jeremy Black describes in detail, editors of newspapers at the time resorted to various strategies for filling their pages with varied, miscellaneous, and even inconsistent material to satisfy a wide variety of consumer-readers on a clocked schedule. Black focuses mostly on elaborating the content of news, which was predominantly of a political nature but also often included accounts of deaths, sporting events, anecdotes, pieces borrowed from other publications, and sometimes even jokes and bawdy pieces. But a telling passage from an anonymous letter printed in a *Berrow's Worcester Journal* underscores one of the main reasons for such inconsistent variety—newspapers were obliged to fill a specific amount of textual space periodically regardless of the richness or scarcity of events:

> In the Nature of a Newspaper, '*non datur vacuum*'—A Newspaper must be as full as an Egg:—It is not like many other daily Vehicles or Stages, which frequently go off half empty, and sometimes without any Passengers at all, but is obliged to set out at the appointed Time, and *must* be cram'd full, Outside and Inside, Before and Behind, Top and Bottom; nay, if there is but *one* empty Place, you are sure to be overset. Since this is the case with those political Vehicles, Newspapers, there exists an absolute Necessity of Plentitude, 'tis no Wonder that the conductors of those Machines are not very scrupulous or nice in the Choice of their Company; but rather than suffer any Vacancy, they imitate the great Man's Servants in the Parable, who went out to the Streets and Highways, collecting the Old and the Young, the Lame, the Blind, the Good, and the Bad; in short, whomsoever they could get to make up the Number of Guests.[9]

Because of their very materiality, newspapers had no choice but to fill every corner of the sheet. There was an "absolute Necessity of Plentitude" that made editors resort to any piece of news they could lay their hands on. Such indiscriminate reporting made newspapers present not just a mixture of important news and trifling reports, but also occasionally a mixture of true and false.[10]

The stagecoach, then, did not work as a straightforward metaphor for describing the experience of communal reading for Fielding, but was, first and foremost, a metaphor that highlighted the problems of reading in an expanding commercial print culture. While the writer of *Berrow's Worcester Journal* articulates this problem using the stagecoach as an analogy, the same concerns were frequently echoed by others. For instance, *The Spectator,* which was published and delivered to readers every day but Sunday, reverses this logic to argue that its periodicity helped solve a moral and social problem by filling the emptiness of time for its readers. Mr. Spectator encourages readers to make the reading of his daily number a ritual practice within their everyday lives; he recommends his daily observations "to all well regulated Families, that set apart an Hour in every Morning for Tea and Bread and Butter; and would earnestly advise them for their Good to order this Paper to be punctually served up, and to be looked upon as a Part of the Tea Equipage."[11] Such encouragement of a ritualized reading practice reminds us of the image of collective newspaper reading that Benedict Anderson asserts is the basis for an imagined community.[12] But for Mr. Spectator, his papers perform functions that go beyond just signifying the passing of time. He initially states that his goal is to cultivate the minds of his readers, which can easily be tainted by the vices and follies of the age. His papers are necessary as prescriptions, since "the mind that lies fallow but a single Day, sprouts up in Follies that are only to be killed by a constant and assiduous culture."[13] As Mr. Spectator lists his intended audience, it becomes clear that his papers perform the work of "filling up" the time and minds of the readers. For "the Fraternity of Spectators who live in the World without having anything to do in it," the paper helps fill their time by guiding their observations of others. For the "Blanks of Society" who are "altogether unfurnish'd with Ideas, till the Business and Conversation of the Day has supplied them,"[14] Mr. Spectator's daily observations help them to fill their minds so that they will have something to converse about. Most important, such daily reading will benefit those in "the Female World" according to Mr. Spectator, who "have so much Time on their Hands." Reading the paper will not only help them fill at least a quarter hour of their day, but also fill their minds with useful reflections so as to divert them "from greater Trifles."[15] *The Spectator* is central to Habermas's theory of the public sphere where citizens may engage in rational conversation, but the world that Mr. Spectator portrays seems plagued with problems of emptiness—of both time and mental activity—that can only be remedied by supplying readers with the virtuous reflections that *The Spectator* provides.[16]

Morally upstanding periodicals like *The Spectator* become necessary in an expanding print culture where readers were not so much participants in a rational-minded public sphere but simple and gullible consumers. The diurnal form was particularly harmful in the form of newspapers that cater to consumer-readers who unquestioningly swallow any information, because they fail to distinguish between what is of major consequence and what is not or what is pertinent to their business and what is not. Avid readers of news, according to a correspondent of *The Spectator,* "read the Advertisements with the same Curiosity as the Articles of Publick news" and "they have a Relish for everything that is News, let the matter of it be what it will." The correspondent is so convinced of the gullibility of these newsmongers who have "a Voracious Appetite, but no Taste," that he believes he will be able to make them swallow the most insignificant reports about a Brompton widow's courtship or a "Tub of excellent Ale" in Fulham.[17] Anderson emphasizes the ritualistic reading of the newspaper as the source of the "imagined community" regardless of the contents of that newspaper, but for the writers above, the contents present a serious problem. They are highly skeptical of the miscellaneous nature of the newspaper's contents, especially because the "Plentitude" of the content is dictated by the blank spaces on paper rather than the quantity of available news. These readers could not take it for granted that the textual form of the newspaper had the straightforward and transparent effect of conjuring calendrical time. Newspapers may have given the public access to more information, but what they accessed by no means helped to establish a shared understanding among readers that would lead to a sense of community. Whereas Anderson considers the textual form of the newspaper as straightforwardly conjuring temporal sequence, the skeptics I quote above are unable to dissociate the form of the newspaper from its contents. For eighteenth-century critics of the newspaper, the newspaper as media seemed to promote commercial interests rather than indicating the operation of time as a neutral and objective medium.

Such critics—including Fielding—faced a paradoxical challenge, since their own works could easily be mistaken for the commercially motivated texts that they critique in their meta-reflections on print culture of the time. Thus, Fielding attempts to distinguish his own novel from newspapers and other print media that operate on the principle of commercial interest by filling whatever space was available. In a print culture where the form dictates the amount of content required to fill the space on a blank page, Fielding asserts that, in his narrative, form follows substance. Thus, the narrator of *Tom Jones* insists that his work is not subservient to the dictates of time as are periodicals or those past histories written by "voluminous historians" who attempt to "preserve the regularity of his series" or "keep even pace with time" (*TJ*, 67). Instead of filling his pages with words in order to measure time, the narrator claims to present substantial content in his series by leaving out the "blanks in the grand lottery of time" (*TJ*, 68). When Fielding expresses such concerns, he is also responding to the above concerns about how commercial textual media can create a false sense of temporal fullness. He anticipates that critical readers will scrutinize the relationship between the textual form of his novel and what substance it presents as they do with newspapers. He cannot, for instance, prevent readers from assuming that "[authors] mean only to swell [their] Works to a much larger Bulk than they would otherwise extend to" by creating chapters, thus increasing the price of their commodities in the same way that tailors increase customers' bills by adding insignificant trinkets.[18] Fielding feels the burden of proving to his readers that he does not participate in the practice of a commercial print culture that creates various forms of time, only to invest them with artificial and miscellaneous "Plentitude" for the sake of profit. In other words, the narrator needs to assure readers that unlike the stagecoach operator who squeezes passengers into the carriage to maximize his profit, he is not motivated by commercial interests.

Consequently, the narrator attempts to distinguish himself from the more commercial historians by emphasizing how his own narrative form reflects the mutual relevance of events rather than artificial plentitude.[19] For example, Tom Jones recovers from a broken head and meets the Man of the Hill; *meanwhile*, Sophia is escaping from her father's house and following his track. Such explanation is necessary "to account for the extraordinary appearance of Sophia and her father at the inn at Upton" (*TJ*, 481). The sense of simultaneity appears enhanced in scenes where characters perform actions unknown to one another despite their physical proximity. Such is the case when Jones hides his paramour, Lady Bellaston, behind his bed curtain while Honour conveys to him a message from Sophia and abuses the character of Lady Bellaston through very ignorance of her presence in the room (*TJ*, 652–53). Indeed, this fine-tuned manipulation of characters within the same temporal continuum provides one of the crucial keys to the novel's central drama when Jones fears that he has committed incest.

The narrator urges his readers to "refresh his memory by turning to the scene at Upton, in the ninth book, [where] he will be apt to admire the many strange accidents which unfortunately prevented any interview between Partridge and Mrs Waters" (*TJ,* 810). If Partridge had seen Mrs. Waters then, he would have identified her as the very Jenny Jones reputed to be Tom Jones's mother, and he may have prevented this tragedy. But this encounter fails to take place as Partridge, who "had been all this time washing his bloody nose at the pump," does not make his way to the kitchen until Mrs. Waters had retired from it (*TJ,* 438). The narrator observes sagaciously that "the greatest events" like the one above "are produced by a nice train of little circumstances" and that further examples of this can be found in his narrative (*TJ,* 811).

By emphasizing the mutual relevance of events, Fielding attempts to establish how time operates as a neutral medium in his narrative. Elizabeth Ermarth identifies both space and time as "continuous, homogeneous, neutral media" in realist representations that "are populated by objects that exhibit certain consistencies of behaviour, regardless of changes in position, which enable us to recognize them as the same."[20] This neutrality of time and space as media, according to Ermarth, is what makes realistic representation possible, and, more to the point, is what makes the world comprehensible to those who see it from their particular vantage points. This makes it possible for "us" to all agree about what happened in the narrative. She asserts that time and space became neutral in the wake of a Renaissance humanism that encouraged people to see things in relation to other things and events in relation to other events, so that history, for example, was no longer written to contrast time and eternity, but to put past and present in relationship to one another.[21] But it is not "continuity in time" that simply and necessarily "makes collective agreements possible" in realist representations. Instead, "the narrator acts as a kind of administrator, coordinating the novel's various moments into a single sequence that confirms the mutual relevance of one moment for another" so that the "consensus" among different voices and perspectives "not only establishes an agreement of meanings; it literally establishes the continuity of time."[22] The narrator, according to Ermarth, has much heavy lifting to do, since "continuity of time" will not be represented successfully in fiction if the narrator fails to corral the various voices and perspectives and show how they agree about the world they inhabit. For Ermarth, such "consensus" is a crucial component of representation in realism because it ensures that the reader can consistently recognize characters as they move through time and perform actions that help to make meaning within the novel.

Fielding attempts to establish such a consensus by engaging his readers in navigating time as a neutral medium in his narrative. Rather than expecting readers to piece together temporal sequence or temporal coincidence, Fielding underscores the sense of "meanwhile" by creating situations that make retrospective explanations of events necessary. Indeed, the narrator boasts, this is what distinguishes his narrative from others, as he explains how Mr. Western came to discover his escaped daughter at Mrs. Bellaston's residence in London: "Though the reader, in many histories, is obliged to digest much more unaccountable appearances than this of Mr. Western, without any satisfaction at all, yet, as we dearly love to oblige him whenever it is in our power, we shall now proceed to show by what method the squire discovered where his daughter was." To understand this mystery, readers are asked to remind themselves of a "hint" that the narrator provided in "the third chapter . . . of the preceding book" that indicated Mrs. Fitzpatrick's intention of reconciling herself to her relatives, the Westerns, by informing them of Sophia's whereabouts. The narrator explains that this information was withheld from readers at that time because "it is not our custom to unfold at any time more than is necessary for the occasion" (*TJ*, 704). Such statements seem to indicate the narrator's authority; he appears to be a figure who coaches readers to learn to read his history correctly.[23] But such commentaries create another effect; by making it necessary to refer back to a chapter in a preceding book, the narrator has occasion to demonstrate the agreement between different moments in the narrative. What was said then, in the current flow of the narrative, and what the narrator says now, in a retrospective moment of the narrative, create overlapping temporal references that work together to confirm the continuity of time and the mutual relevance of succeeding events.

Fielding labors to prove temporal coincidence not only to establish time as a neutral medium but also to establish the commercial disinterestedness of his narrative. These details are not unnecessary fillers, the narrator insists, that are merely there to make up the necessary bulk to commodify his novel. Fielding feels the burden of proving to his readers how every circumstance falls into place to establish his narrative, and how each detail is there for a reason. Alexander Welsh argues that the reason for such abundance of details is evidentiary—each minute detail matters in the same way eighteenth-century courts of law built their cases using circumstantial evidence. As

Welsh details, testimonies by private individuals came to be increasingly distrusted around the beginning of the eighteenth century, and thus theorists of law came to place greater emphasis on facts and evidence—and the ability to combine them into a probable narrative.[24] Circumstantial evidence rested on the ability of prosecutors and judges to put details together in a way that made sense; the presumption was that "a narrative cannot be shaped from circumstantial evidence without considerably more work than goes into most lies."[25] Welsh argues that Fielding arranges his novel so as to demonstrate the possibilities of misrepresenting evidence (by the villainous Blifil), while establishing an elaborate defense of Jones through his own superior mobilization of circumstantial evidence. Tom Jones's character, however, is not the only defendant on trial in Fielding's novel. As my preceding discussion demonstrates, the narrator himself is obliged to demonstrate, circumstantially, that he is not imposing unnecessary information on his readers. The narrator acknowledges that he is, like Jones, subject to the censures of judges, though these judges may only exist in the form of critics, who have overstepped their boundaries and have come to act "as a judge would." Against such would-be judges who, "being men of shallow capacities, very easily mistook mere form for substance" (*TJ*, 182), the narrator must defend his own character and reputation by demonstrating how each circumstance of his narrative is necessary because they are part of a "series of closely connected evidentiary facts."[26]

Time, for Fielding, is not a neutral medium, but one that can be distorted by commercial forms like newspapers that invest time with a false sense of substance, so he labors to prove how his novel is a different kind of media from newspapers, stagecoaches, and other commercially driven forms. Thus, Fielding's formal realism is not so much the transparent manifestation of homogeneous empty time but the result of negotiating it into existence. The success of Fielding's self-defense, in this regard, appears in the critical reception of his work as numerous scholars—especially in the structuralist tradition—have considered Fielding as central to the rise of realist fiction because of his tightly knit plots and the successful adoption of an objective perspective in his narratives. But attending to the anxieties over print culture that inform Fielding's formal negotiations show how he cannot assume that his various readers—from gullible newsmongers to critics who mistake "form for substance"—will arrive at a consensus regarding his narrative. Far from assuming that print culture creates the conditions necessary to establish a virtual community of readers who understand time as a neutral medium and who can evaluate what they read with judgment and taste, Fielding suggests that print culture gives readers limited access to such a community because it is underpinned by commercial institutions and interests.

Problems of Consensus

While commercial media—such as newspapers that deliver content with the regularity of a stagecoach—present an unstable foundation for establishing consensus for a virtual community of readers, according to Fielding, traditional, place-based communities provide an equally unstable foundation for establishing consensus with readers. In short, neither work as straightforward models that enable Fielding to imagine the kind of print-based community of readers who might share a virtual stagecoach journey. The early books of the novel focus on the community surrounding the estates of Mr. Allworthy and Mr. Western in Somersetshire to describe in detail how a community functions without the mediation of printed texts. Such a community—though often overshadowed by historical narratives that emphasize the rise of modernity and print culture—was central to the experience of eighteenth-century men and women. Wolfram Schmidgen argues that the modality of Anderson's "meanwhile" only emerges in the nineteenth century because eighteenth-century Britons registered their experiences not by measuring them in the context of a neutral and purely abstract space and time, but in a more relative, relational context that has been established through their experience of local traditions and customs that have been gradually established surrounding landed estates.[27] Schmidgen convincingly argues that though living in a rapidly commercializing society, eighteenth-century Britons inherit the feudal mentality of the manorial estate that associates authority with landed property and the customs that have become established on that very manor through long continued practice.[28] Indeed, J. Paul Hunter suggests that modernization may have helped to strengthen a sense of attachment to old country communities. He claims that newly migrant Britons who flocked to urban centers came to feel a "kind of loneliness [that] expresses the profound feelings of emptiness and desire for connection that result from physical, emotional, or spiritual isolation but not necessarily from literal solitude."[29] Such feelings of isolation, he claims, were heightened all the more because Londoners had an exaggerated sense of how "generations before them enjoyed a vast and easy social familiarity among themselves and felt deep personal ties with those near whom they lived and with whom they conversed daily."[30]

In detailing the process of mediation in a manorial community, Fielding suggests that while local communities are not undermined by commercial print media, they are plagued by the effects of a social gossip network that produces consensus too hastily in the form of communal opinions. The narrator resorts to descriptions of communal opinion repeatedly in the early books of the novel to demonstrate how the gossip network of a small local community bypasses the evidentiary logic that underpins his own novel. This is made explicit in the rumors surrounding the mystery of Tom Jones's birth and parentage, as well as how the gossip mill creates reputations of various characters. When Partridge is punished for being the father of the foundling, for example, the "justice which Mr Allworthy had executed on Partridge at first met with universal approbation" until "his neighbours began to relent, and to compassionate his case" (*TJ*, 89). It is not merely scandal that triggers the formation of such general opinions. People's characters are also assessed publicly so that "the neighbourhood resounded [Master Blifil's] praises" while "Tom Jones was universally disliked" (*TJ*, 103). The force of such "universal" agreement among neighbors appears most explicitly when the "Somersetshire mob" come together after church to attack Molly Seagrim for her impertinence in wearing a lady's gown (*TJ*, 154). While men and women in the local community of Somersetshire may not avidly read the columns of the newspapers the way a lonely, isolated Londoner would do, they nevertheless have their own information economy. They fill their times and minds with gossip instead of news, and gossip takes on a life of its own to rapidly establish consensus among community members regardless of whether it is true.

Fielding asserts that even the educated elite are not immune to the force of such "universal" opinions in a local community. Mr. Allworthy's understanding and superior social position appear to make him immune to the contagious effects of "general opinion;" his general character is so well known that "scandal . . . never found any access to his table." Indeed, the story of Partridge's intrigue with Jenny Jones and his supposed paternity over Tom Jones never reaches Mr. Allworthy's ears, making him "the only person in the country who had never heard of it" (*TJ*, 84). What happens in the community and what happens within Paradise Hall appear distinct from each other in ways that seem to signify the supposed distance between the "general opinion" of the mob and the mature judgment of the charitable and benevolent squire. Nevertheless, readers find that Mr. Allworthy ends up consenting with the "general opinion" regarding Partridge by unquestioningly accepting Captain Blifil's account. Though Mr. Allworthy does not participate in the gossiping activities of the general public, he is still part of the old, country community, and he often fails to make impartial and independent judgments. He relies on Captain Blifil's account to condemn Partridge, just as he takes Blifil junior's word regarding the conduct of Tom Jones. Having lived with these characters in the same house, and having spent time with them, Allworthy finds no reason to doubt their veracity or to put their testimony through the test of circumstantial evidence. He relies on the information provided by those whom he trusts and those who are familiar to him, so that consensus emerges from a relational context—not a context based on time and space as neutral media.

The novel demonstrates the far-reaching effects of communal opinions and suggests that the dangers of "universal opinion" extend beyond small communities to include participants in the emerging print culture. In the figure of Partridge, Fielding represents a participant in modern print culture—a modern subject who is on the move and relies on texts for a sense of community, even as he continues to embrace a local, communal mindset. He reads not as an objective, rational reader, but as an extension of local gossip-mongering. Partridge, who is wrongfully accused of being the father of Jones in Book Two of the novel, is stripped of his annuity and is eventually forced to flee the country. In his own account, he has moved restlessly from one place to another until he meets Jones resting at an inn until healed of a broken head. Partridge expresses great affection for Jones and decides to accompany him on his quest. But, as the narrator takes care to insinuate, Partridge is not entirely motivated by affection. He is motivated primarily by selfish considerations, the foremost of which is to be "again restored to his native country; a restoration which Ulysses himself never wished more heartily than poor Partridge" (*TJ*, 370). Though Partridge does not take refuge in London as many of his contemporary exiles might have done, he does rely on the same sources of consolation and companionship as the Londoners that Hunter describes. Partridge owns books to keep him company in his spare hours, including, among a miscellaneous collection of classics, religious texts, and periodicals, a copy of *Robinson Crusoe* (*TJ*, 365). In addition, Partridge reveals during the course of his conversation with Jones that he has maintained contact with those from his native country through letters—a form of writing that became the basis for epistolary novels and that, as Hunter puts it, works "as a personal substitute, a frozen version of presence-in-absence" for writers and readers who have lost "human context."[31] Through letters, Partridge maintains contact with others despite his physical absence from the community, and he is able to share, at least virtually, in its events. Thus, he is able to assert that he "has a great respect for" Tom Jones, a person with whom he has no prior acquaintance, because he knows about "the good nature [Jones] showed to Black George," about which he "received more than one letter." Jones's kindness for Black George made him "beloved by everybody," according to Partridge, and Partridge is able to imagine himself a part of that "everybody" despite his physical absence from the community (*TJ*, 363).

Partridge, in other words, appears to be a modern subject—mobile and literate—but maintains the mindset associated with a parochial community. The opinions and ideas that Partridge expresses throughout his journey with Jones reveals that he, too, probably would have made one of the "Somersetshire mob" had he stayed there. He is not only fond of hearing scandal, gossip, and local news, but is easily misled by what others say. His improbable ghost story, he asserts, is "certainly true" not because there is any convincing evidence, but because "the whole parish will bear witness to it" (*TJ*, 398). It is not difficult to imagine that, had Partridge remained in the comfortable and familiar surroundings of his own neighborhood, he would have blissfully remained ignorant of any truths and continued to believe whatever the neighborhood "universally" agreed upon. Away from the neighborhood and on his own, however, he is forced to articulate his own opinion among others who do not always belong to the same gossiping network. While his speech gains currency among inn keepers and other frequenters of various taverns and kitchens, his opinions—even the ones that appear "universal" in one context—often fall flat upon the ears of Jones and others. Partridge's obliviousness to how his opinions are received by others comically accentuates the difference between what counts as relevant within a small community and what might gain credibility in a broader public.

By juxtaposing Jones and Partridge during their journey, Fielding emphasizes this disjunction between the "general opinion" of a local gossiping community and the kind of consensus and mutual understanding that make the print public sphere viable. While Jones is able to converse with others such as the Man of the Hill, the king of gypsies, and young Nightingale regarding general concepts like friendship, social justice, and honor, Partridge is mired in the details of gossip that mainly contribute to what the narrator ironically refers to as "general" or "universal" opinion. Jones, in other words, reminds us of what it meant to belong to an educated class of readers, who can carry on conversation with strangers based on common grounds that include Greek history, Latin texts, logical reasoning, or refined feeling. Partridge, on the other hand, represents a new kind of participant in the expanding print public sphere, whose knowledge is a hodge-podge mixture of book learning and gossip. Indeed, his reading habits are an extension of his penchant for gossip—as both a reader and a gossip, Partridge is like the newsmongers that *The Spectator* critiques, with "a Voracious Appetite, but no Taste." When Partridge intervenes into Jones's conversations with strangers, he also exemplifies how individuals may disrupt conversations in the public sphere by bringing with them biased opinions and ideas rooted in their communal origins. Thus, Partridge's encounter with Jones reveals the limits of sustaining communal consensus in a mobile world.

More important, Partridge's perspective—rooted in his communal origins while participating in a wider public—makes him a bad reader of Tom Jones's story, especially since he does not have the advantage of a narrator to mediate his understanding of the narrative. Partridge imagines himself still a part of the familiar community back in Somersetshire, and thus imagines that he knows the story and motive behind Jones's solitary journey away from home. But his encounter with Jones exposes how his knowledge is based on false assumptions and other misunderstandings. Because Jones's account of his expulsion from Paradise Hall does not add up according to his assumptions, Partridge concludes that "the whole [of Jones's narrative] was a fiction" and that Jones "had in reality run away from his father" (*TJ*, 370). The events do not add up in Partridge's mind because he assumes that Jones is Mr. Allworthy's son. This assumption is nurtured through communal consensus as well as his own experience and misconception. Partridge assumes that "Allworthy had sacrificed him to his own reputation" because "knowing himself to be innocent, [he] could not conceive that any other should think him guilty" (*TJ*, 370). Prior to Partridge's personal experience, however, the community had already deemed Mr. Allworthy guilty of being the child's father. Shortly after Jenny Jones confessed to Mr. Allworthy that she is the mother of the foundling child, another rumor spreads in the neighborhood implicating Allworthy himself: "a whisper soon went abroad that he himself was the father of the foundling child." According to the narrator, this rumor was found so plausible and so convincing—it "so well reconciled his conduct to the general opinion"—that "it met with universal assent" (*TJ*, 51). The irony, of course, is that such rumors can gain "universal assent" without necessarily being true, as the narrator makes explicit in the following paragraph. Thus, Fielding projects onto the character of Partridge the characteristics of a modern reader whose communal mind-set and reading habits prevent an accurate understanding of his narrative.

In a world populated with readers who resemble Partridge, Fielding must not only establish time as a neutral medium to defend the commercial disinterestedness of his narrative but also negotiate shared understanding among readers of various communal allegiances and backgrounds. Hunter argues that "by the mid-eighteenth century, we can see novelists bidding to be a substitute for communality," sometimes by pretending that "they are tellers going over the story with readers in the process of reading."[32] But what does it take to create a sense of community through storytelling, especially when readers bring with them various habits of mind, rules of conduct, and models of interpretation and consensus-making based on their own local communities? As I have argued, Fielding is far from optimistic that the mediating powers of print will necessarily resolve this problem that faces modern authors and readers. Neither is he willing to simply ignore the issue, thus pretending that he possesses a coherent readership. Like the travelers who happen to share a stagecoach, readers of Fielding's novel form a "community" only accidentally and may not share tastes or customs or knowledge—very much like Jones and Partridge who have very little in common. The tension between Jones and Partridge is thus a synecdochic rendition of the tension characterizing print culture: the text's ability to make meaning and create consensus is undermined by the way readers will interpret a text differently based on their social, economic, and educational background as well as their habits of mind established and nurtured in local communities.

Imagining Audience

The narrator of *Tom Jones* famously claims absolute authority over his readers stating that "I am, in reality, the founder of a new province of writing, so I am at liberty to make what laws I please therein. And these laws, my readers, whom I consider as my subjects, are bound to believe in and to obey" (*TJ*, 68). But readers like Partridge—those who get mired in specific pieces of information rather than the big picture and cannot understand the relationship between form and content—threaten to undermine such laws by unwittingly misreading the novel. Despite his own assertion, the narrator of *Tom Jones* does not so much resemble an absolute monarch who tyrannizes over his readers and imposes whatever law he pleases as he does a legislator—or an "administrator," to use Ermarth's term—whose authority is circumscribed by constitutions and contracts; the narrator negotiates rather than assumes the reader's consent and understanding. Indeed, his contradictory metaphors of authority and authorship throughout the novel alert us to the problems of assuming that representations necessarily create certain effects, whether that effect be sympathy, laughter, or indignation. For Fielding, the author has dominion over his representations but not over his readers, who may be skeptical or naive, discriminating or not.[33] No matter how consciously the author tries to create fictional representations that aim at producing certain effects, it is ultimately up to the reader to perceive and to feel those effects.

The narrator manifests this problem using a concrete example when he imagines his own readers as audiences attending a play, who display diverse reactions to a specific scene. He puts a face on an otherwise faceless mass of readers by imagining them as similar to theatrical audiences who witness the scene in which Black George steals Jones's bank bills:

> Those who sat in the world's upper gallery treated that incident, I am well convinced, with their usual vociferation; and every term of scurrilous reproach was most probably vented on that occasion.
>
> If we had descended to the next order of spectators, we should have found an equal degree of abhorrence, though less of noise and scurrility; . . .
>
> The pit, as usual, was no doubt divided: those who delight in heroic virtue and perfect character objected to the producing such instances of villainy, without punishing them very severely for the sake of example. Some of the author's friends cried, 'Look'ee, gentlemen, the man is a villain, but it is nature for all that.' And all the young critics of the age, the clerks, apprentices, &c., called it low, and fell a groaning.
>
> As for the boxes, they behaved with their accustomed politeness. Most of them were attending to something else. Some of those few who regarded the scene at all, declared he was a bad kind of man; while others refused to give their opinion till they had heard that of the best judges. (*TJ*, 285)

The narrator thus presents potential readers in different classes and categories depending on where they might be seated in a theater. Such categorization suggests, on the one hand, that it is possible to anticipate the audience's response by analyzing their social and economic class, habits, and degree of learning. But by dividing the audience into separate categories, the narrator also reveals the difficulty of creating a consensus among them. If readers are like a theatrical audience, and if their response to what they read is preconditioned by their place in society, it seems difficult to envision a coherent image of a single implied reader by consolidating such a wide variety of possible responses.

Fielding's concern about the wide variety of potential readers and their diverse opinions echoes contemporary thinkers' dilemma about the coherence of society in general, rooted in the problem of how men and women can hold diverse and incompatible opinions. In his discussion of the idea of "common sense," for example, Shaftsbury emphasizes how there is no such thing as "common sense" that one can refer to as the standard opinion of society as a whole. He refers to a statement made by a gentleman with whom he was in company to demonstrate the problem of defining "common sense":

> "If, by the word 'sense,' we were to understand opinion and judgment and, by the word 'common,' the generality or any considerable part of mankind, it would be hard," he said, "to discover where the subject of common sense could lie. For that which was according to the sense of one part of mankind was against the sense of another. And if the majority were to determine common sense, it would change as often as men changed. That which was according to common sense today would be the contrary tomorrow, or soon after."[34]

It is difficult to identify a single, unitary public opinion if one considers the constitution of the public. The public is not only a gathering of a wide variety of men and women of different classes and origins, but also a fluctuating mass that never stays steady. For Shaftsbury, then, the public is not brought together by an agreement in opinion, but by a feeling of kindliness and sociability that enables the sharing of opinion in the first place. He claims that "if anything be natural in any creature or any kind, it is that which is preservative of the kind itself and conducing to its welfare and support." Shaftsbury's idea of common sense draws attention not to a particular set of opinions, but to the sense of society as a whole. It is in the interests of members of society to maintain such sense of community for the sake of "the pleasure found in social entertainment, language and discourse," in addition to the benefits of a stable society based on "good correspondency and union."[35] Shaftsbury assumes that the good of society as a whole is in everyone's interest, an interest that can be upheld despite the diversity of people and their opinions.

If Shaftsbury envisions society as a unit held together by mutual goodwill despite a diverse population with various opinions, David Hume later presents a much more specific theory about how such a society is held together by more than just goodwill in "Of the Original Contract." Like Shaftsbury, Hume acknowledges the diversity of people and opinions, but he claims that the force of history brings them together. Because humans do not change generations all at once like "silk-worms and butter-flies," they cannot establish a society "without regard to the laws or precedents, which prevailed among their ancestors." On the contrary, "as human society is in perpetual flux, one man every hour going out of the world, another coming into it, it is necessary, in order to preserve stability in government, that the new brood should conform themselves to the established constitution, and nearly follow the path of their fathers."[36] This "established constitution" provides a guideline that enables a stable government and unified society without relying solely on the volition of its inhabitants. Whereas Shaftsbury's theory of sociability relies on individuals to exert their powers of assessing what is or is not beneficial to society as a whole, Hume's theory of historical precedents obviates the problem of relying on individual judgment by substituting "established constitution" for individual goodwill.

Shaftsbury and Hume both argue that unity can be achieved in society despite diversity, but how might such theories help us consider the dilemma of accommodating diverse readers that Fielding imagines? Hume gives us insight into how his theory of social unity might apply to literary representation when he discusses why people disagree in their assessment of writing and other works of art in "Of the Standard of Taste." Just as Fielding identifies his readers as variously scurrilous, insightful, inattentive, or partisan, Hume admits how difficult it is to control an individual's response in matters of taste. Even if the writer or artist produces a work that is generally considered pleasing, "we must not imagine, that, on every occasion, the feelings of men will be conformable to these rules." Representation, or the work itself, must be considered distinct to some degree from its reception, because the "finer emotions of the mind are of a very tender and delicate nature, and require the concurrence of many favourable circumstances to make them play with facility and exactness, according to their general and established principles."[37] For Hume, the reader or viewer occupies his or her particular context in ways that impact their perception of a work of art. Although nature dictates the relationship between "form and sentiment," or representation and reception, that relationship is often obscured because of the less-than-ideal state of the audience's fancy as well as "all the caprices of mode and fashion, all the mistakes of ignorance and envy." Hume believes that it is possible to account for the unreliability of reception by increasing the range of data and minimizing statistical irregularities. When works are "examined by posterity or by foreigners" who do not necessarily share the same cultural, political, or religious values with the culture in which those works were initially received, it becomes possible to assess what is "durable or general" as opposed to what is merely "a temporary vogue." By studying works that have gained "durable admiration," Hume argues that it is possible to extract "certain general principles of approbation or blame." In principle, then, one might produce pleasing works of art by adopting "particular forms or qualities" that are "calculated to please" and assume that "if they fail of their effect in any particular instance, it is from some apparent defect of imperfection in the organ" of the perceiver.[38] Hume characterizes taste as a universal principle so that the force of "universal beauty" is obscured only by biases particular to small social circles. Hume's theory of taste thus helps to underscore why Partridge is a problematic reader: as a gossip-monger, he subscribes to matters of "temporary vogue" within a small community even as he participates in a broader public where discourse is based on "general principles."

The logical steps that Hume takes to identify such "general principles," however, render his idea of universal beauty dangerously similar to "established constitutions" that are based only on "precedents." A truly universal standard of taste may exist in theory according to Hume, but even he admits that it is difficult to judge "universal beauty," since without ideal conditions that are impossible to obtain, "our experiment will be fallacious."[39] Hence, one can only identify "general principles" by studying works of art that have maintained public approbation in different ages and in different cultures. Hume does not mention the likelihood that men may "conform" their taste to approved standards of art in the same way that they "conform" to the "established constitution" of society except by arguing that they may improve the delicacy of taste through "practice."[40] However, such practice also opens up the possibility that the mind will become accustomed to the objects of beauty presented to them. Such is the force of "custom," which "has two *original* effects on the mind, in bestowing a *facility* in the performance of any action or the conception of any object; and afterwards a *tendency or inclination* towards it."[41] When a person becomes accustomed to something through sheer force of repetition, Hume argues, that object or action will become familiar enough to eventually be pleasing and desirable. While "universal beauty" presents what appears to be a stable aesthetic standard, the unstable alternative implicit in his theory provides us with a way of thinking about how a literary work might establish a certain degree of shared understanding among diverse readers through the force of repetition and custom.

Customary Forms

To counter the problems of the diversity of readers in modern print culture, Fielding builds upon the workings of what Hume calls custom and attempts to present his narrative in a way that is familiar and reassuring to his readers. Fielding puts effort into helping his readers experience "facility" in "the conception of" his narrative. This is made clear, for example, in the discussion that precedes his introduction of Sophia. Prior to his introduction of Sophia, the narrator discusses what appears to be a "universal principle" that helps to "prepare the mind of the reader" for the "reception" of certain characters. "Thus," the narrator explains, "the hero is always introduced with a flourish of drums and trumpets," and "when lovers are coming forth, soft music often conducts them on the stage." These auditory introductions help to prepare the audience and put them into the right mindset by "[rousing] a martial spirit in the audience" to greet the hero or by "[soothing] the audience with the softness of the tender passion" in the case of the lovers (*TJ*, 132). The same principle applies to visual representation, so that the hero or king is always preceded by numerous attendants on to the stage in dramatic representations. It is for this very same reason, the narrator claims, that he shall introduce Sophia with a sublime style of writing that is reminiscent of the way an ancient text may invoke a deity in order to "introduce our heroine with the utmost solemnity in our power, with an elevation of style, and all other circumstances proper to raise the veneration of our reader" (*TJ*, 133). Thus, while Fielding may not be able to ensure that readers will experience positive "inclination" towards his work, he does his utmost to enable "facility" in "the conception of" his narrative. While readers may not agree in their judgment of the character or action within the narrative, Fielding mobilizes customary forms to nudge readers towards a consensus about what is being represented and how.

Throughout the novel, the narrator raises and engages reader expectation by invoking existing literary conventions. At times, the narrator adopts rhetorical models that readers can identify through precedents, such as when he adopts the rhetoric and style of mock-epic when describing the great battle between Molly Seagrim and the villagers in the churchyard, or the amorous battle between Jones and Mrs. Waters over the dinner table at the inn at Upton. At times, the narrator demonstrates his awareness of how readers build their expectations through familiar plots; for readers who are familiar with tragic drama, it seems as though nothing "remains to complete the tragedy but a murder or two and a few moral sentences" at the beginning of book seventeen (*TJ*, 772). In the same chapter, the narrator also explains that his readers must not expect to see the conventions of Greek mythology or oriental romance in his narrative, since his modern production cannot utilize supernatural elements in the same way. Whether by simply adopting narrative conventions or making distinctions from them, the narrator constantly provides clues and markers that indicate to readers what they can expect as they continue to read the narrative.

But, as Partridge again exemplifies, such literary conventions failed to engage readers whose reading habits and education limit their ability to understand such narrative cues. This becomes evident in the scene where Jones takes Partridge, along with Mrs. Miller and her younger daughter, to the theater to see a production of *Hamlet* featuring Garrick. This scene, perhaps most famous for highlighting the effects of Garrick's acting performance on Partridge, also underscores Partridge's inability to pick up on narrative—or theatrical—cues and conventions that are meant to facilitate his understanding of the play.[42] Jones expects Partridge to display reactions to the play that obey "the simple dictates of nature, unimproved, indeed, but likewise unadulterated, by art" (*TJ*, 751). This very lack of "art" makes Partridge mirror the emotions exhibited by Garrick's Hamlet on stage, but without fully understanding the context of such emotions. Lacking prior knowledge of Shakespeare's play, Partridge refuses to acknowledge that the man in armor represents the ghost of King Hamlet, arguing that "ghosts don't appear in such dresses as that" (*TJ*, 752), thus using existing assumptions he holds external to the text to judge its representations. The "number of skulls thrown upon the stage" surprises him without cluing him into the fact that these skulls help to represent the graveyard, and "he did not at first understand" the idea of a play within a play (*TJ*, 754, 753). The representations repeatedly confuse Partridge because he judges them against his own assumptions, and it is not until Jones explains what these theatrical devices mean that Partridge is able to "enter into the spirit" of the play (*TJ*, 754).

The theater scene also suggests the possibility for a different kind of engagement with narrative. While Partridge often misunderstands the play or misses the point of the representations (such as when he denies Garrick credit for his acting performance), he is an integral member of the temporary community of theatergoers who attend the play on that particular occasion. Far from having limited access to a community of theater aficionados, Partridge adds another layer to the communal experience of watching the play by providing entertainment for his companions off stage. He constantly gives rise to laughter through his exaggerated reactions and self-corrects his understanding by seeing others' responses. Thus, he is able to allay his fear of the ghost by stating that "I know it is only a play: and besides, if there was anything in all this, Madam Miller would not laugh so" (*TJ*, 753). Partridge "afforded great mirth" not only to his own companions, Mrs. Miller and Jones, but "to all who sat within hearing, who were more attentive to what he said, than to anything that passed on the stage" (*TJ*, 755). Instead of being marginalized for his lack of understanding and appreciation of the performance, Partridge inhabits and enlivens a space parallel to the stage where the audience members exchange pleasantries, responses, and laughter in ways that create a sense of temporary community that exists in relationship to—but is not contingent on a full understanding of—the play being performed.

Hence, even as Fielding employs literary conventions to facilitate readers' conception of his narrative, he also relies on various popular "customs" and situations that stem more from interactions in a commercial society, with the theater providing one such example. Returning to his preamble prior to introducing Sophia, he mixes literary and non-literary references so that classical texts are not the only models he employs to heighten readers' expectation of what is to come. For instance, "that awful magistrate my Lord Mayor," he imagines, "contracts a good deal of that reverence which attends him through the year, by the several pageants which precede his pomp" (*TJ*, 133). Piling example upon example, Fielding also invokes the "custom of sending on a basket-woman, who is to precede the pomp at a coronation, and to strew the stage with flowers, before the great personages being their procession" (*TJ,* 133). While admitting that the ancients will "certainly have invoked the goddess Flora for this purpose," Fielding gives his readers the liberty of choosing which metaphor they will subscribe to: "those who object to the heathen theology, may, if they please, change our goddess into the above-mentioned basket-woman" (*TJ,* 133).

Throughout the novel, the narrator raises and engages reader expectation by invoking conventions, literary and non-literary, ancient and modern, high and low. Such mixed use of various conventions and references mark out Fielding as a writer who was intensely conscious of the anonymous, mixed audience he was addressing through print.[43] Rather than adopt a classical model to embrace and imitate in a unified manner, Fielding uses both ancient and modern models, classical and current references, and anything else that had the chance to appeal to the reader's experience, knowledge, or fancy. Epic invocations and the basket-woman provide equally valid strategies for raising audience expectations that Fielding can appropriate for the readers of his novel. Using customary forms not only from literary predecessors but also from his culture and society at large, Fielding strives to make his narrative principles accessible to readers despite their various social, cultural, and communal backgrounds.

In doing so, Fielding highlights the possibility of imagining community through commercial spaces, such as the ordinary and the theater, in which diverse groups of people come together for a common purpose. On the one hand, such spaces show how a crowd gathered together with the same aim may nevertheless exhibit very different reactions; some will commend a play while others condemn it, and some will demand boiled beef while others will put up with nothing but mutton chops. On the other hand, such metaphors also help to show how these diverse reactions can be anticipated and controlled through the use of "formal" conventions. The public ordinary displays a "bill of fare" before the meal to prevent diners from disappointment and creates room to accommodate the different tastes and preferences of diners. The theater offers various sections for seating audiences with different rates for entry; while this arrangement distributes audiences according to their economic capacities, it also creates a single space that audiences of different classes and tastes can share, even as they display dramatically different reactions to the same scene. The narrator uses these and analogous conventions to help fold into his narrative the reactions of various readers. Thus, Fielding attempts to give readers access to a sense of print-based community—a community that brings readers together while allowing for their divergent tastes and opinions—by theorizing how communities might be revived, at least temporarily, through modern commercial institutions.

Accessing Community

It is no accident that Mr. Allworthy discovers the truth about Jones away from the influence of his familiar community back in Paradise Hall and in a new environment that forces him to encounter familiar stories in a new light.[44] The London lodging house of Mrs. Miller becomes an important gathering space towards the end of the novel—a space that ultimately stages the novel's dénouement. Unlike the neighborhood of Paradise Hall where neighbors and family members are brought together through spatial proximity and habitual interactions, Mrs. Miller's lodging house is not a place that necessarily produces "universal" opinions. This temporary community established within the commercial space of a lodging house is held together by something else; sharing the same space at the same time, visitors are physically brought together to experience shared space and time and they all have (or come to have) a common interest in the fate of Tom Jones. Furthermore, visitors are subject to a different authority; they must observe the basic social formalities of the lodging house and cannot conduct themselves in their usual, habitual manner. Not only does Mrs. Miller herself act as mediator between Jones and Allworthy, between Jones and Sophia, her house becomes the nexus of communication between otherwise unrelated characters. Taking his station in the dining room of the house, Allworthy meets with a series of visitors—ranging from Partridge and Mrs. Waters to young Nightingale and the lawyer, Dowling. One after another, these characters come to visit him and reveal the real story behind Jones's dismissal, adventures, and birth. Even the letters of Square and Thwackum reach him there, confirming Allworthy's sentiments in favor of Jones. Jones becomes the object of common interest in these rapidly succeeding scenes. And though the interest he attracts varies from one character to another—from love, pity, and sympathy to envy, jealousy, and hatred—Jones nevertheless becomes the center of attention and thus helps to create a temporary community of people who share the same concern in a space where no community existed before. Indeed, this new community is made central to the novel's concluding scenes; characters of various social classes, origins, and occupational interests repeatedly share the same dining table, and ultimately end up living, happily ever after, in the neighborhood of Paradise Hall.

By comparing the space of his narrative to a stagecoach journey where readers and narrators form a temporary community, Fielding belies conventional ideas about what makes stories "realistic." Fielding is not exclusively concerned about providing accessible representations to the people and places seen through the carriage windows or to create a shared understanding among his readers/passengers—in short, he does not insist upon the objectivity of his representations. Rather, the stagecoach itself is an important space in which he negotiates interactions between writers and readers. While his contemporaries debated the nature of the emerging print public sphere that opened up unprecedented possibilities for virtual interactions between men and women of the early eighteenth century, Fielding envisions a more inclusive alternative that accommodates the different reactions of individuals. Like the interior of a stagecoach, his introductory chapters assume the presence of a mixed audience and works as a space that nevertheless helps to connect them to each other by observing each other's divergent responses. Like the gallery in which Jones and Mrs. Miller are seated alongside Partridge who displays comical misreadings of the play, Fielding's introductory chapters are separate from the narrative space but adjacent to it.

Fielding defines and identifies new communal spaces within commercial venues—like Mrs. Miller's lodging house within the narrative or the stagecoach and ordinary to which he refers in his introductory chapters—to make visible the mediating work of his novel. While Laurence Sterne and Tobias Smollett will later call into question the novel's mediating potential by showing how texts circulate along with bodies and things, Fielding theorizes the novel's mediating work as a question of communal meaning-making. His novel, for Fielding, is analogous to real commercial spaces that bring people together for specific occasions—thus creating shared interest among a community of readers, albeit only temporarily. Fielding strives to make his novel accessible to readers, not so much by relying on a formal realism that assumes that time is a neutral medium, but by mobilizing various social and spatial forms that are customary in readers' everyday experience to guide their entry into his narrative. Mobilizing everything from physical spaces like the interior of stagecoaches to social conventions like the Lord Mayor's parade, Fielding makes use of various familiar forms. Unlike newspapers and other media that fill readers' time with false substance without bringing readers together into a shared community, he argues, his novel gives readers access to a community that is just as real as that which they experience when they step into a stagecoach; while their subjective reactions may differ, they share the same time and space, hear the same conversation, and are bound to observe the same basic social formalities. By thus reaching out to readers, he expects that he and his readers can "behave to one another like fellow-travellers in a stage coach, who have passed several days in the company of each other; and who, notwithstanding any bickerings or little animosities which may have occurred on the road, generally make all up at last" (*TJ*, 808).

2

Noisy Vehicles and Oversensitive Readers

Miscommunicating Feeling in Sterne's *A Sentimental Journey* and Smollett's *Humphry Clinker*

In the mid-eighteenth-century culture of sentiment, vehicles feature prominently as a media metaphor as writers speculate how feelings can be conveyed through various channels including the nervous system, commercial circulation, letters, and printed texts. This chapter explores how vehicles emerge as an important transport metaphor that helped sentimental fiction conceptualize affective communication in an expanding commercial society that jumbled together bodies, things, and texts in the course of circulation. This transport metaphor is grounded in a medical discourse that considered the human body as a vehicle for the soul that is imperfect, permeable, and subject to the effects of commercial circulation. Conceptualizing mediation through vehicular metaphors, sentimental fiction grapples with the predicament of readers who have limited access to real feelings represented in texts; Laurence Sterne presents Yorick in *A Sentimental Journey* (1768) as a case in point of how oversensitive readers might respond to the problems of affective communication. Rather than insisting that readers experience perfect sympathy in response to sentimental vignettes, sentimental novels engage the dilemmas of affective communication in a commercial society by representing how affect can be interrupted and rerouted in the process of communication, both face-to-face and in mediated form. Sentimental novels stage these interruptions to affective communication within the pages of the printed text by emphasizing their status as media. In doing so, they also open up an alternative model of reading that creates a feedback loop between text and material reality, where the novel validates—and even invites—a distracted model of reading that prompts readers to seek their own sentimental adventures by hopping onto stagecoaches rather than remaining in their own armchairs to immerse themselves in a virtual, fictional reality.

A strange, frustrating, and quirky set of anomalous novels that sprung up in the mid- to late eighteenth century, sentimental fiction seems to promise readers access to real feeling, but only if readers have the patience to wade through numerous digressions and other obstacles. Because of these characteristics, genealogical accounts of the novel's rise frequently leave out novels of sentiment, leaving the analysis of this popular mid-eighteenth-century genre to its own body of criticism on the culture of sensibility or novels of sentiment.[1] Even within this genre-specific discussion, critics have traditionally found it difficult to reconcile the popularity of sentimental fiction with the frustrating reading experience it imposes, particularly because sentimental fiction continually undermines its own message. While numerous critics have emphasized the utopian potential of sentimental discourse that promises a communal sharing of affect, others have equally urged the need to recognize the solipsistic self-absorption of sensibility.[2] If the former view of sentimental fiction highlights the possibility of fiction bringing readers together through sentimental representations, the latter underscores the comical—even satirical—effect of sentimental vignettes.

Nevertheless, both of these accounts implicitly subscribe to assumptions about reading put forth by Ian Watt's influential account of formal realism—that people read novels because they want to see a pleasing simulation of an individual's experience in a particular time and place, so that they can understand modern selfhood in relationship to a virtual society.[3] That is, critics have often determined the value of sentimental fiction by considering the genre's success in or failure to provide access to real feelings of characters that resemble real people. As I will argue, such a model of reading assumes a stable idea of self—one that stems from John Locke's foundational theory of possessive individualism. But sentimental fiction exposes the instability implicit in Locke's perceptive psychology by focusing on the slipperiness of affect as it travels through various communicative channels. This focus on mediation creates disruptions and ambiguities in sentimental narratives that often draw the reader's attention away from the mimetic illusion and prevent easy conclusions about how fictional protagonists relate to and evolve in society. The most recent critical interventions attempt to synthesize this long-standing debate over the communicative potential of sentiment by emphasizing how novels of sentiment as well as works of moral philosophy theorize mediation.[4] These accounts of mediation in the eighteenth century show clearly why sentimental fiction is so self-reflexive. They also underscore the unique concerns that distinguish sentimental fiction from other novels—to trace emotion is to think about mediation, and to think about mediation is to look beyond mimetic representation to consider the continuity between different mediums from the material to the textual.

Thus, novels of sentiment explicitly theorize what it means to communicate in what Deidre Lynch has called the "world of moving goods"—a culture where commerce increasingly defined the relationships between people and things.[5] These moments of theorizing become most apparent in the way these texts mobilize vehicles, both literal and figurative.[6] From transportation carriages to texts as conveyors of feeling, to focus on vehicles both as thing and idea in mid-eighteenth-century discourse is to explore the tensions between self and other, messages and mediums, spiritual and material communications—the tensions, in short, that characterize novels of sentiment in the eighteenth century. Such tensions surface in novels of sentiment not because characters have feelings, but because they feel compelled to share them, and often fail to do so. Laurence Sterne's *A Sentimental Journey* (1768) exemplifies the problems of communication in such a world, as Yorick seeks to share feelings with others, only to have his attempts undermined by the mediated condition of his existence. More skeptically, Tobias Smollett takes such mediation for granted in *The Expedition of Humphry Clinker* (1771). In contrast with critics who read sentimental fiction's self-consciousness as a sign of the novel's mediating potential, I argue that narrative disruptions and distortions in sentimental fiction gesture towards a historically specific model of reading that encouraged readers to look beyond the immediacy of feeling to revisit the material reality that informs it. By detailing the numerous obstacles to face-to-face communication, sentimental fiction also calls into question the even more mediated act of textual communication. Rather than immersing readers in a cohesive virtual reality, sentimental fiction forces readers back into the "world of moving goods," only to discover or produce further texts. Thus, sentimental fiction promotes a feedback loop between text and material reality that goes against the grain of novelistic realism.

NOISY VEHICLES AND OVERSENSITIVE READERS · 57

The Vehicular State

In the culminating chapters of *The Light of Nature Pursued* (1768), Abraham Tucker speculates on the fate of the human soul after death.[7] He hypothesizes that the human body comes pre-equipped with a built-in escape hatch for the soul, a vehicle so small that it is invisible to the naked eye. This vehicle carries the human spirit away from the corporeal body into the world of spirits, where they can communicate without words. In a chapter titled "The Vision," Tucker presents a dream vision in which his avatar, Ned Search, enters "the vehicular state." Ned, or rather his soul encased in a tiny vehicle, encounters the soul of John Locke (also in his vehicle) who explains that spirits have a peculiar way of communicating with one another:

> we have another language among us we call the Sentient, in distinction from the Vocal. . . . This is carried on by applying our vehicles close to one another and raising certain figures or motions on our outsides which communicate the like to our neighbour and thereby excite in him the same ideas that gave rise to them in ourselves, making him as it were feel our thoughts. This is a much completer way of conversing, being not liable to misapprehension provided the recipient takes care to remove all his own ideas that none of them may confound or interfere with those delivered.[8]

The sentient language bypasses the process of vocalization, enabling "a much completer way of conversing" in which communication depends on feeling rather than intellect. Tucker envisions spiritual communication by eliminating the need to articulate words. Ironically, Tucker's hypothesis substitutes motion for sound and the body of the vehicle for the organs of hearing and speaking, so that communication is just as physically mediated as ever.

As outlandish as Tucker's theory of spiritual communication seems, his posthumously published philosophical text articulates one of the central dilemmas of novels of sentiment: the very words and bodies that express feeling can also get in the way. When the eponymous heroine of Mary Hays's *Memoirs of Emma Courtney* (1796) exclaims, "I wish we were in the vehicular state, and that you understood the sentient language; you might then comprehend the whole of what I mean to express, but find too delicate for *words*,"[9] she not only echoes Tucker's desire for absolute communion between souls but also his skepticism towards words. Hays's voluminous epistolary novel nevertheless proceeds to present letters from the heroine, pouring her heart out onto paper using the very words that she distrusts. This impasse appears even more strongly in Hays's predecessor and Tucker's contemporary, Laurence Sterne. For Sterne, it is not just words that get in the way of feeling, but everything from carriages and bodies to the very texts he reads and writes. Like Tucker's philosophical treatise that spends volumes upon volumes describing various communicative barriers before presenting a brief fantasy of spiritual communication, sentimental fiction expends as many—or more—words depicting the frustrating impasses that prevent sympathy as it does describing the communion of souls. And yet, late eighteenth-century men and women avidly continued to read these frustrated texts, as the numerous imitators of sentimental fiction demonstrate.

Despite his central role in Tucker's philosophical fantasy, Locke himself dared not imagine spiritual communication. Locke assumed that spirits "must needs have . . . a perfecter way of communicating their thoughts," but he was content to say that "of immediate communication, having no experiment in ourselves," we can have "no notion . . . at all."[10] Nevertheless, his philosophy laid the groundwork for a work like Tucker's by contributing to the formation of a culture that craves communication and fantasizes its consummation. John Durham Peters identifies Locke as one of the communication theorists responsible for shaping the sense of "communication as we know it"—that is, "to describe the sharing of ideas between people."[11] Peters points out how Locke's ideas about possessive individualism also inform his ideas about communication so that "the individual (and not society, language, or tradition) is the master of meaning."[12] Under conditions where individuals "possess" unique thoughts and feelings, words are but the means—often very insufficient—of sharing them with others.[13] Shackled by the need for language as a medium, but rooted firmly in the belief that language does not do justice to what really lies inside, "common understanding between individuals," according to Peters, becomes "desperately urgent and highly problematic."[14]

If Tucker's hypothesis is symptomatic of a post-Lockean epistemology of communication, it makes more sense why he needs to fantasize unmediated communication—because communication in real life fails to truly give access to the real feelings of others. It also becomes clear why he needs to place the spirit in a "vehicle." One of the main problems that Locke had with spirits is that they supposedly have no bodies. "We have no idea," he writes, "how spirits that have no bodies, can be masters of their own thoughts, and communicate or conceal them at pleasure."[15] Without a body that creates the distinction between inside and outside, self and other, Locke wonders how it is possible for one to "possess" thoughts. For Locke, a physically defined location in which to store one's ideas is the cornerstone of communication in a world of possessive individualism. By placing departed souls in vehicles, Tucker maintains the sacred separation between self and other that is so central to modern humans. At the same time, Tucker's choice of the term "vehicle" indicates a need to minimize the effects of the body that contains the human spirit. James Chandler observes that, in the eighteenth century, the word "vehicle" would more likely invoke the idea of a medium whose existence mattered little except as a carrier of something else.[16] By imagining human souls in vehicles, Tucker places spirits within something that works as a container, but whose materiality disappears into the background to become the neutral means of conveying the human spirit—or so he hopes.

In response to this conundrum, contemporary medical and philosophical treatises characterize the nervous system as the ultimate communicative agent that can capture and convey even the most ethereal sensory impressions. But they also recognize the challenge inherent in the attempt. How can nerves communicate feeling when they do not extend outside the human body? And how can one guarantee that impressions are not distorted or diluted on their way to the mind when nerves are so intricately embedded in the other fibers of the body? The key to answering such questions was in part rhetorical. Numerous writers rely upon figurative language to resolve or disguise these issues. Most famously, George Cheyne describes "the Intelligent Principle, or *Soul*" as residing "somewhere in the Brain, where all the Nerves, or Instruments of Sensation terminate, like a *Musician* in a finely fram'd and well-tun'd Organ-Case; that these Nerves are like *Keys,* which, being struck on or touch'd, convey the Sound and Harmony to this sentient Principle, or *Musician*."[17] Cheyne's metaphor not only illustrates how the nervous system captures sensations and conveys that sensation to the "Intelligent Principle," but also ascribes agency to the human soul that acts as the "Musician" who creates harmony out of what is otherwise a mere material instrument. Cheyne's auditory metaphor resonates widely with the mid-eighteenth-century rhetoric of sensibility so frequently used in novels.

Like the tightly wound strings of a musical instrument, delicate nerves respond to even the most subtle impressions, and, in turn, create laments or harmonies according to the impression. Such is the effect produced when Yorick "touch'd upon the string on which hung all [Maria's] sorrows," and when, after a time, "The string [Yorick] touched ceased to vibrate" and Maria "returned to herself."[18] Such highly strung instruments can synchronize with others by being struck directly with sensory impressions or by reproducing the same wavelength, enabling subjects to sympathize with one another. Thus, David Hume explains that feelings of virtue are communicated among human beings, creating a wave of sympathy in which all synchronize with the movements of others: "As in strings equally wound up, the motion of one communicates itself to the rest; so all the affections readily pass from one person to another, and beget correspondent movements in every human creature."[19]

Cheyne's metaphor of the musician—and its numerous variations—bypasses the problem of the physical barrier between individuals, but the physical embedded-ness of the nervous system remained a medical fact. To further illustrate the relationship between the human body, the mind, and the nervous system, Cheyne presents "a more gross Similitude" immediately after he presents to his readers the metaphor of the Musician. The "Intelligen [sic] Principle is like a Bell in a Steeple," and nerves are like a series of ropes and hammers.[20] The metaphor exposes the passive role of the sensing self, who merely responds to external stimuli provided by "any Body whatsoever." The length of the "ropes" that represent nerves also represents the distance between one's bodily surface and one's mind so that readers are reminded that the bell cannot synchronize with other bells without the intervention of agents who pull the rope and strike the bell with the hammers. In his attempt to describe the "vehicular state," Abraham Tucker expands and elaborates upon Cheyne's "gross" description of the nervous system so that nerves are not represented as a simple rope, but as a "long contrivance of strings and pulleys" that underscores how distant body parts are controlled through a series of mediating instruments. Cheyne, too, is careful to present such interdependence of bodily parts as a medical fact, though his description avoids literally tracing the process of communicating sensory impressions from one body part to another by interweaving figurative and literal names for bodily parts: "solids," such as nerves and other bodily fibers, "are made use of to communicate the Impression they receive from outward Objects, or the muscular Fibres to the *Sensorium* in the Brain, and by it to the sentient Principle or *Musician,* and from it to the Organs."[21]

What is at stake here—both when Cheyne wavers between literal and figurative descriptions of the body, and when Tucker seamlessly transitions from real to fantastical philosophical speculations—is whether sensing and feeling are matters of the body or the mind, and how directly or indirectly the mind communicates with the external world. As the communicative system linking mind and matter, nerves seem to occupy a figurative no-man's land for these writers. Working within the framework of a mechanistic philosophical tradition, particularly the strain inherited from Descartes that considered the physical mechanism of the body as a substance distinct from the more sophisticated mind, Cheyne "take[s] it for granted, that the *intelligent Principle* is of a very different, if not quite contrary, Nature from this organical Machin which contains it."[22] Cheyne's impulse is to associate nerves more directly with the mind, or "the intelligent Principle" as he calls it, because nerves transmit sensations, and sensations, according to Lockean psychology, are the source of ideas.

But Tucker can only imagine the vehicular state as a postmortem phenomenon because he considers the human body as a cumbersome medium that intervenes between the spirit and the outer world. Thus, in his description of the vehicular state, he contends that "the spirit upon quitting her present mansion does not go out naked nor entirely disengaged from matter" so as to maintain a boundary between the outer world and the soul within.[23] Since spirits must not be visible to mortal beings, he supposes that the spirit carries away only a select portion of "matter"—namely, "organs of sensation and reflection and instruments of action" that enable sensory perception without eyes and ears.[24] In other words, Tucker's vehicle consists of a hyper-sensitive bundle of nerves that communicate with the mind more directly than when they were lodged in the human frame. The sentient language that Tucker describes is thus less spiritual and more physical than one might expect: Locke "thrust out a couple of broad arms or rather flappers, something like the tails of Turkey sheep with which he muffled up my head all round as with the hood of a great coat. I knew my business was only to ruminate on all that had passed in my thoughts from my first arrival, for he would feel the ideas as they rose."[25] Tucker's theory builds upon contemporary medical theories to envision transparent access to others' ideas and feelings, but his very knowledge of the human body also prevents him from imagining a system of communication that extends beyond his vehicle. Tucker assumes that the human body contains a complex network that mediates between one's mind and the external world, and that one can become more sensitive by making the process of mediation as direct as possible. Tucker's philosophical fantasy resonates with novels of sentiment because they both represent the individual as the owner of feelings struggling to communicate them effectively. Tucker's idea of the vehicular state highlights, in particular, the problematic role of the body in the culture of sentiment; bodies are necessary for people to own their feelings, but they also undermine the authenticity of those feelings.

Man of Feeling

Tucker imagined spiritual communication as a possibility reserved for the afterlife, but the discourse of sensibility suggested that some individuals could communicate affect in a more refined way than others. Cheyne, among other physicians, considered melancholy, hypochondria, and other disorders as conditions that can and should be cured through diet and exercise, but they also "insist[ed] upon the over-determined nature of the melancholy 'type.'"[26] "Degrees of sensibility," that is, "the ability to transmit 'sense' via vibrations to the brain," explains G. J. Barker-Benfield, "betokened both social and moral status."[27] The expressive bodies so often featured in novels of sentiment echo contemporary understandings of the nervous system—the crucial medium that "transmit[s] 'sense' via vibrations to the brain," and that distinguishes men of sensibility from others. The nervous system seemed to have the ability to transmit sensations within the body almost instantaneously, and in a way that preserves the subtlety of those sensations. As Barker-Benfield catalogues extensively, writers described the way affect travels within and between bodies by figuratively expanding the vocabularies of the nervous system: "nerves" and "fibres" were "braced," "sensations" warmed bodies, and "vibrations" "thrilled" through one's being.[28] As the medium that conveys sense impressions to the mind, nerves promised access to not just sensation, but also feelings.

Throughout *A Sentimental Journey,* Yorick repeatedly asserts that he belongs to this privileged class of men whose sensitive nerves qualify them to take part in sentimental conversations. Alone in the room with the fair *fille de chambre,* for instance, Yorick finds himself exchanging blushes with her: "I thought she blush'd—the idea of it made me blush myself—we were quite alone; and that super-induced a second blush before the first could get off." Here, Yorick expresses sympathy by mirroring the other person's physical manifestation of emotion. Tears should be reciprocated with tears, blushes with blushes, and smiles with smiles. Like the sentient language that Tucker envisions, sentimental bodies seem to communicate feeling by transmitting bodily motions—and consequently emotions. Yorick finds that "there is a sort of a pleasing half guilty blush, where the blood is more in fault than the man—'tis sent impetuous from the heart, and virtue flies after it—not to call it back, but to make the sensation of it more delicious to the nerves—'tis associated—" (*SJ*, 88). Yorick's nerves, according to his self-observation, receive a "delicious" sensation produced through the sequence of causes and effects within his own body. The "man" has no control over his "blood" that "impetuous[ly]" rushes forth to produce the blush. Yorick indulges in the pleasures of feeling with his entire body, even though that feeling originates in an amorphous nowhere between himself and the *fille de chambre*. Yorick's experience thus seems to confirm the amazingly communicative nature of feelings in the eighteenth century as Adela Pinch describes it. Pinch claims that feelings are portrayed during this period "as transpersonal, as autonomous entities that do not always belong to individuals but rather wander extravagantly from one person to another."[29]

Yorick's subsequent reflections, however, make clear that feelings do not just wander between persons, but between persons and things as well. In the *fille de chambre* episode above, for example, Sterne also emphasizes the potentially solipsistic nature of Yorick's conversation with the *fille de chambre*. He makes us wonder whether the exchange of blushes is indeed a conversation. Perhaps the sunlight is shining through the "crimson window curtains," as it "reflect[s] through them so warm a tint into the fair *fille de chambre*'s face" that she merely appears to be blushing. Perhaps it is not the *fille de chambre*'s blush that induces Yorick to blush, but the mere "idea of it" (*SJ*, 88). Nerves played a central role in imagining how sensibility works, but they failed to bridge the physical gap between bodies. G. Gabrielle Starr asserts that "limits of subjectivity appear as limits of sensation, and the letter emerges as an attempt to cross these bounds" in Richardson's epistolary novel, thus identifying letters as a rare medium that allowed people to share feelings across bodies.[30] But Sterne inhabits the space between individuals with more than just letters. Numerous things—lighting, curtains, his own thoughts and reactions—prevent Yorick from registering the actual sentiments of the *fille de chambre*. This sentimental scene does not depict mutual sympathy between the characters. It merely triggers Yorick's self-observation. As a result, we gain insight into the failures of affective communication; they learn how messages pick up noise during the process of transmission. "Noise," as defined by William Paulson, may involve "the interruption of a signal, the pure and simple suppression of elements of a message, or it may be the introduction of elements of an extraneous message." Paulson considers such noise as an integral—rather than random and accidental—part of the message, since it highlights the transmission process and thus helps to define "a system of communication."[31] When Yorick observes how affect wanders and picks up noise along the way, he is observing the communication system that surrounds him to theorize how affect travels promiscuously between people and things in an emerging commercial society.

The series of mediations that occur within his body, then, are not the only cause of Yorick's communicative dilemmas. An earlier scene in the novel shows that physical movement brought about from external objects can also impact the state of one's feelings. At Nampont, Yorick witnesses a sentimental scene in which an old man laments the death of his ass, who shared with him a toilsome pilgrimage to Spain. While the story of the man and his dead ass puts him in a properly sentimental mood, the movement of his carriage, as he drives away from Nampont, agrees little with the movement of his affect. Indignantly, Yorick claims that the postillion will "go on tearing my nerves to pieces till he has worked me into a foolish passion" (*SJ*, 41). And he does. Since nerves are intertwined with other fibers of the body, they feel sensory input, regardless of whether they contribute to one's sentiments. Things and movements of the material world outside of one's body, then, have a way of interfering with how one feels and how one communicates feeling, making interpersonal communication not just an operation of the human nervous system, but also a process intertwined with eighteenth-century practices of economic and physical circulation.[32]

In addition, the human body itself creates just as much noise as the commodities that Yorick consumes. At the door of the Remise, for instance, Yorick is left holding a lady's hand while awaiting M. Dessein. Physical contact conveys Yorick's thoughts to the lady, in a manner reminiscent of Tucker's sentient language: "The pulsations of the arteries along my fingers pressing across hers, told her what was passing within me" (*SJ*, 20). But Yorick repeatedly feels something other than emotion. One feeling that often intrudes upon Yorick is sexual impulses, creating what Christopher Nagle calls "erotosocial" moments.[33] In a manner that echoes the previous scene in which Yorick is unable to let go of Madame de L's hand in front of the Remise, Yorick is left standing with the *fille de chambre*'s hand in his own, immediately after the exchange of blushes that I have discussed earlier. In this chapter, suggestively titled "The Temptation. Paris," direct physical contact does not just contribute to a silent conversation between the parties but leads to an internal battle in which Yorick attempts to overcome desires that manifest in the form of "trembling" in various parts of the body. In Yorick's own account, sentiments arise through a meandering process, mixing themselves with various impurities as they travel through nerves and bloodstreams. Yorick rarely describes feelings per se, so much as he describes how such feelings travel through society and through one's body, registering the noise created in the process.

Thus, even in the most sublime moments of Yorick's sentimental experience, Sterne's rhetoric slyly reveals how Yorick may be experiencing sensations that arise from the noise of culture and from his own body rather than actually communicating with others. It is possible to observe this inability to clearly envision communication as extending beyond one's self when Yorick praises sensibility, the intertwined workings of affect and the nervous system. Yorick imagines sensibility as something that connects him to the world of spirits par excellence—that is, Heaven:

> —Dear sensibility! Source inexhausted of all that's previous in our joys, or costly in our sorrows! Thou chainest thy martyr down upon his bed of straw—and 'tis thou who lifts him up to HEAVEN—eternal fountain of our feelings!—'tis here I trace thee—and this is thy divinity which stirs within me . . . I feel some generous joys and generous cares beyond myself—all comes from thee, great—great SENSORIUM of the world! (*SJ*, 111)

Religious enthusiasm and secular sensibility appear inextricably tied together as Yorick describes the operation of the divinity in terms of "sensibility" and "feeling." The fragmented exclamations joined together by a series of dashes confuse the distinction between divinity and sensibility so that Yorick seems to feel connections with a larger world of spirits within the confines of his own body. The word "SENSORIUM" appears capitalized along with "HEAVEN," making the communication tower within the human mind a typographical counterpart of a larger world of spirits so that "HEAVEN" seems to be the seat of a larger "SENSORIUM" through which we communicate.[34] This passage, which seems to optimistically represent the communicative possibilities of sensibility, ultimately reveals how Yorick conceives spiritual communication through mixed metaphors and various rhetorical manipulations.

We might consider the discourse of nervous sensibility as one that was struggling on the verge of an epistemological threshold: how can one imagine interpersonal communication when the most sophisticated communication system known to humanity was its own nervous system, and when that nervous system did not extend outside individual bodies?[35] Lacking the ability to imagine connections between individual bodies, Adam Smith is quick to point out that "our senses will never inform us" of what others suffer, since our senses "never did, and never can, carry us beyond our own person." Smith's well-known solution to this dilemma is that "imagination" mediates our feelings for others.[36] By delineating the process of sympathetic feeling, Smith underscores the distance between subjects.[37] Despite his attempt to fantasize direct communication, Tucker shares Smith's conundrum. They both argue that it is possible to feel for or with others, and they both attempt to place this action on epistemologically certain grounds. The need to know how feeling makes it from one person to another leads Smith back into the mind of the empirical subject, while Tucker anchors his theory in human physiology. Neither imagination nor nerves, however, truly works to bridge the gap between individuals in separate bodies. While nerves occupy the center of discourse about communicative fantasies, those fantasies offered no speculations about how people might access each other's feelings more directly. Yorick's attempt at sentimental exchange thus exposes the central irony of eighteenth-century communication—the more one pursues unmediated communication, the more one is forced to acknowledge the obstacles that stand in the way. As I will argue in the following sections, this dilemma also impacts the very texts that attempt to transmit feeling between men and women in the age of commerce.

Circulating Letters

Since late eighteenth-century men and women could not enter the vehicular state or imagine a telegraphic transmission of feeling, many trusted letters as the best available means of spiritual communication. Samuel Johnson, for example, exemplifies this trust in the power of letters in his correspondence with Hester Thrale. "A man's letters," he claims, "are only the mirror of his breast, whatever passes within him is shown undisguised in its natural process. Nothing is inverted, nothing distorted, you see systems in their elements, you discover actions in their motives." Johnson even goes so far as to imagine that his correspondence creates a union of souls resembling what Tucker imagined might be possible in the vehicular state: "These are the letters by which souls are united, and by which minds, naturally in unison, move each other, as they are moved themselves."[38] Unlike Emma Courtney who distrusts words even as she invests her feelings into them, Johnson seems to trust entirely to the power of letters to move and to be moved. Johnson's naïve trust in epistolary correspondence echoes that of his contemporary Samuel Richardson, who claims that the familiar letter is able to convey the characters' feelings "in so probable, so natural, so lively a manner, as shall engage the passions of every sensible reader."[39]

But this tells only half of the story of eighteenth-century letters. The conventional story of the novel singles out Richardson as *the* writer who made it possible to imagine the novel as an effective means of conveying and sharing feeling through the use of familiar letters that acted as so many windows into characters' feelings. The epistolary form seems to promise to its readers a direct access pass to the unsullied, innermost, private feelings of the letter writer, presenting, as it were, an ideal vehicle for delivering and developing the characters' interiority. Yet, as Mary Favret points out, the innocence and purity—that is, the (feminine) privacy—of the letter as a medium seems always already scripted into a plot of foretold tragedy. Violation awaits the letter as soon as it ventures out into "the public."[40] Even within the pages of *Pamela,* the heroine's letters are threatened alongside her person as Mr. B attempts to violate his mother's former maid; in Richardson's second novel, the materiality and manipulability of Clarissa's letters become painfully clear as they become the object not only of Lovelace's desire but also of subsequent editing.

As a novel that mocks epistolary form even while employing it to depict a man of feeling, Tobias Smollett's *The Expedition of Humphry Clinker* rarely appears within discussions about how eighteenth-century Britons strove to share their feelings.[41] But precisely because Smollett brings a more cynical and detached perspective to the culture of sentiment, his novel helps to further highlight the conditions and economies of letter writing that made intimate letters subject to violation in the course of public circulation. The novel presents a series of letters written by family members as they share a journey from their Welsh home to the fashionable bathing places of Bristol and Bath, the capitals of London and Edinburgh, as far as the Scottish Highlands and back accompanied by their eponymous servant, Humphry Clinker. For the most part, the letters are addressed to the writers' respective confidants, and include reports of their journey and observations as well as their feelings in response to varying environments and events. Together, these letters present a narrative, or rather several narratives, of Matthew Bramble's restoration to health, of rediscovering family ties and old friends, and of several love affairs. Individually, many of these letters exemplify the condition of individuals who have become "transient[s]," which Lynch describes as "a modern body [that is] unmoored from the traditional corporate identities associated with the Guilds, Church, and Court, and yet, in new ways, meeting as buyers and sellers, colliding as fellow travelers, and thanks to print technology's capacity to bridge geographical and social distances, convening as a 'public.'"[42] If the letters collectively present a glimpse into the nature of the late eighteenth-century "public" that consists of different classes of men and women with varying degrees of education and literacy, the individual letters and their contents suggest that one of the "new ways" in which these transients established their place within a modern commercial economy is by communicating their feelings and sustaining intimacies, despite distance and despite constant movement and dislocation.

In contrast with Yorick who struggles to sustain intimate relationships by insisting a bit too much on the immediacy of feeling, Smollett's characters are content to communicate with their friends in a more mediated manner through the use of letters. Lydia, for example, often laments the absence of her friend, exclaiming "what a miserable situation it is, to be without a friend to whom one can apply for counsel and consolation in distress!"[43] Yet she is still able to entrust much of her feelings to letters. Her correspondence with her schoolfellow Miss Laetitia Willis is of so intimate and private a nature that she is unwilling, at times, to "venture to communicate by the post." But that does not hinder her from making intimate communications. Frequently, she takes the opportunity to entrust private hands with her correspondence, and to "seize it eagerly to disburthen [her] poor heart" (*HC*, 134). Towards the beginning of her journey, she glories in how "absence serves only to heighten and improve" friendship (*HC*, 38). Later on, even when she is tired of perpetually moving about from place to place and longing for the physical presence of her friend, she is able to put faith in the communicative powers of the letter that enables her still to assert, "with you, my dear Willis, I have no secrets" (*HC,* 308).

These letters, however, reveal more than just the characters' thoughts and feelings. They also confirm how letters need to circulate—along with other goods—to reach their destination. The fate of the letter after it leaves the hands of the writer is made unusually clear in Lydia's and Winifred's letters, as readers frequently witness detailed accounts of how they will be sending their letters and what carriers they have entrusted. Winifred's letters frequently begin with the statement that she has the "opportunity" to write and implies that her writing depends not so much upon her need to communicate, but upon the available methods of delivery. Sometimes, the opportunity of writing presents itself when others help cover the cost of correspondence. Winifred relies upon others to be able to send her letter without cost, such as when "Lady Griskin's botler, Mr. Crumb, having got 'squire Barton to frank me a kiver" (*HC,* 107). By having her letter "franked," her letter can travel without costing herself or her correspondent a penny. She also bypasses the cost of correspondence by piggybacking on others' correspondence. Winifred begins her letter of July 18, for example, by explaining that "The 'squire has been so kind as to rap my bit of nonsense under the kiver of his own sheet" (*HC,* 219). For her letter dated October 4, "Miss Liddy" is the member of the family who "is so good as to unclose me in a kiver as fur as Gloster" (*HC,* 306).

Both Winifred and Lydia take advantage of another kind of opportunity when they entrust their correspondence to private hands for delivery. Winifred takes advantage of the "occasion of my cousin Jenkins, of Aberga'ny" not only to send her fellow servant a letter, but also, "as a token, a turkey-shell comb, a kiple of yards of green ribbon, and a sarment upon the nothingness of good works" (*HC,* 155). Lydia also takes advantage of a "private hand" to send "Bath rings," that is, mass-produced souvenir rings with sentimental inscriptions to her schoolfellows (*HC,* 58). Neither does she miss the chance to communicate private matters when she has "the occasion of Jarvis" (*HC,* 25), who is not only a carrier but also the brother of a Gloucester milliner who mediated her affair with her love interest, Wilson. During their stay in Scotland, furthermore, both Lydia and Winifred encounter an opportunity that Lydia describes as "little less than miraculous—Honest Saunders Macawly, the travelling Scotchman, who goes every year to Wales, is now at Glasgow, buying goods" (*HC,* 257–58). The extended network of transport and trade helps these women maintain private correspondence in unexpected ways. Thus, the letters that presumably give readers direct insight into the characters' feelings also expose the very distance between the writer and reader, highlighting not only the material reality of circulation, but also the economic underpinnings of correspondence.[44]

It comes as no surprise, then, that even as the characters of *Humphry Clinker* utilize letters as a substitute for face-to-face communication, the novel refuses to allow readers to maintain the same blissful delusion. Even before readers encounter the characters' correspondence, they are rudely made aware of how these letters are circulating objects when they are informed of the origin and history of publication in the introductory pages that present the correspondence between a London bookseller and the presumed editor, Jonathan Dustwich. In this exchange, the writers consider the letters as a potential commodity on the same level with manuscript sermons, the "Court-kalendar," and "toasted cheese" (*HC,* 3–4). Moreover, though Jonathan Dustwich will not reveal "the manner in which I got possession of these letters" (*HC,* 2), it is made clear that this potential commodity was not produced for the explicit purpose of being marketed. On the contrary, they are "private correspondence of persons still living" (*HC,* 1). The bookseller demonstrates some concern over potential legal action on the part of the writers whose private correspondence has been co-opted for public use, but Dustwich alleviates this concern by assuring him that "the Letters in question were not written and sent under the seal of secrecy," and that, should any legal action take place, he "will take the whole upon [his] own shoulders, even *quoad* fine and imprisonment" (*HC,* 1).

If these letters are any indication, circulation seems to have a way of detaching content from context and rendering public what is private so that it is not just privacy, but also authorial intention that is subject to violation. As Jerome Christensen details when he describes David Hume's complaint against the book trade, those who control the channels of communication—which, in the eighteenth century also happen to be the channels of circulation—can lay just as despotic a claim on texts in transit as an absolute monarch.[45] According to Christensen, David Hume was incensed with his publisher, Andrew Millar, for passing along to a third party what Hume had sent Millar under the guise of private correspondence. Yet, far from attributing any malicious intention to Millar, Christensen argues that his actions were consistent with "a system which does not distinguish between private and public."[46] That system is the system of the London booksellers, who effectively monopolized the book trade by using the infrastructure for product distribution not only to issue communications to provincial booksellers, but also to gather intelligence about them to prevent the sales of pirated material. The booksellers used the most regular, reliable, and centralized method of transport available by "[riding] piggyback on the newsman and the postman,"[47] distributing advertisements through mail and newspapers, receiving orders through the post, and finally fulfilling the orders through the very same channel. Like the post office, the London Conger did not just facilitate circulation of texts; they claimed it as their collective property through a centralized, dominant authority.

Humphry Clinker dramatizes the same disturbing effects of circulation that Hume encountered and places it in a wider context. The fact that letters can transform into novels through the agency of an unknown editor is a disturbing thought. The idea that writers can lose ownership over the text, too, is disturbing. But even more disturbing is the possibility that these texts will mingle with other texts and goods and become obscured by the overwhelming flow of economic circulation. The London bookseller, for instance, considers the collection of letters in the general category of "letters upon travels" that include "Smollett's, Sharp's, Derrick's, Thickness's, Baltimore's and Baretti's, together with Shandy's Sentimental Travels" and is by no means confident of its success because "the public seems to be cloyed with that kind of entertainment" (*HC,* 2–3). If the bookseller's statement makes clear that the text may become obscured by the sheer quantity of available goods within the same category, some passages within Bramble's and Jery's letters raise yet another concern—not merely of quantity, but also of quality. Bramble is incensed by how "every rancorous knave" takes advantage of the liberty of the press so that "the public papers are become the infamous vehicles of the most cruel and perfidious defamation" (*HC,* 102). In a political climate where party allegiances run high, newspapers cannot be relied upon to carry trustworthy information, so that the public is subject to a stream of information that cannot be trusted. Books are no more reliable than newspapers, according to Jery, who joins a party of writers who "were, or had been, understrappers, or journeymen, to more creditable authors, for whom they translated, collated, and compiled, in the business of book-making." The assortment of "originals" that Jery encounters produce texts that are as confused as their conversation, which "resembled the confusion of tongues at Babel" (*HC,* 126). Their personal characteristics are strangely at odds with their literary productions so that the "Scotch-man" tries to publish by subscription "lectures on the English language," while the author of "a treatise on practical agriculture" has a "horror of green fields" and the author who had completed writing "his travels through Europe and part of Asia" managed to do so "without ever budging beyond the liberties of the King's Bench" (*HC,* 127). The text of *Humphry Clinker,* then, circulates amidst a market awash not only with other goods, but also with other goods that may be false, unreliable, counterfeit, or simply lacking quality.[48]

This problem of bloated economic circulation—one that puts into circulation quality goods along with eventual waste that only clogs the system—is represented most forcibly in the odd assortment of letters that constitute the novel of *Humphry Clinker.* Matthew Bramble's critical observations of London appear alongside his sister's self-interested instructions to the housekeeper, and Jery's coherent narrative of the events that befall his fellow travelers is juxtaposed with Winifred's disjointed rambles. The consequence of such odd juxtapositions, as numerous critics have observed, is that the novel seems to marginalize the correspondence of women—those of Winifred Jenkins in particular, who occupies a lower social class and whose orthography reflects her Welsh origins.[49] While the contrast between the letters is often striking, it is also true that these letters—of various quality, insight, and reliability—all circulate within the same system, sometimes even under the same "kiver." Smollett's novel thus replicates in its very form the condition of textual circulation that it describes and poses questions about how men and women can learn to read within a system of commercial circulation that jumbles together texts of various qualities alongside various consumer goods.

Texts as Vehicles

Both Sterne and Smollett demonstrate that sentiment is problematic because it is never as immediate as it seems. Spontaneous affective responses are not transparent windows into feeling—neither are letters that promise access to the writer's innermost sentiments. Both are subject to meandering processes of transmission and pick up noise along the way, because both circulate within the cacophony of a commercial public sphere. This is also true of Yorick's travelogue. On the one hand, novels seemed to move readers by appealing directly to their feelings. Johnson, for example, claims that novels (like letters) possess a "power of example so great as to take possession of the memory by a kind of violence, and produce effects almost without the intervention of the will."[50] On the other hand, novels themselves were products of economic circulation, since they were handed through the hands of editors, printers, carriers, and numerous other agents, as Smollett highlights in his fictionalized framing apparatus. Sterne highlights this tension between the seeming immediacy of novelistic representation and the problematic status of the novel as media by dramatizing how circulation pressures—and distorts—novelistic form. To some extent, the novel seems as if it should resemble Tucker's spiritual vehicle; the novel as a vehicle carries its contents safe and whole to the reader, without interfering with how the text communicates. But Sterne illustrates how the novelistic vehicle is riddled with the problems of noise, just as the human body interferes with spiritual communication.

The sequence in which Yorick discovers "The Fragment," which records the sentimental tale of an anonymous notary, exemplifies Sterne's concern over the fate of texts as material objects. La Fleur brings Yorick a bit of butter on "a currant leaf," but since he was afraid that the butter would melt onto his hands, he "begg'd a sheet of waste paper to put betwixt the currant leaf and his hand." This waste paper provides Yorick with an unexpected source of entertainment: "When I had finish'd the butter," Yorick writes, "I threw the currant leaf out of the window, and was going to do the same by the waste paper—but stopping to read a line first, and that drawing me to a second and third—I thought it better worth; so I shut the window, and drawing a chair up to it, I sat down to read it" (*SJ*, 97). When Yorick first considers throwing the waste paper out the window, he regards the text as just another thing, like the currant leaf; there is no sense that the text contains a message or that it is the vehicle of a sentimental narrative. If it is a vehicle, it is only a temporary container for the butter, and as soon as it completes its purpose, it becomes "waste" again. "The Fragment," like other rescued manuscripts that appear in sentimental fiction, is a mere object amidst a sea of other things that circulate in a commercial society. Like the numerous it-narratives of the eighteenth century with which Sterne's novel shares strong affiliations, "The Fragment" finally finds its voice and reveals the story it has to tell after a life of circulation.[51] What distinguishes it, and what enables it to recover its status as text, is Yorick's ability to be moved by this transient object.

Perhaps such awareness of the materiality of texts helps explain why sentimental fictions—the very genre that presumably sets out with the mission of gaining readers' sympathy—often refuse to disappear into the background as good vehicles should. Not only did Richardson's career famously originate in a letter-writing manual, his epistolary novels become increasingly self-reflexive so that letters are not just transparent windows into heroines' inner feelings; they become letters about letters and letters about how to compile, organize, and edit letters. Henry Mackenzie's *The Man of Feeling* is famously fragmentary, because the curate used parts of the manuscript as gun wadding.[52] And Sterne's *A Sentimental Journey* draws explicit attention to the mediating function of his writing by characterizing his sentimental travelogue as a new kind of "vehicle" (*SJ*, 13). Whereas Johnson emphasizes the powerful, agency-depriving effects that novels have on readers, these sentimental novels insist upon their own powerlessness. Thus, as I have already argued, even as Richardson insists that the epistolary form of his novels gives readers direct access into the characters' mind and heart, his novels constantly remind readers—perhaps unwittingly—that these heart-felt letters are subject to violation as they enter the world of circulation in an attempt to reach their addressees.[53] But such possibilities did not disillusion readers. Instead, Richardson's works, for instance, triggered a cult of reader participation in which readers did not just write about his novels in their own letters, but also abridged, anthologized, compiled, and indexed them. Leah Price speculates that this reader participation stems not only from the sheer volume of the novels, but also "through the surplus of signatures built into the epistolary novels."[54] Rather than belonging to a single author, the names of various editors, compilers, and publishers suggested that these manuscripts are circulating objects that are up for grabs by any discerning or indiscriminate readers who choose to lay their hands upon them—very much like Jonathan Dustwich who appropriates private correspondence to "edit" the text of *Humphry Clinker*.

A Sentimental Journey explicitly acknowledges that letters are not the only things that are up for grabs by readers. The idea that his text will eventually circulate in public puts pressure on Yorick and distorts the narrator's attempt at communication, even as the writer puts his pen to paper. To begin with, the preface is itself a problematic vehicle. In an early chapter titled "Preface In the Desobligeant," Sterne shows Yorick seated within the stationary desobligeant (a single-person carriage) in Monsieur Dessein's coach yard, writing the preface for a journey that has hardly commenced. Using the conventional device of a preface, Yorick addresses his readers in an attempt to interest them in his journey, which he asserts "will be altogether of a different cast from any of my fore-runners" (*SJ*, 13). Yet, his preface begins dispassionately, in a detached, matter of fact manner that is hardly engaging (exemplified in the passive "it" that begins the first two paragraphs of the chapter: "It must have been observed" and "It will always follow" [*SJ*, 11]). While laying claim to the title of a "Sentimental Traveller," Yorick's preface lacks any expression of sentiment or feeling—that is, until the very end of the preface, when the increasingly frequent dashes indicate how Yorick gradually works himself up to a pitch of agitation, finally addressing his readers emphatically: "Where then, my dear countrymen, are you going—" (*SJ*, 14). However, the opportunity for a direct communication from the author/character to his readers fails to develop any further as the writer's mental agitation translates into the physical agitation of the vehicle in which he writes. At this juncture, Yorick's writing itself is interrupted as his "dear countrymen" appear outside the chaise, pulling Yorick and his readers away from the textual space where Yorick presents himself as the author and back into narrative space in which he is a character.

When Sterne turns Yorick's imagined audience into an embodied presence within the narrative, he also literalizes the pressures that the expanding print public sphere puts upon the relationship between writers and readers—and consequently, upon forms of writing that mediate such a relationship. The ease and abruptness with which Yorick turns away from the Englishmen—the very specimen of his presumed audience, his "dear countrymen"—seem to indicate that they are not all that "dear." Yorick does not see that the countrymen he appeals to in his preface and the men who stand before him have a metonymic relationship and are, to some extent, one and the same. Sterne dramatizes the disjunction between the act of addressing a wider public and the act of communicating face-to-face, a disjunction that seems prescribed the moment he chooses to address his readers in a preface. The preface itself is squeezed in awkwardly after the commencement of Yorick's journey so as to underscore the artificiality of the device—a frame that physically precedes the given body of work yet that follows it chronologically because it is usually written after the fact to better orient readers. If the act of presenting a book to a faceless, anonymous mass of readers necessitates a preface, Yorick's failure to write a competent one suggests that the form itself is ill suited for the purpose of his composition. By categorizing different kinds of travelers in a quasi-philosophical manner, Yorick pretends to account for the reasons why Englishmen insist upon engaging in "sentimental commerce" despite the likelihood that they will be more at ease back home. But just as his fellow Englishmen will travel beyond the confines of their own country against all rationality, so too will Yorick stray from the category he has assigned himself by demonstrating the ease with which the "Sentimental Traveller" can become the "Vain Traveller" (*SJ*, 12–13). The pressures of circulation unsettle both people and writing in Sterne's world. A preface may work adequately to present a philosophical system rigidly set in stone, but Yorick's attempt fails to accommodate a genre that captures Englishmen on the move, whimsically diverging from their paths, encountering accidents, and experiencing accidental encounters.

"Preface In the Desobligeant" provides an outlet for neither physical nor emotional movement. Yorick's preface very much resembles the vehicle in which he writes that text; it fails to accommodate the purpose of Yorick's journey/writing. Within the preface, the movements that characterize the "Sentimental Traveller" constantly threaten the boundaries set by the preface as though seeking escape, just as the stationary desobligeant rocks back and forth, creating an odd spectacle in the coach yard. Yorick appears to recognize the need for a space in which to hold human intercourse when he acknowledges that the preface "would have been better . . . in a *Vis a Vis*" (*SJ*, 14). When Yorick turns away from the solitary vehicle and towards one more suitable to face-to-face conversation, he also shifts the grounds of his own writing so that face-to-face encounters, not faceless prefaces that address an anonymous, virtual audience, lie at the heart of his sentimental travelogue.[55] But the initial sequence in which Yorick chooses the wrong vehicle resonates throughout his text as he continues to describe affect gone awry; feelings transform as they travel through his body and sentimental texts become indistinguishable from waste in the course of circulation. For Sterne, face-to-face communication does indeed provide a model for novelistic form—the novel registers through its form the kinds of noise that adulterate sentimental exchange, even in person.

If we return once again to Abraham Tucker and his fantasy of the vehicular state, it becomes possible to identify an underlying purpose for his "vehicle." His desire to achieve direct communication through nerves also demonstrates an implicit need to escape the vagaries of circulation. Yorick, on the other hand, stages his own novel as a vehicle that performs the instability of a literary text in a world of circulation. Sterne confronts the problems of communication in a commercial economy head-on by registering the noise of circulation through form and representation—a task that Smollett also engages in, albeit with a much less naïve attitude. Sterne's textual vehicle and Tucker's fantasy of the vehicular state thus occupy two sides of the same coin; Sterne revels in what Tucker seeks to avoid. Together, they highlight the broad spectrum of things—from physical bodies to textual bodies—that mediate communication in the eighteenth century. Both these texts, then, present an object lesson in what it means to inhabit a world of mediation. It is impossible to distinguish what is and is not mediated, because even the most intimate feelings and sensations travel through communicative networks. Hence, there are only degrees of mediation.

Accessing Material Reality

Far from functioning as a secure compartment that carries literary meaning across space and across time to various readers, Sterne's *A Sentimental Journey* appears to be a defective vehicle; it fails to disappear into the background to allow the content—the sentiment—of the novel to shine forth. Whereas Smollett satirizes the impact of commercial circulation on letter writing and on the practices of editing, Sterne consciously shows his entire textual vehicle buckling under the pressure of physical and economic circulation in the rapidly developing commercial culture of eighteenth-century Britain. Sterne's text thus provides insight into the period's consciousness of the blurry boundaries between subject and object, messages and mediums. Such "knowingness," Christina Lupton argues, is characteristic of the literary culture of the mid-eighteenth century that reveled in the powers of print media through self-reflexive representation and found delight in the powerlessness of the writer and reader, who both submitted to the playful tyranny of print.[56] By implicating the knowing subject in the network of feeling, novels of sentiment thrust readers into a profusion of mediating objects, minimizing the distance between the observing self and the surrounding world. For Sterne, readers and novels are physically part and parcel of their media environment so that the world that novels represent and the world they inhabit are extensions of each other. Novelistic representation, for Sterne, does not have a distinct ontological status that separates it from reality; instead, he suggests that readers may move back and forth between the two so that representation and reality mutually feed upon each other.

As a case in point, "The Fragment" that I discussed above leads to a further adventure in which Yorick as the reader takes center stage. The fragment—precisely because it is a fragment that fails to conclude a narrative—prompts Yorick to ask, "And where is the rest of it, La Fleur?" (*SJ*, 100). This simple query on Yorick's part sends his servant on a fruitless scavenger hunt. La Fleur, it turns out, had used the two remaining sheets of the fragment to wrap a bouquet of flowers that he presented to his mistress. Within minutes of taking his farewell, "his faithless mistress had given his *gage d'amour* to one of the Count's footmen—the footman to a young sempstress—and the sempstress to a fiddler, with [Yorick's] fragment at the end of it" (*SJ*, 101). The circulation of text-as-thing takes Yorick and his readers through a catalogue of the lower classes of society, so that the act of reading in an isolated chamber imperceptibly leads back into the world of people and things.

To read and write sentimental fiction in such an environment, Sterne suggests, is to exercise one's ability to see the continuity between a world of textual representation and a world of material objects.[57] Sterne certainly exaggerates the found manuscript convention in this particular scene, but other novels in the sentimental tradition also reinforce this reciprocity between text and material reality. Mackenzie's *The Man of Feeling* begins with the narrator and a curate on a hunting expedition, encountering the estate where the protagonist, Harley, used to live. The scenery reminds the curate that he has a manuscript detailing the history of Harley, given to him by one of his parishioners. But that manuscript is torn because the curate—who sees no value in the manuscript—used it as gun wadding. The readers not only see the manuscript's connection to a specific place and specific people but are also constantly reminded of the manuscript's own history through missing chapters and passages. By reading such texts, readers are taught to look out for similar incidents in their own life—or, at least sentimental fiction gestures towards this possibility. Thus, Mackenzie describes how a Frenchman discovered the original manuscript of *Julia de Roubigné;* he "desired a sight" of papers that an errand boy was trying to sell to a grocer on the off-chance that the writing might be worth reading.[58] Novels of sentiment encourage readers to keep a lookout in their everyday lives in case they may hear a tale of woe, discover tearful letters, or find trinkets with a sentimental history behind them. The next bird one encounters may be Yorick's starling; this is possible, according to Yorick, since "it is impossible but many of my readers must have heard of him" during the course of its extensive circulation in society (*SJ*, 72).

Despite contemporary critiques that *A Sentimental Journey* promoted self-indulgent wallowing in sentiment,[59] it was followed by hordes of imitators, perhaps because the very act of reading the text turned the eyes of readers back to their physical environment, which in turn led to the further production of texts.[60] Sterne's novel did more than produce readers who were vicariously moved by Yorick's sentimental encounters; it also worked as a how-to manual for writing sentimental journeys. Once identified, the torn manuscript, the forgotten trinket, or the unusual pulsation in one's body may finally fulfill its task of communicating a sentimental story. But these sentimental encounters are never unmediated. Sterne's imitators frequently begin their journeys in pursuit of sentiment by hopping onto carriages; more often than not, the vehicles they happen to choose dictate the people, things, and feelings they encounter. George Keate's *Sketches from Nature* begins in media res with a conversation with a lady inside a carriage.[61] Samuel Pratt's *Travels for the Heart* begins with the narrator ruminating on a physical journey, indulging in an imaginative journey, and having his nerves torn up by a carriage ride on his way to the physician who prescribed traveling for his condition.[62] George Thompson's *A Sentimental Tour* begins with the narrator walking on foot through the landscape of Cumberland, but quickly has him on board a mail coach.[63] These travelers rely on such vehicles to physically carry them onward on their sentimental journeys; the textual vehicles that convey their chronicles, in turn, inspire readers to seek their own sentimental adventures.

Sterne's text in particular—and sentimental fiction more generally—thus suggests an alternative relationship between novels and reality. Sterne does not present the cohesive virtual reality that the traditional rise-of-the-novel discourse, following Watt, considered central to the emerging novel. Readers are not allowed to immerse themselves in a world that resembles (but is distinct from) their own. They are not permitted the experience of living vicariously through the novel's hero and heroine, sympathizing with their dilemmas and rejoicing in their happiness. Instead, Sterne's novel works to create a dynamic feedback loop between readers, texts, and the numerous things that populate commercial society. Rather than giving readers access to a pleasing imitation of reality, the narrative interruptions in sentimental fiction force readers back into the world of things. Sentimental fiction is, for Sterne, not a copy of reality, but an extension of it. Walter Scott would later compare the experience of reading *Waverley* with a carriage ride where the passenger-reader seeks picturesque scenes from within the safe confines of the vehicle. But more often than not, Sterne suggests, travelers encounter accidents and carriages are prone to break down, so that passengers are forced to step out of the carriage—especially when a dead ass blocks the way. Sterne's textual vehicle works not just to convey sentiment, but also to draw readers' eyes towards the very journey that it has taken. The novel of sentiment is a vehicle that comes with the figurative equivalent of mud splashed on its panels, the baggage strapped up behind, the repaired pin attaching a wheel, or the forgotten fragment of a letter amidst the seat cushions.

3
Local History for Distant Readers
Narrative Transmission in Scott's *The Tales of My Landlord*

Walter Scott's historical fiction features mail coaches as transport metaphors that afford insight into how readers who consume printed material across the nation have limited access to local, historical narratives. Focusing on Scott's use of mail coaches as a media metaphor symbolizing a national network of transportation that nevertheless failed to reach remote localities in Scotland, this chapter explores how Scott theorizes narrative transmission by negotiating the national and the local, the fashionable and the historical, print culture and oral narratives, and the mobile networks of transportation and the immobile monuments in country churchyards. Conceptualizing mediation as both spatial and temporal, Scott identifies how readers have limited access to authentic history from remote Scottish origins and are instead trapped in a cycle of consuming popular narratives perpetuated by the print market. Postponing the main narrative to an introductory framework that relates the fictional origins of each historical narrative, Scott uses the frame narrative to engage readers who are conditioned by common narratives circulated by print culture and asks them to imagine themselves instead in the context of a mediating network that bridges the national and the local, coined reproductions and authentic history. Scott not only suggests that the writer and editor assume a key role in this process of mediation but also envisions an alternative model of reading, evaluating, and preserving literary texts. Rather than pitting novels of ephemeral interest against those of enduring value, Scott imagines how narratives can survive and be transmitted for posterity by the very virtue of their extensive circulation and popularity.

Scott's concerns about mediation appear immediately in the opening passage of *The Heart of Midlothian* (1818), where the narrator, Peter Pattieson, asserts that the "times have changed in nothing more . . . than in the rapid conveyance of intelligence and communication betwixt one part of Scotland and another."[1] Here, Pattieson confirms the crucial role that the speed of print distribution played in Romantic print culture, particularly in relation to time-sensitive reading material such as periodical publications, political pamphlets, and statements by various corresponding societies.[2] Indeed, the rapidity of the mail coach that enabled up-to-date communication is crucial to our understanding of the Romantic period as an age that became particularly cognizant of history as an ongoing process, forming, as it were, what Benedict Anderson characterizes as a "historically clocked, imagined community."[3] Scott's readers would have been more than familiar with mail coaches that were established in the 1780s and had cut travel time in half by achieving unprecedented speed.[4] And yet the first half of Pattieson's sentence reveals ambivalence about such change; while he admits that there has been dramatic increase in the speed of communication, he also asserts that "nothing more" has changed. Despite the presence of "the new coach, lately established on our road," Pattieson considers the village of Gandercleugh as otherwise unchanged, since it still offers him the opportunity to collect local, historical tales that will eventually be published as *The Tales of My Landlord* (*H,* 14). This representation of communication infrastructures in *The Tales of My Landlord* series does not so much confirm the thorough penetration of a national print-based imagined community as it exposes how this national infrastructure existed uneasily alongside pockets of traditional, local communities, thus confirming the uneven access that characterized mail-coach routes in Scotland and Wales that Ruth Livesey meticulously details.[5]

This uneven access to local history is thematized in the very reception of Scott's historical fiction. Time and time again, Scott has been accused of manipulating his representations of Scotland and its people in ways that cater to the mainstream—that is, English—reading public in his historical fiction. Such accusations started to appear soon after the first publication of his novels when, as Ina Ferris details, some of Scott's contemporaries objected to his depiction of Covenanters in *Old Mortality* (1816).[6] The accusations continue to this day as critics argue that Scott essentially commodifies Scotland for the consumption of English readers in his historical novels.[7] Given such a critical tradition, it seems hardly worthwhile to discuss how authentic Scott's historical representations are;[8] in the same way that sentimental fiction represents the difficulty of pinpointing real feeling as I have discussed in my previous chapter, Scott's portrayal of history elides judgment about authenticity. Scott's passion for collecting authentic historical artifacts—ranging from ballads and legends to various historical knickknacks and, of course, documents—is well chronicled, but recent scholars have convincingly argued that Scott's own pursuit of authentic history creates irony and indeterminacy so as to leave his representation of history imperfect and his vision of the nation unstable.[9] Yoon Sun Lee and Livesey show how this indeterminacy is heightened by attending to how Scott's pursuit of authentic history is emmeshed with the workings of commerce that crossed English-Scottish boundaries, whether in the form of antiquarian commodities or of expanding mail-coach routes.[10] Livesey, for instance, argues that "Scott's fiction rarely lets the implied reader forget that the medium he or she is about to be immersed in is as much a thing made by practices of communication and mediation as the mail coach itself."[11] Pursuing similar lines of inquiry, this chapter imagines Scott grappling with the question of how one might access local history, especially through printed texts, when commerce and other forces of modernity were starting to change the face of the nation to create an increasingly unified idea of Great Britain.

But rather than focusing on the power of the local to unsettle or transcend the national as Lee and Livesey do, I argue that Scott traces the continuity between the national and the local by imagining how existing processes of mediation might make local history accessible to readers in a national print culture—despite some inevitable distortions along the way. Far from relying on realistic representation to make historical narratives accessible to readers, Scott conceptualizes a mediating process through which narratives from obscure Scottish villages might reach his readers hands; by mapping the delivery of historical narrative from the local to the national, Scott also situates historical fiction at the intersection of local, historical romance and mainstream realist fiction.[12] The opening passage to *The Heart of Midlothian* exemplifies Scott's own sense of the contradiction inherent in taking a historical narrative transmitted within a local Scottish community and circulating it throughout the British Isles. In the following discussion of *Old Mortality* and *The Heart of Midlothian,* I examine how Scott attempts to negotiate and bridge the gap between isolated local communities and a print-based imagined community by theorizing narrative transmission within his frame narratives. For Scott, the national imagined community, which continues to extend its reach as roads are built and mail-coach routes are instituted, does not so much incorporate localities into a national network of communication as subordinate them. This subordination has dire consequences for the literary health of the nation, since the national print market brainwashes readers with mass-produced narratives that merely reproduce conventional patterns, while authentic historical narratives remain entrapped within individual local communities. In the first two installments of *The Tales of My Landlord* series, Scott explores how an authentic historical narrative might be recovered from obscurity and put into national circulation without losing its authenticity. This exploration results in a series of renegotiations—between circulation and stability, between reproductions and originals, between spatial and temporal transmission—that help to establish a modern conception of literary value that lays the groundwork for institutionalizing the novel as a genre.

Transmitting *The Tales of My Landlord*

In the introduction to *Old Mortality,* Jedediah Cleishbotham, the fictitious editor of *The Tales of My Landlord,* presents himself as an armchair traveler. Having spent the last forty years sitting "in the leathern armchair, on the left-hand side of the fire, in the common room of the Wallace Inn, winter and summer, for every evening in my life," Cleishbotham claims that he has "seen more of the manners and customs of various tribes and people, than if [he] had sought them out by [his] own painful travel and bodily labour."[13] For Cleishbotham, the centrally located town of Gandercleugh is also the center of information where he can access news from all corners of the globe. He presumes that the knowledge of the world will be gained efficiently by remaining stationary like the "tollman at the well-frequented turnpike" (*O,* 6). Circulation may put people, things, and information in motion, but Cleishbotham asserts that individuals may benefit from the effects of circulation if they place themselves in a privileged—that is, central—position to observe and to gather information. In doing so, he reverses the logic of cultural capital represented in eighteenth-century novels of social circulation in which protagonists gain experience by circulating throughout the nation and exchanging narratives with various characters like innkeepers.[14] Cleishbotham suggests instead that an innkeeper has as much claim to a knowledge of the world as the customers he serves. He asserts that sitting still at the Wallace Inn contributes to the "enlargement of my views of the ways and works of the present generation" (*O*, 5)—a qualification that, in his opinion, demonstrates his capacity to write novels like the following narrative of *Old Mortality*, which he "could have written . . . if [he] would" (*O*, 9).

Cleishbotham's claims about his superior knowledge of the world, however, expose his misrecognition of genre. His introduction underscores how oblivious he is to the contents of the following narrative. The plot of *Old Mortality* revolves around the seventeenth-century struggles between the Covenanters and the Loyalists, culminating in the battle of Bothwell. The novel follows the vicissitudes of the hero, Henry Morton, who becomes part of the Covenanters' army from circumstances rather than from choice. Much of the succeeding narrative revolves around the precarious position that Morton holds within the Covenanters' army, and the fates of the various characters as they experience the shifting political alliances brought about by the Glorious Revolution. Cleishbotham claims that he could have written this narrative because he has sufficient knowledge of the world today, but that would hardly help him write a historical novel that narrates these events that occurred more than a century ago. The criteria that Cleishbotham uses to establish his ability to write such a narrative is based upon the precedence of writers such as Henry Fielding, who claims that an author needs a "true knowledge of the world [that] is gained only by conversation."[15] It is not that Fielding's claim is outdated. Novels of manners may continue to depict the manners of the present time, but the historical novelist, whose characters are clothed in garbs of past generations, must look beyond manners and describe "those passions common to men in all stages of society."[16]

Cleishbotham fails to assess the genre of the tale he introduces because he does not understand the relationship between genre and circulation. The novel of manners gathers its material from the realm of social circulation; it capitalizes on people who circulate in the fashionable world, their dresses and knick-knacks that circulate as commodities, and their stories that circulate in the form of gossip and "that part of a newspaper entitled the Mirror of Fashion."[17] Gathering such objects in the amusing form of narrative, novels of manners place them back into the realm of circulation through the print market so that the world they represent and the world they inhabit reciprocally inform each other. Such, however, is not the case with *Old Mortality*. This historical narrative does not take its ingredients from the world of circulation but from history, and its relationship to circulation differs from that of novels of manners. Historical novels circulate in the print market like novels of manners or periodicals, and they are delivered into readers' hands by way of the very mail coaches that Scott mentions. But they do not gather their materials from the synchronic realm of economic circulation. Cleishbotham himself gestures towards two distinct functions of circulation when he states that travelers at Wallace Inn would tell "news that had been gathered in foreign lands, or preserved from oblivion in this our town" (*O, 8*). Here he identifies two distinct functions of circulation—gathering and preserving. While he attempts to establish his authority based upon the former function of circulation, the narrative that follows his introduction works upon the latter principle of preserving stories that may otherwise remain in oblivion. Cleishbotham overlooks this latter function of circulation not only because he is too busy asserting his cultural authority, but also because he is not the real author of the historical narrative. The reader finds in the two final pages of Cleishbotham's introduction that the tales were not written by him, but by his deceased employee and Gandercleugh schoolteacher, Peter Pattieson, whose "papers have been left in [his] care" (*O, 9*). It is Pattieson, then, and not Cleishbotham, who is responsible for preserving the following historical tale from oblivion.

The introduction to *Old Mortality* dramatizes the intersection between temporal and spatial transmission to situate the genre of the historical novel at the juncture of an isolated local community where historical narratives remain buried in oblivion and an information economy that extends far and wide. Historical narratives, it seems, are difficult to access even in the days of rapid communication, and Scott demonstrates this through what Livesey calls "serio-comic thresholds" that confront readers before the main narrative.[18] Although Cleishbotham mistakes the nature of his agency, he nevertheless participates in a cultural mechanism that preserves local history through the functions of modern circulation. By the Romantic period, writers and readers were already able to assume that literature—and poetry in particular—had powers of preservation. William Wordsworth, for instance, was able to envision his poetry as a vehicle that could "summon back from lonesome banishment" the "plenteous store" of "yet remembered names" and "make them inmates in the hearts of men / Now living, or to live in times to come."[19] Rather than following Wordsworth's lead and taking it for granted that it is the nature of literature to withstand the corrupting and obscuring forces of time, Scott labors, first of all, to situate his text within a process that enables literary texts to preserve obscure narratives in the first place. In the succeeding pages of *Old Mortality*, Scott proceeds to outline such a process of preservation by staging the origin of the narrative within a communal network of transmission that preserves the narratives of the dead. If Cleishbotham's introduction tells us how the narrative entered the commercial marketplace, Pattieson's introduction tells us how the narrative was initially recovered from obscurity by conversing with those who travel off the beaten track or those who adhere to local tradition.[20] His process of discovering the tale of *Old Mortality* educates readers that to access obscure historical narratives, one must recognize that the process of transmission involves oral as well as print culture and objects as well as subjects.

Pattieson's introduction to *Old Mortality* begins by meditating on unchanging, stationary monuments, as though to distance the narrative from a society characterized by the rapid communication enabled by mail coaches. By doing so, Pattieson highlights what John Durham Peters calls "time-binding media," that is, monuments "such as statuary or architecture, [that] are durable and 'bind' distinct moments across great spans of time."[21] In one of Pattieson's favorite haunts in the village of Gandercleugh, there is a little cemetery that contains some monuments erected in honor of Covenanters who fell in battle. While Pattieson initially observes that "those who sleep beneath [these monuments] are only connected with us by the reflection, that they have once been what we now are," his succeeding descriptions make clear that one may gain access to the buried through textual inscriptions (*O*, 27). Despite the state of decay, these monuments still function as texts that offer information about those whom they memorialize. The monuments of the "doughty knight" and the "nameless bishop" bear various signs—such as armorial bearings, miters, and pastoral staff—whose values are verified by "tradition" (*O*, 27). But there is yet another monument that signifies nothing of status, has no sculptured ornaments, and shows an inscription that consists simply of "rude prose, and ruder rhyme" (*O*, 27). This tombstone, which belongs to "the class of persecuted Presbyterians who afforded a melancholy subject for history in the times of Charles II. and his successor," is referred to merely as a "stone," as opposed to the "monument" of the knight or the "tomb" of the bishop (*O*, 27). The stone and its inscription may both be humble, but "the history of those who sleep beneath them" can still be "read" on this solid text (*O*, 27).

While this passage seems to confirm the time-binding nature of monuments as media, this role of monuments is immediately problematized as it becomes clear that history is not quite dead, and that it still has relevance to those still alive. Pattieson does not need to decode obscure inscriptions, since "the peasantry" continue to reverence these relics as memorials of "victims of prelacy," and as emblems of their faith and principles (*O*, 28). By pointing back to the memory of the deceased, the religious faith of the Covenanters lives on from generation to generation: "when they point [the tombstones] out to their sons, and narrate the fate of the sufferers, [they] usually conclude, by exhorting them to be ready, should times call for it, to resist to the death in the cause of civil and religious liberty, like their brave forefathers" (*O*, 28). Monuments work as material counterparts to the narratives that are passed on from father to son and from generation to generation. While a visitor from afar may gather very little history from these monuments, the local peasants have many stories in store regarding those very monuments that say so little to outsiders. Monuments are valuable not because they function as time-binding media that tell stories of their own, but because they remind people to tell and retell the stories they already know.

This symbiotic relationship between monuments and stories is exemplified in the title figure of Old Mortality. The featured historical narrative, Pattieson tells us, comes from the titular character, an itinerant who has devoted his life to visiting the numerous monuments of Covenanters who fell under the persecution of government. He "regulated his circuit so as annually to visit the graves of the unfortunate Covenanters," and his visit involved "cleaning the moss from the grey stones, renewing with his chisel the half-defaced inscriptions, and repairing the emblems of death with which these simple monuments are usually adorned" (*O*, 30). He considered this a "sacred duty," which also enabled him to renew "to the eyes of posterity the decaying emblems of the zeal and sufferings of their forefathers, and thereby trimming, as it were, the beacon-light which was to warn future generations to defend their religion even unto blood" (*O*, 30–31). Old Mortality is dedicated to the preservation of time-binding media, but readers find that it is Old Mortality's skill as a narrator, not the tombstones, that provides material for Pattieson's succeeding narrative. Pattieson emphasizes the almost novelistic nature of Old Mortality's communications when he describes how realistic his narratives are: "One would almost have supposed he must have been their contemporary, and have actually beheld the passages which he related, so much had he identified his feelings and opinions with theirs, and so much had his narratives the *circumstantiality of an eye-witness*" (*O*, 32; emphasis mine).[22] But Old Mortality was not an eyewitness to the events he narrates; he was able to gather these narratives through his annual circulation through Scotland. As an itinerant figure, Old Mortality is at once a collector and a distributor, who is "profuse in the communication of all the minute information which he had collected concerning [the Covenanters], their wars, and their wanderings" (*O,* 32). Old Mortality's storytelling ability supplements the silent textual status of monuments, while his narrative itself becomes enriched as he gathers "minute information" from others.

Old Mortality circulates stories to supplement the mere presence of texts and transmits historical memory from one generation to another. But his model of circulation is distinct from the kind of circulation that informs Cleishbotham of "the ways and works of the present generation" at inns alongside coach routes. Indeed, Old Mortality travels off the roads frequented by the infamous mail coaches. Thus, he neither extends the reaches of the stories he tells nor ensures that the stories of Covenanters will hereafter become part of a more general national history. The distinction that Régis Debray draws between communication and transmission helps to highlight what is at stake in Old Mortality's activities. For Old Mortality, storytelling is not simply a matter of producing and disseminating information, or what Debray calls "communication." Old Mortality's storytelling is a means of "transmission," which is distinct from communication in that its aim is to ensure the survival of beliefs that are important to his particular cultural group. Old Mortality's lone struggle to renew "to the eyes of posterity the decaying emblems of the zeal and sufferings of their forefathers" thus makes him a part of "people establishing membership in a group . . . and to coded procedures signaling that group's distinction from others," as Debray puts it.[23] The memory of Covenanters, unsanctioned either by antiquarians or by the nation at large, resides obstinately within the small compass of local peasants scattered across the country, institutionalized as history only in the memory of those who follow an anti-institutional religious sect. Old Mortality's stories as well as the tombstones whose inscriptions he renews transmit cultural memory among the peasants, but they matter to these peasants only because they are already part of their culture. This group, which includes Old Mortality himself as well as the peasantry to whom Pattieson refers earlier in the passage, distinguishes itself through shared historical narratives, even from other cultures within Scotland and within the locality of the village of Gandercleugh. Old Mortality's work, Pattieson supposes, was inspired through religious enthusiasm in the first place; it is that very religious motivation that leads him to seek shelter from fellow Covenanters, to listen to their stories, and to propagate them in turn. Old Mortality perpetuates historical narratives for the Covenanters, and reaffirms their faith, community, and shared history. Old Mortality's narratives are thus confined to a closed circuit and remains inaccessible to outsiders; the audiences and narrators are already initiated into a consensual understanding of the sufferings of their ancestors.

Scott's novel attempts to break this circuit and to put into national circulation what, for the Covenanters, is the stuff of tradition. Old Mortality circulates among various Covenanters' communities and freely exchanges stories with them so that no single person claims an authority over these stories; rather, these stories act as currency that implicitly set the consensual standard of values within a community. By encouraging Old Mortality to narrate these stories to an outsider, Pattieson breaks a closed circuit and mediates the narratives' entrance into the wider realm of national print circulation—with some controversial results, as Ferris's account of the novel's reception shows.[24] As Pattieson himself discloses, such mediation also distorts the narratives themselves. "Far from adopting either [Old Mortality's] style, his opinions, or even his facts," he claims to "have endeavoured to correct or verify them from the most authentic sources of tradition, afforded by the representatives of either party" (O, 34). After a long-winded introduction of Old Mortality, fleshing out the life and character of the itinerant storyteller, Pattieson buries that very embodied voice under a mass of historical documentation. He claims to balance Old Mortality's partial narrative by consulting the descendants of Loyalists, mainly through local lairds, their gamekeepers, and non-juring bishops. Old Mortality's partial perspective as a dissenter is also supported, "much in the taste and spirit of the original," by "packmen or pedlars" as well as weavers and tailors who "may be considered as possessing a complete register of rural traditions" (O, 34–35).

When Peter Pattieson thus explains his method of historical writing, he reveals how differently the historical writer and communal agents handle these narratives. The historical writer gathers narratives and arranges them so that the narratives are like so many objects put into relief to highlight the central image within a larger picture. Not so for the "representatives of either party," both dissenters and loyalists, that Pattieson consults. For both parties, the narratives continue to be handed down like family heirlooms or other objects of value. Within such communities, each narrative, each rural tradition is valuable for its own sake. For Pattieson to lay claim to objectivity and to synthesize these narratives is for him to wrest the narratives from the original context, and to present them as curiosities within an antiquarian's cabinet of collections. If history writing is about collecting narratives from various communities so as to eradicate partiality, it also involves "the reframing of objects within a world of attention and manipulation of context."[25] What Susan Stewart claims to be the nature of collecting objects may illustrate the threat that Pattieson's historical method poses to the local community: "Like other forms of art, [the collection's] function is not the restoration of context of origin but rather the creation of a new context, a context standing in a metaphorical, rather than a contiguous, relation to the world of everyday life."[26] Most disturbing to those to whom the narratives originally belonged, the collection presents "a world which . . . has banished repetition and achieved authority."[27] While attempting to rescue and preserve local narratives (unlike Cleishbotham, who focuses solely on narrative circulation in a commercial economy), Pattieson nevertheless participates in a mediating process that distorts local narratives as they enter national circulation.

Insides and Outsides

When James Buzard characterizes Scott's turn to novel writing as a self-conscious shift towards an autoethnographic model of writing, he provides another set of terms for discussing the dilemma of accessing authentic history that Scott, Cleishbotham, and Pattieson all encounter in varying degrees and forms. "Jedediah Cleishbotham and the other avatars Scott employs in his fiction," Buzard argues, "imply that they can apprehend and salute a 'Scottish culture' entire only from a position 'outside' or 'above' any particular locality within Scotland or any mentality belonging to one of that nation's religious or political factions—whose bloody conflicts have constituted much of Scottish history."[28] The discontents that Scott's representations of history provoke arise from the fact that the narrator positions himself as an outsider, who presumes to "have endeavoured to correct or verify" Old Mortality's anecdotes. This position of the outsider is even more strongly claimed by Cleishbotham in the introduction to *The Heart of Midlothian:* "I . . . claim a privilege to write and speak of both parties with impartiality. For, O ye powers of logic! when the Prelatists and Presbyterians of old times went together by the ears in this unlucky country, my ancestor . . . was one of the people called Quakers, and suffered severe handling from either side" (*O*, 11). Buzard urges us to acknowledge how Scott constructs an outside vantage point towards Scottish (and particularly Highland) culture, marketing his Scottish novels "within the framework of United Kingdom internal colonialism."[29] Cleishbotham not only corroborates Buzard's argument, but also adds a tongue-in-cheek element to it by praising the "powers of logic" that help him create a position outside what is represented in the novel. Cleishbotham's invocation prompts readers to further consider how the position of the "outside" is created—not only in geopolitical space, but also in the space of writing.

The narrative framework of *Old Mortality* that I have been discussing demonstrates Scott's attempt to incorporate what lies "outside" of a narrative within the body of the text itself. By detailing the conveyer belt–like process through which the story is handed from one person to another, Scott portrays the friction that occurs at each stage of narrative transmission; Pattieson recontextualizes Old Mortality's narrative by consulting the descendants of Loyalists, and Cleishbotham introduces Pattieson's tale with various caveats and marks of disapproval. These additional layers of narratives accumulate as sediment that tells the history and transmutations of the story, and they indicate that there is no smooth process that enables local, authentic narratives to enter national circulation without additions, distortions, or recontextualizations. Is it possible for communal and individual histories to enter the realm of national circulation and become accessible to participants in the ever-expanding print market without losing their authenticity? What does such a transition entail? And how might a writer of historical novels like Scott conceive of his own agency when performing such a task?

The concluding pages of *Old Mortality*, as well as the introductory frame of *The Heart of Midlothian*, provide some clues that help us to begin answering these questions. Scott famously begins *Waverley* and *Ivanhoe* with introductions that explain the principles of writing a historical narrative, focusing on issues of realistically representing unfamiliar manners of past historical eras. But in the framing narratives of these two novels in *The Tales of My Landlord*, Scott shifts his focus away from issues of representation and more towards those of mediation as he describes what we might call the infrastructure of the Romantic reading public—from the mail coaches that deliver new periodical publications to assumptions about genre that underpin Romantic readers' encounters with the novel. However, in describing these mechanisms that sustain the kind of print-based imagined community that Benedict Anderson theorizes, Scott by no means claims a central position within a predominantly English reading public—and hence outside the provincial vantage point of an internally colonized Scotland. Rather, Scott suggests that both the material and the conceptual infrastructure of the nation perpetuate their own closed circuit of communication in ways that exclude the circulation and preservation of local, historical narratives. By contrasting his own work with others that participate in reading institutions such as the circulating library and periodical journals, Scott claims the position of a mediator between local and national circulation by staking out a position that lies not only outside of Scotland, but also outside of the increasing array of hegemonizing English cultural institutions.

The circulating library appears as the foremost example of an institution that trains readers to expect certain formal elements in a novel. A conversation between Pattieson and Miss Buskbody in the concluding frame of *Old Mortality* underscores how Scott's own work both satisfies and defies expectations raised by the circulating library. Miss Martha Buskbody is "a young lady who has carried on the profession of mantua-making at Gandercelugh and in the neighborhood, with great success, for about forty years" (*O*, 455). In addition to supplying consumer goods, she is herself an avid consumer of fictional texts—from the circulating library. "Knowing her taste for narratives of this description," Pattieson states, "I requested her to look over the loose sheets the morning before I waited on her, and enlighten me by the experience which she must have acquired in reading through the whole stock of three circulating libraries, in Gandercleugh and the two next market towns" (*O*, 455). Pattieson is particularly interested in consulting her about the ending to his narrative, in which he "had determined to wave the task of a concluding chapter, leaving to the reader's imagination the arrangements which must necessarily take place after Lord Evandale's death" (*O*, 455). Pattieson's novel ends by portraying Henry Morton reunited with his beloved over the dead body of Lord Evandale, who had just been killed in a fray. Lord Evandale was on the verge of marriage with Edith Bellenden, who had been obliged to him for both protection and sustenance after the events that had ended in Morton's exile from his homeland. Lord Evandale's death, just at the moment of Morton's return, is at once an ending and a beginning; while his death signifies the end of one series of events, it also suggests the beginning of the reconciliation and eventual marriage between the two lovers by absolving Edith of her engagement to him. This ending, for Pattieson, has the recommendation of convenience. However, he is concerned that "precedents are wanting for a practice which might be found convenient both to readers and compilers" (*O,* 455). And he is right. Miss Buskbody cannot understand the suggestive ending that Pattieson substitutes for a conventional one. Like a habitual novel reader, she presses Pattieson to provide satisfactory knowledge concerning the fate of every character. For Miss Buskbody, it is incumbent upon Pattieson to "redeem this gross error by telling us all about the marriage of Morton and Edith, and what became of the other personages of the story, from Lady Margaret down to Goose-Gibbie" (*O,* 456).

While the inclusion of this conversation demonstrates Scott's familiarity with genre conventions, the fact that Pattieson's conclusion fails to satisfy Miss Buskbody suggests that Pattieson's narrative is distinct from other novels. Miss Buskbody calls Pattieson's narrative experiment a "gross error" because her reading habits have already confirmed her idea of what a novel should be and how it should end. Pattieson's historical tale is regarded by this reader alongside Eliza Haywood's *Jenny and Jemmy Jessamy* (1753) and Henry Mackenzie's *Julia de Roubigné* (1781)—the former, a novel that Scott held up as an example of bad novels, and the latter, a novel that Scott praised for its depth of feeling.[30] Such an indiscriminate pairing of texts only confirms the readers' impression that Miss Buskbody is a questionable authority. Her gender, moreover, confirms the contemporary opinion that "women, especially impressionable young ladies, were [the circulating libraries'] main customers," as William St. Clair attests.[31] So far from gaining authority from having read "the whole stock of three circulating libraries," such a reading habit shows that Miss Buskbody is a promiscuous reader who prefers "formulaic" reading material provided by "producers trying to commodify the texts textually as well as materially by implying that they were broadly similar, within quite narrow limits, both in subject matter and in the ideologies they advocated."[32] As an avid reader of three circulating libraries, then, Miss Buskbody is assessing Pattieson's work based not so much on judgment and wide-ranging information, but based on the narrow, perhaps ill-formed, literary standards that were institutionalized by the circulating library.

Even beyond the gender-coded institution of the circulating library, novels were still considered to work "within quite narrow limits," as the next installment of *The Tales of My Landlord* demonstrates. *The Heart of Midlothian* picks up where *Old Mortality* left off, focusing on a heroine

LOCAL HISTORY FOR DISTANT READERS · 95

whose father had settled into a modest agricultural life after experiencing the Covenanters' wars. The story focuses on Jeanie Deans's heroic journey to London to obtain pardon for her sister who had been found guilty of child murder. In the introductory frame of this novel, Scott stages a discussion between Pattieson and two Edinburgh lawyers about the Heart of Midlothian, the architecture of the Edinburgh prison that looms over the first half of the novel. Hardie, one of the lawyers, begins the discussion by mentioning that the prison is to be demolished, and that it should have its "Last Speech, Dying Confession, and Dying Words" just like the criminals it has contained (*H,* 20). The lawyers suggest the publication of the "*Causes Célèbres* of Scotland" (*H,* 22), claiming that the narratives culled from "State Trials, or in the Books of Adjournal" will produce narratives in which "you read new pages of the human heart, and turns of fortune far beyond what the boldest novelist ever attempted to produce from the coinage of his brain" (*H,* 21–22). Hardie chooses to publish this narrative in a form reminiscent of criminal biographies, because he does not want them to resemble novels that are manufactured reproductions like coins and perpetuate their own signifying system without necessarily reflecting reality. Hardie is forced to choose between the two genres, since the sources of his narratives—the State Trials and the Books of Adjournal— are hardly appealing to the general public and will likely remain in the lawyers' bookcases. Given the choice between novels and criminal biographies, Hardie considers criminal biography as the most appropriate vehicle for transmitting the narratives associated with the prison, because that genre will best distinguish the factual basis of the narratives: "The true thing," he states, "will triumph over the brightest inventions of the most ardent imagination" (*H,* 22). The difference between the "true thing" and fiction are differentiated by how fiction falls into a cycle of conventions, since it is difficult for authors to "hit upon characters or incidents which have not been used again and again, until they are familiar to the eye of the reader" (*H,* 22). Hardie considers fiction as a product of economic circulation, a manifestation of how the print market recycles the same conventions over and over again. The print market does not just produce novels; it also reproduces them.

Thus Scott describes how mainstream novels are trapped within conventions and boundaries imposed by society, just as obscure, local narratives remain in their confined circle as I have discussed earlier. Scott most vividly captures this parallel when he traces the origin of Jeanie Deans's story, which is associated with the Heart of Midlothian. The Edinburgh prison physically contains a restricted society and encloses within its boundaries a narrative community. Economic theorists conventionally used the metaphor of the circulation of blood to describe the circulation of wealth throughout the nation, but the "Heart" of Midlothian does not pump blood to a larger body; it is an isolated body politic, whose economy extends no further than the prison walls.[33] The Edinburgh Tolbooth has an internal economy that circulates money, goods, and narratives. Not only is the prison "a world within itself" that "has its own business, griefs, and joys, particular to that circle," it also has an isolated system of economic hierarchy so that "there are degrees of wealth and poverty among them" (*H*, 20). Parallel to this monetary economy exists a narrative one, confined to those who live within its walls: "Jails, like other places, have their ancient traditions, known only to the inhabitants, and handed down from one set of the melancholy lodgers to the next who occupy their cells" (*H*, 26). The narrative transmission in the Heart of Midlothian remains within the physical confines set by the prison walls, in a way that parallels the confined transmission of narrative among Covenanters in *Old Mortality*.

Scott contrasts this isolated community of the Heart of Midlothian with a nationwide information economy that has been expanding rapidly over the past generation. The opening chapter to *The Heart of Midlothian* begins by illustrating the transportation infrastructure that connects the village of Gandercleugh to the rest of Scotland and Great Britain. The vehicles that pass through the village enable "the rapid conveyance of intelligence and communication betwixt one part of Scotland and another" (*H*, 13). The slow but safe conveyances in the form of cumbersome stagecoaches have been replaced by lighter, speedier vehicles; thus, Pattieson observes, "mail-coach races against mail-coach, and high-flyer against high-flyer, through the most remote districts of Britain" (*H*, 13). This infrastructure of communication that characterizes modern Scotland, however, by no means works to fully integrate isolated, local communities within its network. Rather, such a network reinforces its own image of a centralized system of uninterrupted circulation, one that subordinates rather than incorporates local communities. Like the image of the post office that Mary Favret describes, rapid conveyances "figured a general restructuring of society in the nineteenth century, a restructuring that squeezed the irregularities of correspondence out of the public sphere."[34] It creates readers who, like Pattieson, expect "by the coach a new number of an interesting periodical publication" that

LOCAL HISTORY FOR DISTANT READERS · 97

enables them to participate in the reading public (*H,* 14). But that public is far different from the public sphere that Habermas envisions as an arena of exchange for rational conversation.[35] The reading public that Pattieson participates in is located along a one-way street, not because conversation is discouraged, but because communication occurs so quickly. The coaches deliver the new periodical publications so rapidly that there is no time for mutual exchange—the coach guard would "[skim] forth for [Pattieson's] grasp the expected packet, *without the carriage checking its course for an instant*" (*H,* 15; emphasis mine). It is perhaps counterintuitive to imagine that rapid circulation hindered rather than facilitated the exchange of ideas. In a technological society, we are conditioned to think that reliable, smooth, and fast access to one another through sound technological infrastructure enables good communication.[36] Scott, however, implies that rapid circulation merely produces passive consumers who are perpetually exposed to objects of mass production—like Miss Buskbody.

If developments in the transportation system extended the reach of a print-based imagined community to further consolidate a British national culture, it would seem difficult to step outside of its influence and to turn one's eyes towards forgotten authentic narratives of local, isolated communities that do not circulate in the print market. It is telling, then, that Scott stages the introduction of the tale of *The Heart of Midlothian* as an accident—an accident that creates a narrative space "outside" the national system of circulation. Pattieson never receives his periodical publication, and instead witnesses the overturn of the carriage. After safely extricating "the *insides* by a sort of summary and Caesarean process of delivery" from "the womb of the leathern conveniency," Pattieson proceeds to rescue the "*outsides*" who were tossed into the river from their elevated situation (*H,* 15–16). The outsides—two Edinburgh lawyers and a man recently released from the Heart of Midlothian—who are refused conveyance because of their wet garments, resort to the village inn with Pattieson, where they share with him various legal anecdotes that become, under Pattieson's pen, the narrative of *The Heart of Midlothian.* Contrary to the expectation raised by the metaphor of birth and reproduction in this passage, the "insides" who were "delivered" from the carriage move on to the next stage of their journey without contributing to the production of Pattieson's narrative.[37] Instead, it is the outsides, who have been disabled from continuing the previous mode of travel, who communicate the incidents regarding the Edinburgh Tolbooth, signifying the break between the kind of "communication" that would have conveyed to Pattieson "a new periodical publication" and the narrative that follows.

"The True Thing . . . Will Triumph"

True to the message conveyed in the novel's frame narrative, the central plot of *The Heart of Midlothian* explores the prevalence and shortcomings of "coined" narratives and contrasts them with the fate of a "true" story that gains authority in the end despite the initial difficulty of circulating beyond local boundaries and gaining a broader audience. The novel revolves around the trial and condemnation of Effie Deans, who is accused of murdering her own child soon after birth. What ultimately condemns Effie is that she failed to disclose her situation to anyone before the birth of her child and cannot clearly remember what happened immediately after childbirth. In short, the central problem of the novel is that Effie did not, will not, and cannot tell her own story. The subsequent pages of the novel detail how various characters attempt to overcome the crucial lack of Effie's oral testimony. While her lawyer depends very much on evoking the sympathy of the jurors, her lover, George Staunton, tries to recue Effie by plotting schemes that rely on moving the passions of others. Yet, the attempt that proves successful at the end is that made by Effie's sister, Jeanie, who unwillingly helps to condemn Effie by telling the truth that Effie never disclosed her pregnancy to her sister. After Effie's sentence is handed down, Jeanie walks all the way to London to personally plead royal authority for Effie's pardon. The very adherence to truth that condemns Effie at the beginning of the novel prevails in the end when Jeanie obtains a pardon from the queen—with some storytelling tips provided by the Duke of Argyle. If Jeanie's truthfulness proves that "the true thing . . . will triumph" in the end, the heavy-handed editing of the Duke of Argyle suggests that the truth may have to be modified or tweaked for such a truth to become accessible.

The case of Effie's child murder is a peculiar one that revolves around issues of communication—or the lack thereof. As Bartoline Saddletree, the would-be lawyer, puts it, Effie's case is "a beautiful point of presumptive murder" (*H*, 53), which is "a murder of the law's inferring or construction, being derived from certain *indicia* or grounds of suspicion" (*H*, 54–55). The law, in other words, "constructs" the story of a woman who disguises her pregnancy in order to do away with her child based on certain "grounds of suspicion." Effie provides grounds for legal action by confessing to having given birth to a child. However, she cannot account for anything else. Her child is missing, and she can give no account of its whereabouts. She had been silent to her family and friends about her pregnancy. And she cannot positively identify the woman who helped her give birth. All the clues Effie provides turn out to be dead ends, so the legal authority is forced to fill in the blanks, thus creating its own version of Effie's story. The law does not construct its story by taking into account the particular circumstances of Effie's case; rather, it constructs a story based on past precedents and judges how Effie's case fits into a pattern in common with many other women who have concealed their pregnancies and given birth in secret.[38] In the eyes of the law, the death of the offspring is "an event most likely to be the consequence" of concealing one's pregnancy (*H*, 217–18). Scott underscores how the impersonal "law" gains a certain kind of authorial agency through Saddletree's personification of his beloved law and Mrs. Saddletree's rebuff. "The crime is rather a favourite of the law, this species of murther being one of its ain creation," Saddletree explains. Mrs. Saddletree retorts, "Then, if the law makes murders . . . the law should be hanged for them" (*H*, 55).

The law gains authority over Effie's story, because Effie herself has no convincing version of her own story to tell. It is hardly surprising, then, that different versions of Effie's story are told and retold repeatedly within the novel by different characters for different purposes. As a case in point, Scott consciously employs the rhetoric of storytelling when representing the speech of Mr. Fairbrother, the counsel for the prisoner. Mr. Fairbrother begins his account of Effie by stating that "his client's story was a short, but most melancholy one." This explicit characterization of Effie's case as a "story" resonates in the subsequent parts of his speech; he attempts to "carry his whole audience with him" by mobilizing sympathy with the characters of his tale. The lawyer sets Effie up as the tragic heroine, and even digresses into the story of the infamous criminal George Robertson to account for Effie's silence regarding her seducer. If the law fills in the blanks of Effie's narrative to construct the story of child murder, Mr. Fairbrother fills in those same blanks with different material to construct an alternative story about a young woman who kept her condition secret in the hopes of redeeming her reputation through marriage with the father of the unborn child. The effect of the lawyer's construction of Effie as a tragic heroine becomes particularly obvious in the audiences' reactions. When Mr. Fairbrother expresses his desire to spare the judge "the most painful duty" of condemning "a creature so young, so ingenuous, and so beautiful," his "address seemed to affect many of the audience, and was followed by a slight murmur of applause" (*H,* 220). Mr. Saddletree claims that his wife is not an adequate witness and complains that the lawyer is misguided in bringing "a woman here to snotter and snivel" (*H,* 226). But it appears that tragedy, and the snottering and sniveling that come with it, is precisely the order of the day, as even the presiding judge must "repeatedly [wipe] his eyes" and admits that "he had felt no less than they had done from the scene of domestic misery which had been exhibited before them" (*H,* 232, 235).[39]

Mr. Fairbrother's story may be associated with those genres of print that Scott characterizes as products of generic reproduction within the frame narrative that precedes the novel. Mr. Fairbrother's representation of Effie as a tragic heroine resembles the romances to which Hardie refers, despite its more proper judicial and historical place in the State Trials. But rather than making Effie's case new or surprising, Mr. Fairbrother weaves it into a familiar narrative of seduction and betrayal—one that people might "read from habit and from indolence, not from real interest," one that makes them "read and swear till . . . the end of the narrative" and no further; one that, according to Hardie, resembles "the new novel most in repute" (*H,* 21). Hardie's assertion of the temporary nature of how fiction affects the reader is reflected in Mr. Fairbrother's case as well, since the audience, though highly affected by the trial, return to their usual state as soon as they flock out of the court so that they "soon forgot whatever they had felt as impressive in the scene which they had witnessed" (*H,* 239).

If Mr. Fairbrother's rendering of Effie's story reminds us of romances and novels that cater to the indolent appetite of consumer-readers, George Staunton's leading role in the Porteous Riot is reminiscent of how the radical press enabled readers to participate in ongoing public debates. Staunton explains his role in the Porteous Riot, describing how his own interest, his own passions, and the anger of the crowd fed each other to form a plan in his mind: "the general rage excited among the citizens of Edinburgh on account of the reprieve of Porteous, suggested to me the daring idea of forcing the jail, and at once carrying off your sister from the clutches of the law, and bringing to condign punishment a miscreant, who had tormented the unfortunate Wilson even in the hour of death" (*H,* 330). This plan, according to Staunton, was acted upon immediately upon the spot in which it was conceived. He explains that he "flung [himself] among the multitude in the moment of fermentation—so did others among Wilson's mates, who had, like me, been disappointed in the hope of glutting their eyes with Porteous's execution" (*H,* 330). Staunton attributes his plan of action to the crowd itself, and yet, as the representative and leader of that crowd, it becomes unclear whether Staunton is speaking *for* the crowd or inciting the crowd to a course of action that they otherwise may not have pursued. Staunton's manner of appealing to the crowds' volatile passions appears similar in nature to what Robert Southey considered as the "inflammatory harangues" that were "sold through the manufacturing districts at a halfpenny or penny each."[40] Like the radical publications of Scott's time that worked to virtually—and sometimes physically—convene crowds, Staunton feeds on the passion of the Edinburgh citizens to gain his own end.[41]

Not so with Jeanie. Having led a sheltered life under the guidance of her strict Cameronian father, away from the scenes of politics and commerce, Jeanie possesses little knowledge of the world. Unlike Mr. Fairbrother and George Staunton, she neither attempts to sway the masses, nor is she aware that there are conventional means of doing so. And when she is presented with the opportunity of creating an "effect" in others by using a story, she conscientiously avoids taking advantage of her audience by such means. While she, too, intends to tell her story to gain authority—that is, to influence the king to reprieve her sister's sentence—she relies not on coined rhetorical strategies that are already in circulation and are thus familiar to her listeners. She relies, instead, on the simple strategy of presenting the truth directly to the king and queen who have the authority to save Effie. Jeanie's plan to walk to London to present herself and her story to the king and queen sounds all but impossible; the Laird of Dumbiedikes thinks that "the lassie's demented" (*H,* 256), and even her lover, Reuben Butler, calls her plan a "wild dream" (*H,* 267). And yet, Jeanie's resolution does not falter. She believes that the directness of her personal appeal, not just the message itself, will help reach the heart of the monarch. She objects to trusting her message to a letter because "a letter canna look, and pray, and beg, and beseech, as the human voice can do to the human heart. A letter's like the music that the ladies have for their spinets—naething but black scores, compared to the same played or sung. It's word of mouth maun do it, or naething" (*H,* 267). It seems unlikely that Jeanie would draw an analogy between a music score and a letter, since her social class and habits of life would likely make her unfamiliar with ladies' accomplishments. Yet the very uncharacteristic nature of the analogy highlights how Scott emphasizes Jeanie's aversion to things that are only copies and are thus dead and mute representations of living messages. In such a context, Jeanie's heroic walk to London takes on additional meaning; it helps to heighten the authenticity of Jeanie's story by distinguishing her narrative from those that rapidly circulate using the latest carriages. As Livesey puts it, Jeanie Deans represents "rootedness, contiguity, and localized knowledge" that becomes "a paradoxical source of power, free mobility, and speech in Scott's writing."[42]

Jeanie, however, cannot entirely avoid mediation. The Duke of Argyle plays a crucial role as a mediator, not only by making Jeanie's interview with Queen Caroline possible, but also through his narrative interventions.[43] At times, he works as the translator, who clarifies Jeanie's Scottish dialect, explaining that "five and twenty miles and a bittock" means twenty-five miles "and about five miles more." At other times, he intervenes more heavily into Jeanie's method of storytelling, preventing her from scrupulously listing, for instance, every "easement" she received during her pedestrian journey to London, such as "the cast of the cart" and "the cast of a horse" (H, 368). The duke's interventions tend to aim for narrative effect, making sure that Jeanie will not "say more or less than just enough" (H, 370), whereas Jeanie, if left to her own devices, would have aimed at a full and perhaps tedious disclosure of the truth. The duke's narrative intervention helps to mold Jeanie's story into a form and style more accessible to the queen—a mode characterized by "that precision and easy brevity which is only acquired by habitually conversing in the higher ranks of society, and which is the diametrical opposite of that protracted style of disquisition, 'Which squires call potter, and which men call prose'" (H, 366). While Jeanie and the duke both hope that Jeanie's plea will "find an advocate in [the queen's] own heart" (H, 366), not all modes of expression can easily access that advocate.

If the opening scene of *The Heart of Midlothian* demonstrates how an obscure, local tale might enter the broader realm of circulation accidentally, the character of the Duke of Argyle within the central narrative helps to show how a qualified agent can facilitate such a process. The narrator labors to emphasize how the Duke of Argyle is a peculiarly suitable mediator for Jeanie's story. He is familiar with the conventions of the English court, but his private virtues and public position both seem to guarantee that he will not sacrifice the truth of Jeanie's story and the authenticity of Jeanie's voice to the conventions of mainstream discourse. Not only is he "free from the ordinary vices of statesmen, falsehood, namely, and dissimulation," but he is also able to "[soar] above the petty distinctions of faction," thus maintaining a position of independence, respectability, and popularity (*H*, 344). In describing the Duke of Argyle, Scott is doing more than just portraying an honored historical figure of Scotland.[44] He is also portraying an author figure, not of those romances that are "coined" from authors' brains, but of "the true thing" that "will triumph over the brightest inventions of the most ardent imagination." Jeanie may be able to tell her story "with a pathos which was at once simple and solemn" (*H*, 370), in "tones so affecting, that, like the notes of some of her native songs, provincial vulgarity was lost in pathos" (*H*, 366). But it is the Duke of Argyle who stages Jeanie's appearance and ensures that she is heard at all.

Circulation and Literary Value

Argyle's presentation of Jeanie mirrors Scott's representation of the origins of his own narratives; they both originate in obscure localities of Scotland, and they both require a rather unconventional series of mediations to gain an audience. Most important, they are both able to touch the audience's heart because of their authenticity—a literary version of what Walter Benjamin calls "the aura of the work of art."[45] Benjamin's ideas about what makes a work of art unique are uncannily similar to the way Scott situates his own narratives in *The Tales of My Landlord* novels; a work of art has an aura when it has a "unique existence at the place where it happens to be" and "this unique existence of the work of art determined the history to which it was subject throughout the time of its existence."[46] By identifying the origins of narratives in the close confines of the Heart of Midlothian or within the community of Covenanters, Scott renders their existence unique. Unlike Benjamin, however, who believed that "by making many reproductions, [the technique of reproduction] substitutes a plurality of copies for a unique existence," Scott attempts to reconcile the "unique existence" of his stories with the problems of economic circulation such as reproduction and mass marketing.[47]

Scott negotiates this conflict between economic circulation and historical authenticity by participating in and building upon a broader cultural awareness that the infrastructure of the print market impacts how readers think about the value of a printed text. I argue that writers and readers of the time started to theorize the idea of "best sellers" in a way that prefigures the institutionalization of best sellers as a commercial term and mechanism. The print culture of Scott's generation was characterized by a burgeoning awareness of how the print public sphere worked to create literary value in ways that departed from classical conceptions of literary value held by previous generations. As I will suggest in my conclusion to this chapter, Scott builds upon these fluctuating conceptions of literary value to construct an idea of authenticity and of literary history that works as an alternative to Benjamin's—one that is based on a dialectical relationship between space-binding media and time-binding media, between circulation and stability, and between reproductions and originals.

Unsurprisingly, it is Scott himself who works as the best case study for observing the effect of rapid circulation in the print culture of his generation. St. Clair asserts that "during the romantic period, the 'Author of Waverley' sold more novels than all the other novelists of the time put together."[48] Such statistical analysis gives us a vivid sense of the popularity of the Author of Waverley in comparison to other novelists of the age. Implicit in these statistics is the assumption that copies of *Waverley* were consumed more quickly than other novels, since rapid sales are a precondition for the achievement of a higher cumulative sales statistic within a given time frame. If statistical analysis helps to establish the rapid circulation of the Waverley Novels as a fact, the two following review articles help to illustrate the effects of rapid textual consumption. According to *The British Critic, Waverley* circulated throughout the nation so quickly that it turned the relationship between reader and reviewer topsy-turvy: "So rapid is the circulation of those works, to which the public attention has been by anticipation directed, that it is our province rather to confirm or correct a judgment already formed, than to direct it to a new and undiscovered object."[49] The situation hardly improves as Scott publishes more and more novels. In October 1821, *The Quarterly Review* published a review of *Rob Roy* (1817), *The Heart of Midlothian* (1818), *Bride of Lammermoor* and *Montrose* (1819), *Ivanhoe* (1819), *Monastery* (1820), and *Kenilworth* (1821), in which the reviewer confesses his own powerlessness as a critic. Similar to the *British Critic,* the language of the *Quarterly Review* article reveals a confused but nascent recognition that when texts circulate faster, assessment of literary value shifts away from the hands of select critics to an anonymous mass of readers. Indeed, the *Quarterly* can hardly pretend to accomplish much of what it considers to be the objectives for a standard review article. It cannot "draw the public attention to works, which are bought, and borrowed, and stolen, and begged for, a hundred times more than our dry and perishable pages;" it cannot presume to provide feedback and criticism to an author whose pen outstrips the pace of periodical reviewers; it cannot guide public opinion that had already been formed so that "our praise or blame cannot well be heard among the voices of the whole nation."[50] The rapid circulation of the Waverley Novels, the *Quarterly* suggests, contributes to the forming of a "voice" in which the "whole nation" is united so that the critical acumen of the reviewer, instead of guiding the public, follows it.

In describing the rapid circulation of the Waverley Novels, these review articles analyze the effects of consumer democracy on literary texts that will come to manifest itself later on in the form of "best sellers." The term "best seller," according to the *OED,* first came into use in the late nineteenth-century United States.[51] The best-seller list can be traced back to its embryonic state in a London-based monthly periodical titled *The Bookman,* established in October 1891 by William Robertson Nicoll (1851–1923). The periodical catered to those involved in the business of book selling, publishing, and printing. Early issues of *The Bookman* included a section titled "Behind a Bookseller's Counter" that contained ruminations on the current state of the book market and offered analysis of trends that will allow the bookseller to help customers who are overwhelmed by the variety of reading options. This section eventually developed into a section titled "Monthly Report of the Wholesale Book Trade" that included a prototype of the best-seller list.[52] While these early versions of the best-seller list were geared towards booksellers rather than readers, they already serve the same function that best-seller lists perform today. As Laura Miller puts it, "best-seller lists are powerful marketing tools that book professionals use to sell more books"—the more powerful because "they appear to be straightforward devices that objectively provide us with interesting information about the actions of culture consumers."[53] Best-seller lists, of course, are not without their detractors. Yet the very fact that one cannot completely ignore the best-seller list testifies to the condition of the modern reader—as long as literary texts appear in the context of a commercial culture, it is difficult to distinguish the text that is valuable because of its intrinsic qualities, from the text that is valuable because of its popularity.

The writer of the aforementioned *Quarterly Review* article encounters this very problem of distinguishing intrinsic literary value from that conferred by popularity and resolves it by concluding that current trends themselves are worthy of being recorded *as* history. The *Quarterly* declares that "one of our duties is, to give a literary history of the times we live in—to tell those who follow us what were the subjects and the writers which chiefly engaged the attention of our contemporaries."[54] He participates in the recording—if not the construction—of literary history through his "perishable pages."[55] If contemporary readers cannot benefit from the publication of such book reviews, perhaps "those who follow us" can.[56] Just as *The Tales of My Landlord* records how Jeanie Deans and Old Mortality both circulated at one point in history and memorializes the value of such circulation in the form of fiction, the *Quarterly* invests value into the object by recording the very fact that such a thing did indeed circulate at one point in history.

For many writers and readers of the previous century, however, the *Quarterly's* willingness to use the rapid circulation of the Waverley Novels as evidence of their value would have been puzzling, if not outrageous. For much of the eighteenth century, writers and readers were trying to reconcile themselves to both the quantity and frequency of print circulation. Their skepticism of circulation was often associated with the material form of the publications. While the larger folio volumes were considered stationary occupants of the library, lighter, speedier forms of distributing information such as periodicals and newspapers were regarded as ephemeral and less dignified. In a number of *The Spectator,* for instance, Joseph Addison illustrates this idea by representing how the degree of respect and dignity accorded to different forms of print translate into "Rank and Precedence" among authors:

> I have observed that the Author of a Folio, in all Companies and Conversations, sets himself above the Author of a Quarto: the Author of a Quarto above the Author of an Octavo; and so on, by a gradual Descent and Subordination, to an Author in Twenty-Fours. . . . The most Minute Pocket-Author hath beneath him the Writers of all Pamphlets, or Works that are only stitched. As for the Pamphleteer, he takes place of none but of the Authors of single Sheets, and of that Fraternity who publish their Labours on certain Days, or on every Day of the Week.[57]

While the order of books is dictated by relative size in a straightforward manner, Addison's manner of sorting the remaining publications is perhaps less so. The main criterion that distinguishes pamphlets from periodicals is the minimal binding of "stitches" or the lack thereof. But the final clause emphasizes the periodicity of the publication rather than its materiality; periodicals lack dignity not only because they are scantily dressed, but also because they get around a bit too much.

LOCAL HISTORY FOR DISTANT READERS · 107

Later in the century, George Crabbe presents a similar conceit in verse, though the occupants of the lowest ranks reflect changes in print culture:

> Lo! all in silence, all in order stand;
> And mighty folios first, a lordly band,
> Then quartos, their well-order'd ranks maintain,
> And light octavos fill a spacious plain;
> See yonder, ranged in more frequented rows,
> A humbler band of duodecimos;
> While undistinguish'd trifles swell the scene,
> The last new play and fritter'd magazine.[58]

For Crabbe, the dignity of the different kinds of binding and print does not just hold a superficial resemblance to social class as it does for Addison. The size of the book has a direct correlation with the dignity of its contents, and a reverse correlation with the amount of circulation. Hence, "in these times," the folio volumes remain "untouch'd, . . . / And slumber out their immortality," experiencing no circulation despite their contribution to the knowledge of "Our patient fathers."[59] On the contrary, current readers seek "lighter labours" to such an extent that they are "Cloy'd with a folio-Number once a week."[60] Crabbe's elegiac account of *The Library* reproaches modern readers who absorb information only through frequent consumption of small printed matter, in the form of "cuts and comments."[61] Such a situation is particularly dire in Crabbe's view, since he hardly trusted these "*number'd*" vehicles of information.[62] Echoing Henry Fielding's concerns that I have described in my first chapter, he imagined that writers of periodicals merely wrote enough to satisfy the spatial and quantitative requirements imposed on periodicals, so as to "join / As many words as make an even line" and "As many lines as fill a row complete" and so on, until they filled the entire sheet.[63]

This does not mean that all widely and rapidly circulating texts had no authority and no value. Indeed, *The Spectator,* which was published daily excluding Sundays, managed to establish literary value at the time. As a writer of a daily paper, Mr. Spectator ranks lowest on the social scale of authors that he himself describes. He gains status among his fellow writers, not because his papers circulate more, but because his writing is transformed from a single-page periodical to bound volumes: "I never presumed to take [the] Place of a Pamphleteer till my daily Papers were gathered into those two first Volumes, which have already appeared."[64] Unlike the reviewers of

Scott's novels, Addison does not believe that circulation itself speaks to the value of the publication. Literary value, for Addison, comes with the sense of permanence represented by the materiality of the bound volume. Even for writers such as Samuel Johnson, who wrote periodical essays such as *The Rambler* and *The Idler,* the idea of literary value remained classical in the sense that it aimed to produce lasting fame that can continue to thrive in Parnassus like "oaks of towering height" and "laurels of eternal verdure."[65] An author who accomplishes such a feat, in Johnson's imagination, "writes upon general principles, or delivers universal truths," and "may hope to be often read . . . at all times and in every country, but he cannot expect it to be received with eagerness, or to spread with rapidity."[66] Writings that experience "quick circulation," on the other hand, are those that "take advantage of present incidents or characters which strongly interest the passions, and engage universal attention."[67] By necessity, works that experience "quick circulation" are not qualified to continue to occupy Parnassus after its season has passed. It is only the tombs that contain universal truths, according to Johnson, that endure to become literary classics.

Accessing Local History

Johnson's ideas about literary value did not disappear with the coming of the nineteenth century. But the distinction between enduring "universal truths" and writings that experience "quick circulation" that was so very clear to Johnson seems to become less so for Scott's readers, since the changing infrastructure of the print market exposed them generally to a more rapid circulation of texts. Scott captures this very ambivalence in *The Heart of Midlothian* by establishing Jeanie Deans in the valley of Roseneath, secluded from extended society and the forces of history, after she has made her remarkable journey to London; her temporary fame brought about by circulation gains for her a permanent home. Likewise, the reviews of Scott's novels exemplify how the line becomes blurred between what is permanent and what is temporary, what transmits ideas and expressions of value through time and what transmits them through space. Thus, the reviews choose to reconcile the two by adopting a more historically attuned attitude generated at the intersection of a reading public and consumer democracy that values literary popularity for what it is—a historical record of trends.

Scott demonstrates how he participates in and builds upon this historicizing of literary trends in the editorial matter of *Ballantyne's Novelist's*

Library. Along with other anthologies of novels compiled and published during the decades immediately before and after 1800, *Ballantyne's Novelist's Library* gathered novels of previous generations and consolidated them in a standardized collection. While some anthologies focused on making these novels available to a wide variety of readers through cheap serial publication, *Ballantyne's Novelist's Library* provided a historical outlook on these novels through the prefatory material written by Sir Walter Scott.[68] When we study the contents of *Ballantyne's Novelist's Library,* and when we read Scott's biographical discussion of each author, we find that Scott by no means saw enduring value or universal truth in each and every novel. For instance, his discussion of Charles Johnstone's *Chrysal* makes explicit that he considers his work merely as a curious relic of a past generation. But he also makes clear that the novel's past popularity—the fact that it circulated and was read by many—is a sufficient reason for its inclusion in the library.[69] The idea of the best seller, then, is folded into the novel's history as it is being institutionalized during the Romantic period. When Homer Brown points out that various novels of the eighteenth century "have now taken on a lasting solidity in these magnificent sets" of *Ballantyne's Novelist's Library,* he emphasizes the anthology's kinship to tombs and monuments that work as time-binding media.[70] The idea of "solidity" that is embodied in the materiality of the books thus echoes Johnson's and Crabbe's ideals of the enduring literary classic. And yet that enduring quality may be achieved not just through the intrinsic value of the novel, but also through its history of circulation. In the process of institutionalizing the novel, then, transmission through space ("quick circulation") and transmission through time ("lasting solidity") enter a sort of dialectic so that circulating texts are given a permanent place, which allows them to continue to circulate in posterity.

The institutionalization of the novel, then, is a process that both presupposes and entails circulation and reproduction, leaving no means to access Scott's authentic histories that originate outside the realm of mass marketing. Or does it? Scott later suggests that it is worth sacrificing some degree of authenticity if that is what it takes for stories to be included in this process of cultural transmission, allowing a wider audience to access these narratives in the first place. One may trace narratives to their unique origins later on, as long as they are preserved and transmitted in the first place. In the additional preface to *The Heart of Midlothian* that Scott wrote for the Magnum Opus edition in 1830, Scott reveals "that the information [that inspired the novel] was conveyed to him by a late amiable and ingenious lady,"

110 · LIMITED ACCESS

who communicated by letter a brief narrative about her acquaintance with a humble and obscure Scottish woman, Helen Walker (*H*, 3). Her history is so remarkable that Scott's correspondent Mrs. Goldie "once proposed that a small monument should have been erected to commemorate so remarkable a character." She proceeds, "But I now prefer leaving it to you to perpetuate her memory in a more durable manner" (*H*, 5). Scott's correspondent suggests that literary works are "more durable" than material mediums like monuments. Mrs. Goldie's assessment of the monument-like function of print proves partially true. Though Helen Walker became better known by the name of Jeanie Deans, her history was preserved in a way that it would not have been had it remained memorialized in a "small monument" in an obscure churchyard. As it turns out, Helen Walker's history is authenticated retroactively as her biographical information is recorded in the chronicles of local history—after the publication of *The Heart of Midlothian*.[71] While Scott's novels may not, in fact, originate from a quiet cemetery in a hidden corner of Scotland where relics of the past generation will narrate to strangers the history of those who lie under stones with obscure inscriptions, they show that such scenes—and the authenticity that comes with them—may be constructed retroactively. Perhaps it is with such intention that Scott, at the end of his preface, assures Mrs. Goldie's daughter that he will honor Helen Walker's memory by erecting an actual monument *in addition to* the novel—a monument that can become a site of pilgrimage for readers of *The Heart of Midlothian*, whether they visit it using mail coaches or, later, the railway.[72]

4

Information Overload in Industrial Print Culture

Shortcuts to Knowledge in Dickens's *The Pickwick Papers*

Charles Dickens's *The Posthumous Papers of the Pickwick Club* (1836–37) mobilizes transport metaphors implicitly by taking the name of the titular protagonist from a famous stagecoach proprietor and by mirroring the formal characteristics of eighteenth-century stagecoach novels. Focusing on Dickens's use of stagecoaches as an implicit transport metaphor that dramatizes the tension between eighteenth-century models of narrative and an industrial print culture, this chapter explores how stagecoach metaphors help Dickens conceptualize the mediated nature of knowledge production. Dickens draws attention to how readers have limited access to knowledge despite the abundance of information circulating in society through a Pickwickian journey full of misadventures, misunderstandings, and misreadings. In doing so, he stages the disorienting effects of an industrial print culture that overwhelms readers with information without providing either the time or the know-how to synthesize that information into useful knowledge. Dickens imagines knowledge-making as a mediated activity that does not depend solely on media by drawing attention to both information distribution and readers' ability to mentally process the information they receive. Dickens suggests a solution to this problem by introducing the character of Sam Weller, who presents an alternative model of reading and knowing; using analogical thinking, Sam bypasses systems of knowledge-making to suggest that analogies and other decontextualized comparisons can open up democratic access to knowledge.

Best known as Dickens's first serial fiction and the work that propelled him into popularity as a novelist, *The Pickwick Papers* presents a landscape and a model of traveling that was on the cusp of becoming obsolete for contemporary readers.[1] As Jonathan Grossman and Ruth Livesey have emphasized, Dickens was writing at a time when railways have yet to develop into a full-blown national network, and travel by stagecoach was in a highly developed and flourishing state.[2] Dickens associates his novel implicitly with this coaching network by naming the titular protagonist after a prominent stagecoach proprietor—Moses Pickwick, who ran stages back and forth from his headquarters at the White Hart in Bath.[3] But he also adapts the form of eighteenth-century stagecoach novels, relying on a narrative form that belonged to a less fully developed era of stagecoach travel when roads were not yet macadamized, while setting the action in a recent past of the 1820s.[4] This dizzying historical orientation of *The Pickwick Papers* is further complicated by situating it in the history of the novel as a genre; it heralds the coming of the golden age of Victorian serial fiction, but it was barely recognized as a novel when it was first published because it more closely resembled sporting prints or magazines.[5]

Because *The Pickwick Papers* is both forward- and backward-looking, and because it pushes the bagginess of the novel form to the extreme by gathering the narratives and observations of Cockney protagonists propelled into a world of which they can make no coherent sense, it creates a sense of disorientation that comes from observing a world on the move from a vantage point that, too, is constantly shifting.[6] Scholars have approached this disorienting effect of the novel in two ways: it signals the condition of modernity or it is a problem that needs to be resolved in the course of the narrative. Grossman advocates for the modernity side of the argument by claiming that *The Pickwick Papers* provides a way to imagine the synchronous movement of passengers within a network, moving along and pursuing their own ends alongside, across, and distinct from others. For Grossman, *The Pickwick Papers* is not a novel about the past but about creating "a modern awareness of one's times as fleeting, passing, always-in-the-process-of-becoming-what-it-was, into a sense of community."[7] Livesey, on the other hand, argues that this sense of disorientation stemming from dislocation is staged and resolved in the pages of *The Pickwick Papers* by showing how knowledge and affect remain obstinately localized. Challenging Grossman's idea of a uniform temporality, Livesey draws attention to the unevenness of local time and experience, ultimately upholding the novel as a vehicle that turns localities like Dingley Dell into a portable memory embodying the affect of locality for readers.[8] I build on both their arguments in this chapter to consider, instead, how *The Pickwick Papers* conceptualizes disorientation itself as an effect produced not just by temporality but also by a series of disjunctions in the process of mediation—between vehicle and infrastructure, between narrative form and epistemology, and between the conditions of material production and cognitive processing.

By mobilizing stagecoaches as an implicit metaphor for a contemporaneous transportation network and a formal attribute from novels of the past century, Dickens highlights the tension between early Victorian information culture and the models of knowing promoted in an Enlightenment era of systems. Writing in an information society whose industrial infrastructure distinguished it from that which characterized the Enlightenment, Dickens shows how the old infrastructure of narrative presented in eighteenth-century novels buckles under the pressure of information overload. By negotiating old narrative forms and the new infrastructure of industrial publishing, Dickens highlights the shifting conditions of mediation that underpin realism. *The Pickwick Papers* provides evidence of how stories are consumed differently in industrial society; the serial publication format shows Dickens himself as a writer relating to readers contemporaneously on a massive scale, while the characters within the novel demonstrate how readers may be overwhelmed by the sheer quantity of the stories they read and hear. But Dickens also conceptualizes how mental processes like reflection play a key role in mediating information by showing how his protagonists struggle to process the information presented to them at a rapid rate. Unlike the protagonists of stagecoach novels of the previous century, the Pickwickians fail to achieve a superior knowledge of the world not only because of shifts in media technology but also because they lack cognitive strategies for processing information. When individuals are prostrated in the face of information overload, they must resort to alternative methods of knowing the world. Sam Weller exemplifies a possible alternative by practicing analogical rather than systemic thinking throughout the novel. In doing so, he undermines the Enlightenment assumptions that made knowledge accessible only to the educated and well-to-do. In Sam Weller's world, knowledge is accessible even to those in the lower classes of society so long as they practice a modified empiricism that maps things they already know onto new situations. While rejecting the model of knowing presented by eighteenth-century stagecoach novels as obsolete, Dickens nevertheless asserts the value of revisiting novels from previous generations by featuring

Sam as a reader of literature who gains value from old texts through decontextualized reading.

Publishing in Numbers

In an early episode of *Cranford* (1851–53), Elizabeth Gaskell contrasts the aging and distinctly feminine community of Cranford with the newfangled stuff of the current age represented in the character of Captain Brown.[9] One of the major offenses that Captain Brown commits against the community of Cranford is the introduction of Charles Dickens's *The Pickwick Papers*. Captain Brown calls Mr. Boz's production a "Capital Thing!" but Miss Jenkyns refuses to admit its literary merit.[10] Fancying herself literary, she takes the captain's recommendation as an affront, and pits the famous Dr. Johnson against Mr. Boz. For Miss Jenkyns, Dr. Johnson's fiction is dignified, and his style is "a model for young beginners," but Mr. Boz's productions fall far short of such dignity.[11] Unlike Walter Scott who sought to negotiate the popularity of texts with enduring literary value as I discussed in my previous chapter, Miss Jenkyns accords no value to the wildly popular fiction written by Boz. The only solid critique she has, however, is that "I consider it vulgar, and below the dignity of literature, to publish in numbers." Her logic is flawed, of course. Captain Brown retorts accordingly: "How was the 'Rambler' published, Ma'am?" For Miss Jenkyns, the act of publishing in numbers is overlooked for Johnson, whereas it is distinctly a memorable, vulgarizing characteristic of *The Pickwick Papers*.[12]

Precisely because *Cranford* is a text accorded a unique status in the scholarship of Victorian fiction as a work that draws attention to things—and texts as things—as well as alternative ways to imagine temporality, the appearance of *The Pickwick Papers* within its pages works as a powerful historical marker that highlights the epochal status of Dicken's first serial fiction in Victorian information culture.[13] If Gaskell connects the village of Cranford to an imperial network of information through the "slit" of the post box when Mary Smith posts her letter to Peter Jenkyns,[14] the number of *The Pickwick Papers* that Captain Brown holds in his hands implicates the society of Cranford in an industrial print culture that was part and parcel of Victorian information culture. Moreover, through the figure of Captain Brown, Gaskell also associates *The Pickwick Papers* with a parallel development in industrial capitalism: the emergence of railways. It is appropriate that Captain Brown introduces this modern production to Cranford with enthusiasm, since he is already associated with the move towards industrial modernity that Cranford resists; he moved into Cranford after he "had obtained some situation on a neighbouring railroad, which had been vehemently petitioned against by the little town." *The Rambler* may have been published in numbers, Miss Jenkyns might say, but at least it was written before the days of "the obnoxious railroad."[15] The association between the railroad and *The Pickwick Papers* is further strengthened in Miss Jenkyns' mind when the unfortunate Captain is killed by a steam engine; according to various witnesses as well as the local newspaper, "the 'gallant gentleman was deeply engaged in the perusal of a number of 'Pickwick'" immediately before the accident.[16]

Through her very selective critique, Miss Jenkyns draws attention to how *The Pickwick Papers* performs the unstable relationship between message and medium, content and format of literary texts in the context of a Victorian information culture underpinned by industrial print culture. *The Pickwick Papers* was not necessarily associated with the railway, but to the system of coaching that reached its zenith in the 1830s, as Grossman and Livesey amply demonstrate. Indeed, there are only very few hints within the text that clue us into the fact that *The Pickwick Papers* was written during years of rapid industrialization and railroad construction.[17] But Gaskell also reminds us that *The Pickwick Papers* was associated with the emerging railroads implicitly—in ways that are invisible to us twenty-first-century readers. Though readers only see glimpses of the railway in the text of *The Pickwick Papers,* Victorian men and women were sure to be reading elsewhere about the construction of new railway lines or even hearing the thundering of railway carriages in the background as they read in their homes. *The Pickwick Papers* neither thematizes railways extensively nor relied upon a full-fledged railway network for its delivery to readers, but its mode of production and the specific way in which it implemented the serial format were distinctly informed by industrial capitalism—despite a plot structure that recalls to readers' minds the stagecoach novels of eighteenth-century authors like Henry Fielding and Tobias Smollett.

Several elements of the *The Pickwick Papers* remind readers of mideighteenth-century novels by Fielding and Smollett, as numerous critics have remarked.[18] In the same way that eighteenth-century "fictions of social circulation" present heroes who circulate throughout the nation discovering new characters and scenery, the members of the Pickwick Club peregrinate throughout the country endeavoring to gain further insight into men and manners of the current age.[19] Thus, the form of *The Pickwick Papers* resembles a stagecoach novel—an updated version of the picaresque—that characterizes the eighteenth rather than the nineteenth century. The incidents represented in the plot are often of a comical nature, and Mr. Pickwick's quixotic benevolence may remind readers of a Parson Adams or Matthew Bramble. The narrative is highly episodic; the Pickwickians alternately pursue leisurely journeys, experience extended encounters, and chase after other characters. Such narrative form is reminiscent of the various encounters and near-misses that characterize Tom Jones's and Sophia Western's journeys to London. During the first half of the text, this narrative structure goes hand-in-hand with the method of travel that the Pickwickians adopt; stagecoach routes determine characters' destinations and consequently their encounters, and carriages are upset with remarkably good (or bad) timing. And last but not least, the object of their journey is to carry "the speculations of that learned man [Mr. Pickwick] into a wider field, from extending his travels, and consequently enlarging his sphere of observations, to the advancement of knowledge, and the diffusion of learning" (*PP,* 3). Deidre Lynch explains that fictions of social circulation revolve around protagonists who travel throughout the nation, gathering observations and experience in various parts of the country among various classes of people. Ultimately, such knowledge and wisdom acquired through circulation become the prerequisite for heroes of such novels to gain gentlemanly status in the novels' dénouements.[20] Putting the cart before the horse, Dickens makes the accumulation of knowledge the stated goal of the Pickwickians' peregrinations rather than the unintended outcome; an overdetermined character fated to circulate, it is no wonder that the titular protagonist bears the name of a famous stagecoach proprietor.

Dickens claims to have adopted the form of stagecoach novels not only as an extension of his own career as a writer of sketches in periodical publications, but also in the process of reproducing the narrative form that he dimly remembered in "certain interminable novels in that form [shilling numbers], which used to be carried about the country by pedlars" as he states in the preface to *The Pickwick Papers* written in 1836 (*PP,* xxvii–xxviii). Dickens never specifies which novels he had in mind, but perhaps they may have been part of Cooke's Pocket Library series, whose edition of *Tales of the Genii* fascinated the young Dickens, as Peter Ackroyd describes. Other novels published in a collection such as Cooke's Pocket Library series would have included those written by Smollett, Fielding, and Defoe as well as Oliver Goldsmith's *The Vicar of Wakefield* along with some translated texts such as *Don Quixote* and *Gil Blas*.[21] It is worth noting, too, that these standard novels (or what William St. Clair calls "the old canon") were also published in periodical format, such as *The Novelist's Magazine* published between 1780 and 1788.[22]

Dickens's stagecoach novel begins by upholding the ideal of such fictions of social circulation and proclaims the goal of achieving the same end of obtaining what John Barrell calls an "equal wide survey" of English society.[23] But without gaining the same results. Indeed, it may be difficult for Mr. Pickwick to travel peacefully and productively when "travelling was in a troubled state," and when "stagecoaches were upsetting in all directions, horses were bolting, boats were overturning, and boilers were bursting" (*PP,* 6). Far from gaining a synthesized understanding of society and its inhabitants, Mr. Pickwick, at the end of the narrative, remains just as naïve and just as unversed in the ways of the world as when he first commenced his journey. Indeed, he would hardly get along without the help of his trusty servant, Sam Weller. Sam, whose peculiar "eddication" consists of having been let loose to "run in the streets when he was wery young, and shift for his-self" (*PP,* 255), acts as a well-qualified guide who helps Mr. Pickwick and his companions navigate the trappings of society from the intricate streets of London to the malicious intentions of other men. While Mr. Pickwick's naïveté and benevolence are emphasized from the very beginning of the narrative, Sam's patronizing care of his master underscores how Mr. Pickwick is destined to remain innocent and gullible. For Sam, Mr. Pickwick is like an "angel in tights and gaiters" whose benevolence enables him to do much good (*PP,* 598), but that benevolence is accompanied by an implicit trust in the people he encounters so that the more practiced members of society can easily "eat him up alive" (*PP,* 567). While Mr. Pickwick "hopes" that his adventures have contributed "to the enlargement of [his] mind, and the improvement of [his] understanding" (*PP,* 742), the closing scene that records his installment in a country house is not the triumphant moment that marks the well-earned elevation or regaining of social status of a Tom Jones or a Roderick Random. Rather, it is a "peaceful retirement" during which he hopes that "none of [his] adventures will be other than a source of amusing and pleasant recollection to [him] in the decline of life" (*PP,* 741–42). The ramblings and adventures of Mr. Pickwick do not equip him with the knowledge of the world. They merely provide personal "recollection" for amusement in his years of retirement—recollections that may become nostalgic narratives told to youths of the next generation (a theme I will discuss in my next chapter).

Such failure to gain the end of a typical stagecoach novel signals how *The Pickwick Papers* uses the form of the stagecoach novel not to reproduce novels of the previous century, but for different purposes of its own such as the need to accommodate the peculiar publication format. The narrative structure of *The Pickwick Papers* is ideally suited to accommodate its mode of publication.[24] The well-known story of the origin of *The Pickwick Papers* tells us that Chapman and Hall, the publishers, originally envisioned the publication as a series of illustrations accompanied by brief, comical prose, resembling sporting prints that were popular at the time, rather than a full-blown narrative accompanied by illustrations.[25] The young Dickens, who by then was becoming well known as the author of *Sketches by Boz,* was pitched upon as the appropriate second to the famous illustrator, Robert Seymour. Prior to Dickens's participation, it had already been determined that Seymour's illustrations were to present comical scenes of sporting activities in the English countryside, and that his illustrations were to provide direction and plot for the series of publications. After agreeing to this initial arrangement, or so the story goes, Dickens managed to overturn the relationship between illustration and prose; his prose would occupy a larger proportion of each installment, and it would also provide plot and direction, engaging subject matters that extend beyond sporting. Seymour's premature death soon after the launch of the series provided further impetus for Dickens to take the reins and to dictate the future direction of the project. As N. N. Feltes reminds us, however, one must not be too hasty to attribute the subsequent explosion of the popularity of *The Pickwick Papers* to Dickens's genius or to the business acumen of Chapman and Hall. In the process of detailing the historical circumstances that made possible the first mass-produced, mass-consumed literary text, Feltes underscores how Chapman and Hall owned the means of production, while Dickens occupied but the position of a laborer.[26] Robert Patten further elaborates the process of negotiating the serial publication form in the early stages of the venture to highlight the constant negotiations between the author and publisher. For instance, while Dickens successfully changed the relationship between illustration and prose, such an arrangement also increased Dickens's responsibility each month in providing longer manuscripts.[27] The format of serial publication in shilling parts was one of the conditions of production predetermined by the capitalist rather than the laborer, by Chapman and Hall rather than Dickens, by the printing press rather than the author's pen. The narrative structure of *The Pickwick Papers* presents a series of encounters on the road, and this narrative structure, in turn, helps to accommodate publication in serial format.

As it turns out, Miss Jenkyns and Captain Brown are both right; publishing in numbers is by no means a new practice, but it also took on new challenges and new possibilities in the context of industrial publishing. Tom Keymer sketches a brief history of how writers, editors, and publishers like Samuel Richardson, Edward Cave, Tobias Smollett, and Laurence Sterne experimented with serial publication during the previous century.[28] Keymer argues, on the one hand, that these examples in the mid-eighteenth century show that serial publication is by no means a uniquely Victorian literary phenomenon. On the other hand, he also notes that his examples "provide several cases in which serialization came under an unusually high degree of authorial control, thus standing apart from the later tendency of the form to constrain as much as it enabled, or to subordinate the creative freedom of the individual novelist to the relentless measures and schedules of an industrialized publishing machine."[29] Eighteenth-century serial fiction, then, works as both precedent and exception; writers before Dickens wrote fiction in serialized format, but these writers of the previous generation were not forced to accommodate and adapt to the format in the same way. While the previous forms of serialization to which Keymer refers appeared within magazines or in separate volumes of fiction, *The Pickwick Papers* took neither form—it was a standalone publication unlike magazines that featured literary works among other pieces of writing, but each number was too short to be considered a volume of fiction. As it turns out, these shilling numbers were priced low enough for mass distribution of fiction, but this very format, according to Kathryn Chittick, initially caused much confusion about how to categorize *The Pickwick Papers*.[30] In the pages of *The Sun*, it was not reviewed as a novel, or even as "Literature," but as a "magazine," even though there was only one contributor. It was associated more with "sketches" and "miscellanies" that adorned the corners of newspapers and other periodical publications than with installations that would eventually form a "novel."

Information Overload

Despite its ambiguous literary status during the years of its publication, *The Pickwick Papers,* at least in hindsight, came to be considered a novel, as Chittick concedes.[31] Chittick, however, seems troubled by the narrative form of *The Pickwick Papers* and qualifies her argument by suggesting that "the principle of miscellany" may inhere in the novel as a genre after "Dickens improvised it."[32] But the miscellaneous representations of snippets and tidbits can be said to have been part of the novel's history long before the advent of Dickens. Interpolated tales such as "The Stroller's Tale" and "The Convict's Return" are interspersed within the pages of *The Pickwick Papers* just as "the History of the Man of the Hill" and "The Memoirs of a Lady of Quality" appear within the pages of *Tom Jones* and *Peregrine Pickle.* The Pickwickians visit new locales and witness various events, thus producing sketches of places and things. But so are the descriptions of London and Edinburgh presented in the letters of Matthew Bramble in Smollett's *Humphry Clinker*—descriptions that functioned so well as independent "sketches" that they were excerpted and reprinted as standalone pieces in periodical publications.[33]

But Dickens also extends "the principle of miscellany" to highlight how industrial print production creates the conditions for information overload.[34] Characterizing the Pickwickians as avid information-mongers who are eager to record everything from the cabman's account of the longevity of horses to "romance[s] of real life" narrated by various characters, Dickens imagines a world abounding in information of all sorts. By staging the Pickwickian world as a world of information, *The Pickwick Papers* works as an example of how "Victorian fiction, with its tendencies toward extended narrative, multiple plotlines, and experiments in serialization, was well suited for the enterprise of imagining a course through the vast Babel-like, Babbage-esque library of a world that was also information," as Richard Menke argues.[35] While the novel does not focus on specific information technologies, it does imagine how culture mediates information and how, specifically, it overproduces information so that information management and processing became an urgent issue.

The text thematizes overproliferation of information from the very outset. Alfred Jingle, the adventurer whom Mr. Pickwick seeks to punish in the first half of the novel, for instance, produces stories at such a rapid rate that he fails to fully articulate them. His narrative of a conquest over a Spanish lady, for example, proceeds thus: "Don Bolaro Fizzgig—Grandee—only daughter—Donna Christina—splendid creature—loved me to distraction—jealous father—high-souled daughter—handsome Englishman—Donna Christina in despair" and so on (*PP,* 13). His strange "system of stenography," as Mr. Pickwick notices, consists of "rapid and disjointed communication" (*PP,* 86). It almost mimics the effects that a reader might have when skimming a book by piling up important bits of information, one stumbling on top of the other, without any attempt at connection or transition. Scribbling down Jingle's narratives without sufficient scrutiny or understanding, the Pickwickians swallow his fictions whole without having the time necessary to digest the narrative or to evaluate its merits.

Jingle, of course, is not the only character that contributes to the (over)production of words and texts. The *Eatanswill Gazette* and the *Eatanswill Independent* engage in a never-ending battle over print defending their respective party's opinions (*PP,* 150). Even Mr. Pickwick himself unwittingly participates in this system of excessive production by publishing his discoveries. When he discovers the curious stone with a strange inscription in the village of Cobham, he publishes pamphlets and presents lectures that "entered into a variety of ingenious and erudite speculations on the meaning of the inscription" found upon this antiquarian discovery (*PP,* 142). When Mr. Blotton, a refractory member of the Pickwick Club, denies the antiquity of the inscription, he triggers an immense scientific discussion characterized, first and foremost, by the amount of text it produces: "Hereupon the virtuous indignation of the seventeen learned societies, native and foreign, being roused, several fresh pamphlets appeared; the foreign learned societies corresponded with the native learned societies; the native learned societies translated the pamphlets of the foreign learned societies into English; the foreign learned societies translated the pamphlets of the native learned societies into all sorts of languages; and thus commenced that celebrated scientific discussion so well known to all men, as the Pickwick controversy" (*PP,* 143). Readers are here told of the immense quantity of correspondence and pamphlets that had been produced as Mr. Pickwick's account of his discovery triggers an enormous controversy. But readers also remain ignorant of what this textual production helps to accomplish. Ultimately, the production of texts fails to accomplish anything, and instead creates a state of limbo. Such description may remind readers of the Chancery Court in *Bleak House* or the Circumlocution Office in *Little Dorrit,* where the victims of an unjust system remain suspended in a state of uncertainty. In his later works, Dickens often describes such pointless and excessive proliferation of texts as the peculiar function of bureaucratic institutions. However, in *The Pickwick Papers,* texts breed more texts and lies produce more lies more generally throughout society—in scientific circles, in club rooms, in public houses, and in publications such as newspapers.

Ironically, the very success of *The Pickwick Papers* is predicated on a principle of production similar to that which it satirizes. When Feltes characterizes *The Pickwick Papers* as a commodity text, he draws our attention to how *The Pickwick Papers* "marks the transition . . . from the petty-commodity production of books to industrial capitalist production of texts."[36] Such transition mirrors the more general transition towards a full-fledged industrial capitalist mode of production and enables us to recognize the publishing industry itself as a "sub-ensemble" within a wider constellation of industries. Feltes characterizes *The Pickwick Papers* as a commodity text because it has two distinctively industrial capitalist traits: first, the publisher controls the labor process by predetermining the serial format as I have discussed earlier, and second, the product acquires greater surplus value through the very process of production that allows "the bourgeois audience's ideological engagement to be sensed and expanded."[37] Feltes draws our attention to the changed relationship between the production process and the market that consumes the product. Rather than simply identifying a preexisting market and satisfying its needs, industrial capitalism creates and expands the market in which to dispense the perpetual stream of goods it produces. Likewise, *The Pickwick Papers* expanded its sale and increased its readers by feeding off of their engagement, a process made possible by the serial publication format. Dickens was particularly adept at establishing intimacy with readers; Patrick Brantlinger argues that the "instances in which Dickens altered his novels in the middle of their serial publication because of sales figures or, even more dramatically, because of fan mail or direct reader response are evidence that, at least for himself and several other successful novelists, the relations between reader and writer could be dialogical, almost conversationally familiar."[38] Furthermore, the very indeterminacy of *The Pickwick Papers* invited so much fan mail that an address had to be issued, asking readers to desist from sending letters to the publisher.[39] The explosion of *The Pickwick Papers* can thus be seen as a phenomenon reinforcing the sense of textual overproduction represented within the novel. Readers read about characters consuming stories, one after another, only to look forward to the next new story. In the meantime, readers voraciously read each number of *The Pickwick Papers,* which, in turn, made them look forward to the following number and perhaps to write fan mail making suggestions about the fate of their favorite characters.

By using the miscellaneous form of stagecoach novels to accommodate a distinctly industrial capitalist mode of publishing, *The Pickwick Papers* underscores the friction between old forms and new material realities, between familiar vehicles and unfamiliar infrastructures. Such friction was by no means unique to the world of print. Back in 1802, long before passenger railways had become part of everyday life, Richard Lovell Edgeworth proposed a curious method of using this newfangled technology called the railway.[40] For Edgeworth, the railway had obvious promises—by eliminating much of the friction and unevenness caused by conventional roads, rails would enable more efficient and speedy traveling. He proposed that rails should be laid to provide infrastructure for travel, but rather than conveying passengers en masse in carriages built for the purpose, railways should build platforms upon which coaches and chaises can be loaded. Once loaded upon these platforms, the horses can more smoothly pull the carriages, individually, to their destinations. Edgeworth's proposal comes to be partially adopted in the transition years of the railway. While horses were not commissioned to pull individual coaches on railway platforms, mail coaches made use of partial railway lines by being loaded onto flatbeds that formed part of the railway ensemble.[41] Edgeworth was obviously one among the many who had yet to experience the paradigm shift that railway technology necessitated, but his ideas, nevertheless, provide important insight about Dickens's novel. Like the coach-railway hybrid that Edgeworth proposed, *The Pickwick Papers* appears to be an odd hybrid. It is based on the new infrastructure of industrial print capitalism that Feltes describes, and yet it continues to use formal attributes from past novels, leading critics like Chittick to ponder the difficulty of categorizing its genre.[42]

The consequence of this mismatch between the vehicle and infrastructure can be seen in the form of *The Pickwick Papers* in two ways: not only does the novel move away from the fictional apparatus that stages the narrative as a record of information provided by the traveling Pickwickians, it also increasingly downplays stagecoach journeys as an organizing principle of the plot. While the first half of *The Pickwick Papers* portrays the Pickwickians in the position of consumers who are always eager for the next story and the next encounter, avidly collecting narratives while only passively understanding them, the latter half of the novel betrays the limits of such information-gathering. When Mr. Pickwick enters Fleet Prison as a debtor who refuses to pay legal costs, he is initially eager to learn the peculiarities and conventions of the prison. He meets new characters, views the horrors of poverty in the "poor side" of the prison, and sympathizes with a worn-down Chancery prisoner. Towards the beginning of his incarceration, he is interested enough in the new scenes surrounding him to look "good-humouredly around" and to observe, "'Curious scene this, is it not, Sam?'" as he surveys the narrow grounds and observes the prisoners lounging about (*PP*, 599). He "wandered along all the galleries, up and down all the staircases, and once again round the whole area of the yard." After a while, however, his curiosity begins to wane, and he becomes disinterested in the sights and stories of the prison. He is overwhelmed, not with a variety of characters and stories, but too large a dose of the same: "the great body of the prison population appeared to be Mivins, and Smangle, and the parson, and the butcher, and the leg, over and over, and over again. There were the same squalor, the same turmoil and noise, the same general characteristics, in every corner; in the best and the worst alike." Such repetition of sameness prostrates Mr. Pickwick rather than enabling him to classify different characters and to comprehend the microcosm of the Fleet.[43] Inundated with worthless characters and stories of injustice, Mr. Pickwick retires to his private room, declaring that "my head aches with these scenes, and my heart too. Henceforth I will be a prisoner in my own room" (*PP*, 601). As Mr. Pickwick's range of circulation narrows to the confines of Fleet Prison, sameness and repetition overwhelm him until he decides to remain in his room and refuses to circulate at all; he admits defeat, both mentally and emotionally, in the face of overwhelming repetition of "the same general characteristics," which he experiences "over and over, and over again." A more benign version of this symptom appears during the Pickwickians' visit to Bath, where they engage in a "very pleasant routine, with perhaps a slight tinge of sameness" (*PP*, 473). Such repetition fails to produce useful empirical data for Mr. Pickwick and merely induces fatigue like a factory worker going through the same repetitive motions and looking at the same redundant objects day in and day out, producing the effect that Clifford Siskin and William Warner call "saturation," which happens when "the sense of difference generated by initial proliferation becomes more of the same."[44]

The fear over the relatively large quantities of circulating material—information or otherwise—is a persistent theme in literary history and is by no means a uniquely Victorian phenomenon. Indeed, it is the fear of excessive circulation of empty polemic that characterizes Jonathan Swift's *The Tale of a Tub,* and it is the fear of being unable to trace commodities back to their origin that motivates Daniel Defoe to pen *A Tour Through the Whole Isle of Great Britain.* In my previous chapters, I have described how the novelistic genre engages these fears by detailing Smollett's and Sterne's concerns about their messages becoming lost in a tide of commercial economy, and by analyzing Scott's attempt to overcome the homogenizing effects of national circulation. Thus, while each generation of writers experiences fear or anxiety over circulation because of different historical and material conditions, the concerns they express are, in many ways, a variation on the same theme.

But *The Pickwick Papers* presents a variation on this theme by associating narrative excess with the predicament of early Victorian information culture that Menke describes in full detail. On the one hand, Menke points out, the early nineteenth century witnessed how "this conception of knowledge contributes to the Whiggish belief that producing and spreading it would bring not simply material but moral progress."[45] For Menke, this belief is borne out by the establishment of institutions like the Society for the Diffusion of Useful Knowledge (SDUK) as well as the penny post. Such institutions aimed to make "knowledge" available to a broad audience cheaply and in accessible formats in the form of encyclopedias, instructional essays, and other publications—texts that can be categorized under what Alan Rauch calls "knowledge texts."[46] One the other hand, however, such naïve belief in the power of spreading knowledge butted up against new realities. Building on well-established arguments, Menke claims that "new modes of rapid communication and ramped-up data collection threatened to exceed any capacity for diffusion, assimilation, or use."[47] In an attempt to spread knowledge using the latest tools for communication and dissemination, Victorians unwittingly proliferated information. If knowledge implied a cohesive and unified understanding of the world, information indicates potential material for knowledge that remains scattered and inert. Detached from their original context, what counts as knowledge for the authors turns into mere information for consumers, who end up accumulating decontextualized facts without coherence. Ruth Livesey provides a vivid indication of what such information overload entailed; in the years that witnessed the publication of *The Pickwick Papers,* correspondence increased to such an extent that passengers were gradually being squeezed out of mail coaches by excess paper—an excess produced by the very organizations like the SDUK. Livesey aptly observes that "the much-vaunted 'march of the intellect' across Britain at the time Dickens was writing *Pickwick* threatened to overturn the coach system altogether."[48]

Dickens parodies the Pickwick Club's—and by association the SDUK's—aspiration to enlighten society through a wide distribution of knowledge in an industrial print culture by drawing attention to the potentially irresponsible nature of such a project. This is evident in the narrator's own self-characterization as the editor of *The Pickwick Papers.* The numerous other fictitious editors I have analyzed in the previous chapters assert authority in various ways, whether by making claim to truth, historical accuracy, or their right to property in the manuscript. The narrator of *The Pickwick Papers,* on the other hand, uses a distinctly industrial language to describe himself as a mere link in the chain of knowledge production. His role is like that of a capital corporation whose work it is to process resources and to deliver the resulting product to the consumer: "The labours of others have raised for us an immense reservoir of important facts. We merely lay them on, and communicate them, in a clear and gentle stream, through the medium of these numbers, to a world thirsting for Pickwickian knowledge" (*PP,* 43–44). The "labours of others," in many cases, refer to the never-ending scribbling and note taking that occupies the Pickwickians throughout their journey. And since the "facts" that the Pickwickians record are numerous, miscellaneous, and indiscriminate, so, too, does the "clear and gentle stream" consist of numerous, miscellaneous, and indiscriminate incidents. Even when the chronicle fails, it is not because of the lack of resources or because there are no records to draw upon. Quantitatively, the narrator assures us, there is a massive amount of information. The only problem is that not all the sources can be deciphered or understood clearly. Such is the case when "Mr. Snodgrass, as usual, took a great mass of notes, which would no doubt have afforded most useful and valuable information, had not the burning eloquence of the words or the feverish influence of the wine made that gentleman's hand so extremely unsteady, as to render his writing nearly unintelligible, and his style wholly so" (*PP,* 91). Throughout *The Pickwick Papers,* the "most useful and valuable information" that "no doubt" exists seems almost within reach—of the characters, the narrator, and the readers. But they ultimately remain elusive, leaving the occupants of Dickens's fictional world in a state where they must get by without ever attaining a full and comprehensive view of the world they inhabit.

The Mediating Mind

While Dickens parodies the SDUK and its aspirations to widely disseminate knowledge through textual (over)production, he also alerts us to another crucial component of knowledge-making: how readers mentally process information. He implicitly critiques the industrial capitalist mode of print production for its irresponsible proliferation of so-called knowledge both directly (in the passage above) as well as indirectly (by associating information production with Jingle, the adventurer, or with pointless scientific debates). But he also highlights the gullibility of the Pickwickians in taking information at face value. The Pickwickians exemplify readers who consume information without reflection or judgment, and their lack of mental processing highlights how the human mind is part of a mediating process that digests information and turns it into knowledge. John Brown and Paul Duguid distinguish information from knowledge by arguing that knowledge cannot exist apart from the subject who internalizes and systematizes information to create a way of knowing the world.[49] While the distinction between information and knowledge is unstable during the Victorian period when the concept of information was just beginning to emerge, the distinction is useful for drawing attention to the full range of mediation required for information to become meaningful. In other words, knowledge-production is a process that requires not only the production and dissemination of information but also the cognitive tasks of understanding, interpreting, reflecting, evaluating, and imagining that make particular pieces of information integral to knowledge.

The lack of mental information processing on the part of Pickwickians becomes clear, once again, by juxtaposing them with protagonists of eighteenth-century stagecoach novels. While the distinct episodes in the novels of a Fielding or a Smollett are framed by the judgment and reflection of the protagonists who use the stories they hear as a means of gathering observations and gaining maturity, the Pickwickian events and inset narratives fail to impact the development of characters for the most part because they fail to produce meaningful knowledge. *The Pickwick Papers* is distinct from these previous forms of fiction not only because the narrative is more miscellaneous in ways that suggest overproduction of information but also because it shows characters who struggle to synthesize information into knowledge.

For instance, when Fielding describes Tom Jones and Partridge listening to the interminable "history" of the Man of the Hill, the narrator makes sure to clue readers into the character-audience's reactions that show how characters listen to, reflect upon, and evaluate the story they hear. Not only are readers made to understand Jones's verbal reactions to the history itself, but they are also notified of moments when Jones "smiled at some conceit" of the Man of the Hill.[50] Moreover, the history ends not merely with a simple thanks on the part of the listeners but with an extended dialogue in which Jones points out the "error" that the Man of the Hill commits when he takes "the character of mankind from the worst and basest among them."[51] Such dialogue show that listening to the stranger's story is one of the experiences of life that the protagonist learns valuable lessons from and also helps to incorporate the inset narrative more firmly into the moral and narrative fabric of the entire novel by making the knowledge gained from these lessons a part of the protagonist's outlook onto the world.

In *The Pickwick Papers,* however, no such dialogue takes place to demonstrate how the protagonists learn lessons—moral or otherwise—from the various stories they hear. In some cases, circumstances conspire to prevent readers from gaining valuable Pickwickian insight. Immediately after "The Stroller's Tale," for instance, "Mr. Pickwick was on the point of delivering some remarks which would have enlightened the world, if not the Thames," the narrator conjectures, had he not been interrupted precisely at that moment by some visitors entering the room (*PP,* 40). Some other stories, such as "The Convict's Return" and "The Story of Goblins Who Stole a Sexton" end along with the chapter so that readers gain no insight into the reaction of the character-audience. In yet other instances, readers simply see the protagonists enjoy a story, only to walk away from it without a response, as does Mr. Pickwick when he finishes reading "The True Legend of Prince Bladud." He "yawned, several times, when he had arrived at the end of this little manuscript: carefully refolded, and replaced it in the ink-stand drawer: and then, with a countenance expressive of the utmost weariness, lighted his chamber candle, and went up stairs to bed" (*PP,* 478). Dickens never clearly attributes such absence of reflection to a particular cause; the Pickwickians may not engage in reflection because they don't have time, because of information overload, or because of their middle-class Cockney background. The novel, however, deliberately limits moments of reflection as though to intentionally leave inset narratives suspended within the narrative without a clear framework for interpreting them.

It is not just the characters' ability or inability to learn from hearing stories that is at stake here. What is at stake is the epistemic shift that is represented through characters' changing relationship to stories. Both Mr. Pickwick and Roderick Random work as agents for gathering narratives, and both Mr. Pickwick and Tom Jones encounter numerous strangers on the road. But while Roderick Random and Tom Jones are characters who help to synthesize the narratives and incidents in the novel into systemic knowledge of the world, Mr. Pickwick by no means helps us conceive of a coherent world that makes sense in the same way. In the world of Fielding and Smollett, villains are punished and the protagonists profit permanently from life experiences that constantly remind them to stay on the right moral path to happiness and prosperity as respected gentlemen. In the Pickwickian world, Dodson and Fogg still continue to prey on the naïve and innocent, and life experiences function merely as memories of a happy past.[52]

The Pickwick Papers shows a world lacking the kind of overarching "system" that Clifford Siskin argues characterized Enlightenment thought. Siskin considers system as a genre that mediates knowledge by providing a framework for organizing and explaining observations or, in turn, constraining them.[53] Tom Jones and Roderick Random, on the one hand, can be considered as agents of the Enlightenment. As characters who gather stories and experience from various ranks of society and extensive parts of the nation, they carry out the Enlightenment project of collecting and cataloguing their fictional surroundings. They represent, in other words, the encyclopedic impulse—the desire to catalogue the entire world so that it can be understood coherently and systematically—that characterizes the Enlightenment.[54] Mr. Pickwick, on the other hand, demonstrates the lack of a useful mental framework when he attempts to describe Rochester and the towns surrounding it: the fictional editor writes, "'The principal productions of these towns,' says Mr. Pickwick, 'appear to be soldiers, sailors, Jews, chalk, shrimps, officers, and dockyard men. The commodities chiefly exposed for sale in the public streets are marine stores, hard-bake, apples, flatfish, and oysters'" (*PP*, 15). Adopting the style of a travelogue, Mr. Pickwick attempts to reduce his observations to a catalogue of the town's commercial productions and in the process jumbles together professions, ethnicities, and commodities and collapses the distinction between stores and what they sell. The catalogue reflects neither a sense of hierarchy (stores > goods) nor categories (population demographics, employment, minerals, and source of animal protein). Such a catalogue can hardly be explained except as the result of writing down what he saw in the order in which they caught his attention. While the Pickwickians have access to the means of physical mobility that enable them to see various locales and deliver their letters, they do not have access to conceptual tools—that is, systems—necessary to make meaning out of what they see and hear.

The publication process of *The Pickwick Papers* very much resembles the Pickwickian attempt at knowledge-making—haphazard and opportunistic, with very little time to engage in reflections that help to generate a systemic worldview. Detailing the process of issuing the first few numbers, Patten vividly brings to life the manic pace of production and the uncertainty of what *The Pickwick Papers* will look like for both author and publisher. Chapman and Hall, of course, had multiple engagements, including *The Library of Fiction* to which Dickens also contributed. Dickens's commitments were staggering; he continued to be a reporter for the *Morning Chronicle*, had promised two triple-decker novels to two other publishers, and continued to produce new sketches for *Sketches by Boz*, among other things. Amidst this whirlwind, both author and publisher attempted to fulfill the advertised promise that *The Pickwick Papers* would appear to the public in a certain format—namely, monthly numbers that include four prints accompanied by twenty-four pages of printed prose. At least initially, Dickens not only struggled to meet the deadlines (which were set early enough to give the illustrator plenty of time), but also struggled to "write up to" a comic incident appropriate for illustration.[55] The constraints imposed by the format also meant that lengths of chapters needed to be somewhat controlled.[56] Patten thus concludes that "all the parties involved in getting out the first number of *The Pickwick Papers* were working together to produce a 'something' that no one had complete control over."[57] The publication format was later adjusted to include only two illustrations and thirty-two pages of letterpress, thus giving Dickens room to develop more complex scenes and plots. But the fact remains that Dickens continually struggled to fulfill the stated goal of the publication as advertised, just as the Pickwickians struggled to fulfill their declared intention to create and diffuse new knowledge. Both seem to be striving for "a 'something' that no one had complete control over."

Grossman suggests that this "something" is the idea of a network that can replace the idea of an overarching system that was no longer useful in the post-Enlightenment context. Reading Dickens's first novel in light of the networked society made possible by rapid public transport, Grossman convincingly argues that "what matters about the serialization of the nineteenth-century novel is that it materializes through its story's serial delivery the novel's formal capacity to express individual fates collectively networked as they proceed from a shaping past toward an unwritten future."[58] Just as the public transport system allows individuals to pursue their own purposes by traveling through its channels, *The Pickwick Papers* formally enacts the possibility of taking stories that appear miscellaneous and haphazard while understanding how they are networked nevertheless. Grossman proceeds to argue that *The Pickwick Papers* helped to negotiate the "meaning of serialization," and in doing so, "far from merely leading to a slew of imitative serialized coaching adventures, *Pickwick* thus ushered in serialization . . . as the format for a whole variety of realist novels."[59]

If serial fiction performs the network's ability to show how miscellaneous bodies and stories are united—albeit unintentionally—through an interconnected web, it also has the potential to downplay the cognitive agency of individuals. Faced with information overload that was symptomatic of Victorian culture, the Pickwickians lean towards what psychologists have called information bias. That is, they seek more and more information, even if further information is not very relevant or only adds to their confusion. The end of the Pickwickian journey is to make observations, gain knowledge, and diffuse it to others. But that agenda is never realized as they end up seeking information for its own sake—that is, before they give up their efforts in the face of saturation. The Pickwickians are caught up in a network that puts both bodies and information into circulation without giving individuals within the network the ability to see a coherent whole.[60] *The Pickwick Papers* not only represents how the Pickwickians are surrounded by an over-proliferation of stories, but also exposes the unrealistic expectations inherent in their attempt. They cannot gain a coherent and synthesized understanding of the world simply by accumulating more and more stories, especially without a cognitive process for mediating large amounts of information. But by making Sam Weller the moral center of the novel,

Dickens presents a more realistic way to mentally process information—an approach that sees the world for what it is without attempting to systematically record and understand everything—that can be shared by his readers.

Thinking Analogically

In contrast with the Pickwickians who tend to be clueless, bewildered, or overwhelmed, Sam Weller possesses a knowing attitude and a familiarity with the ways of the world. It is perhaps no coincidence that he is familiar with various stories, particularly relating to the urban environment of London; these stories help him better understand and remember various places and people, and thus enable him to safely guide Mr. Pickwick in his adventures. Sam not only physically guides Mr. Pickwick through the intricate streets of London, but also provides accompanying narratives whenever possible. He does not just answer his master's query, "Which way?" but is also "always especially anxious to impart to his master any exclusive information he possessed" (*PP,* 394–95). Thus, quite a few anecdotes originate from Sam and are narrated in his voice—such as the story about the man who was killed by his very own invention of "the patent-never-leavin'-off sassage steam ingine" that occurred "at a house they were passing" (*PP,* 395). While Mr. Pickwick and his friends indiscriminately take in stories without ever referring back to them, Sam seems to have collected a wide stock of narratives and is able to recall them when the occasion demands.

The familiarity with such narratives gives Sam a knowledge of the world superior to that of the Pickwickians, even though his knowledge seems peculiar and miscellaneous. Some of his stories seem to elucidate a moral point or the workings of society. For instance, while observing an election at Eatanswill, Sam narrates an account of how his father's stagecoach filled with voters for one party was mysteriously upset—just as the committee-man of the other party had predicted. The story is, in essence, a simple story of election-time bribery (the coachman, his father, had been paid by the committee-man), but Sam calls it a "miraculous circumstance" and thus downplays the story's function as an exposé (*PP,* 159). Many of his other narratives, however, do not even pretend to have any practical value and tend to present mysterious urban legends mostly for strangeness's sake. The story of the man who was killed by his own sausage-making steam engine is one such example. His account of the pieman who uses kittens to substitute for veal is another (*PP,* 240). The stories that constitute Sam's repertoire, then, are by no means stories that show representative examples of humanity or society. They focus, rather, on the oddball symptoms of diseased modernity that appear in the nooks and crannies of society.

Nevertheless, Sam is able to mobilize his stories to make sense of the world around him. Like his knowledge of the city of London, his knowledge of human life is "extensive and peculiar" (*PP*, 253). Many of his stories and comparisons draw attention to the bleak and brutal aspects of modern life that are out of the way and hidden, perhaps, in the by-ways of life. They tend to be stories of cheating tradesmen and canting hypocrites, the suicidal and the violent, and it is only his comic demeanor that prevents readers from labeling him a skeptic who only sees the dark side of human nature. Despite the peculiar stories he draws upon, Sam manages to artfully navigate the events within the narrative whether they pertain to the mundane activities of everyday life, celebratory occasions of a holiday, or adventures of romantic interest. As Mr. Pickwick observes, Sam is often "in the right . . . although his mode of expressing his opinion is somewhat homely, and occasionally incomprehensible" (*PP*, 203). Sam is often "in the right" because he is able to compare situations to those with which he is already familiar.

But unlike the protagonists who inhabit the novels of Fielding or Smollett, Sam does not assess the actions of himself or others using an abstract and universal moral measure. Rather, Sam follows commonplace observations with a supplementary comment to support his claim through analogy, thus creating what became popular as "Wellerisms." Both Sam and his father Tony consistently employ Wellerisms that consist of three distinct parts: first, a general remark relating clearly to the situation at hand; second, an "as" clause that attributes the general remark to a character type unrelated to the current context; and finally, the circumstances that made the fictitious character utter this remark. When he recommends sleep to Mr. Pickwick, for example, he states "there's nothin' so refreshin' as sleep, sir, as the servant girl said afore she drank the egg-cupful o' laudanum" (*PP*, 199). While the initial comment recommending sleep to refresh himself is perfectly apt in this context, Mr. Pickwick is nothing like a servant girl, and definitely not a servant girl contemplating suicide through self-poisoning. In response to Serjeant Buzfuz's interrogation—"Little to do, and plenty to get, I suppose?"—about the place he occupies under Mr. Pickwick, Sam not only answers that there is "quite enough to get, sir," but elucidates it with yet another hypothetical circumstance. He adds, rather needlessly, "as the soldier said ven they ordered him three hundred and fifty lashes." In the court of law, such additional information is unnecessary; as the judge warns Sam, "you must not tell us what the soldier, or any other man, said, sir, ... it's not evidence" (*PP,* 453). Contrary to the judge's assessment, readers found Wellerisms so humorous that they took on a life of their own, as Laura Kasson Fiss details, making Sam Weller a prominent character in newspaper excerpts of *The Pickwick Papers* on both sides of the Atlantic. Wellerisms may appear distracting by diverting readers away from the original context. But Fiss argues that by layering multiple contexts on top of one another, Dickens "digressively re-contextualizes" the general statement so that this "pivot is not only crucial to the Wellerism's humor but also connects the joke to its larger contexts in the novel and beyond."[61]

By worrying the line between analogy and dis-analogy, then, Wellerisms create and expand spaces in which knowing can take place. Sam's verbal tics demonstrate how he participates in the larger epistemological project of analogical reasoning, which produces meaning through comparisons rather than through systems. Stemming, in part, from Aristotelian logic, analogical reasoning appears frequently in scientific inquiry. Joseph Priestley, for example, is famous for having employed analogical reasoning in his study of electricity by drawing an analogy between how electricity works and how gravity works.[62] Unlike Priestley, Sam uses analogies without attempting to envision a coherent scientific system and is satisfied with partial comparisons. In this sense, Sam's analogical thinking is evocative of what Devin Griffiths calls "harmonic analogies" that "work from the bottom up" and "allow significant shared features to emerge through contact between two different domains placed in serial relation."[63] Because harmonic analogies bring together two disparate things, Griffiths argues that they are fundamentally imaginative processes—one that is central to the way literature works.

Both Mr. Pickwick and Sam travel within their respective spheres of activity collecting stories and experience, but Sam seems to engage the fictional world in a realistic manner by using analogical reasoning, while Mr. Pickwick remains a quixotic outsider in pursuit of comprehensive knowledge. In characterizing Sam's relation to the fictional world as "realistic," I draw upon Elizabeth Deeds Ermarth's observation that "in ordinary usage we say that someone is 'realistic' who is able to sift relevant from irrelevant considerations and so to act in a manner appropriate to the situation." Even more tellingly in the context of my discussion about Sam, Ermarth proceeds to explain that "while this 'realism' can be seen as moral or political cynicism, a rejection of any fixed standards, in fact it implies a faith in some kind of rule according to which something can be judged irrelevant and would be so judged by anyone with the same perspective."[64] As comical and at times strange as Sam may appear, readers are frequently able to agree with his sagacious remarks and to feel that they can share "the same perspective" with him, whether admiring Mr. Pickwick's benevolence or condemning the villainy of Dodson and Fogg. As Ermarth clarifies, this agreement or "consensus" of the kind shared between Sam and his readers is made possible because the neutrality of space and time enable modern subjects to understand that "any position would reveal the 'same' world with as much validity."[65] More specifically, Wellerisms reinforce such consensus by engaging readers and forcing them to fill in the gap, to experience "not only the pleasure of a cognitive leap but also the pleasure of belonging."[66] Sam, in other words, helps mediate the novelistic world for the readers of *The Pickwick Papers,* enabling them to intuitively understand the world through specifics. Mr. Pickwick, on the other hand, cannot "step back from particulars in order to grasp them,"[67] and thus he remains lost in the labyrinth of his own observations by accumulating details without gaining insight about the world he inhabits.[68]

This contrast between Mr. Pickwick and Sam helps to illustrate the importance of what Ermarth calls "the horizon" in nineteenth-century realist fiction and art. Realist fiction, according to Ermarth, creates a "horizon" that assures readers that "what cannot be seen will be very much like what can, in terms of the fundamental laws of operation."[69] In the same way that one can see the horizon far off in the landscape and yet believe that the world does not end there, realistic representation depends on the belief that a similar world continues to exist beyond the boundaries of representation. Sam is presented throughout the narrative as a character who understands that though his experience may be limited, it will likely help him navigate whatever new sphere of life he is placed into. This method of knowing is by no means perfect, of course. At times, Sam becomes the victim of "gammon," but then he learns his lesson and proceeds to the next order of business. Indeed, his repetitive statements about how "such a one said" something indicates the conscious process through which Sam extends his limited perspective by borrowing from others so as to strive towards a more expansive view of the world.

In making Sam a medium of consensus, Dickens tacitly challenges the class politics that implicitly associate the synthesizing perspective of a Tom Jones or a Roderick Random with their (potential) status as gentlemen. In *The Pickwick Papers*, the man of leisure and observation no longer monopolizes the ability to partake of what Ermarth calls the "realist consensus" so that, by extension, readers of broader social classes can theoretically participate in such consensus.[70] Mr. Pickwick and Sam, the man of leisure and his servant, are both subject to the same conditions of a modern industrial society that continues to produce overwhelming quantities of commodities and texts. Since neither can ever really know the entirety of the world they inhabit, it seems that those who are able to stop gathering stories and begin projecting the knowledge that they have are better able to understand the workings of society.

Accessing Knowledge

Given his upbringing, it makes sense that Sam Weller would have more street-smarts than the Pickwickians, and that he can think on his feet to come up with quick analogies that help him engage the situation at hand. Curiously, however, Sam is also the one who displays superior literary knowledge throughout the novel. It is not the educated and literate Pickwickians, but Sam who consistently makes references to the literature of the previous age. Sam refers to various texts from the legends of Faust and Bluebeard to George Lillo's *The London Merchant* and Laurence Sterne's *A Sentimental Journey*. Such references, to be sure, are brief and barely pertain to the plot of the novel. His reference to Sterne, for example, takes place within a conversation in which Sam wonders about the labor-intensive lives of post boys and donkeys, asserting that "no man never see a dead donkey, 'cept the ge'l'm'n in the black silk smalls as know'd the young 'ooman as kep a goat; and that wos a French donkey, so wery likely he warn't wun 'o' the regular breed" (*PP*, 667). Sam's method of reading is unique, to say the least. He tends to decontextualize scenes from the novel as a whole, focusing mostly on distinct characters or episodes and putting them in comparison to real-life situations. In the example above, the fact that *A Sentimental Journey* is a novel of sentiment hardly matters, nor how the scene to which he refers is an opportunity for Yorick to display sympathy for the old man who lost his donkey. For that matter, the fact that it is a piece of fiction does not prevent Sam from using the example to discuss the rarity of dead donkeys in real life.

And yet, far from considering Sam a "bad reader," such scenes add to his reputation for knowingness. Grossman observes that Tony Weller (Sam's father and stagecoach driver) can be seen "as a self-assured, metropolitan hero whose speech commands respect." Despite Tony Weller's penchant for strange orthography and coach metaphors, Grossman argues that "readers rightly credit this coachman with imaginative perceptiveness and not incompetence or insularity" because his authority is associated with the stagecoach system.[71] The coachman's street vernacular is elevated in the novel and gains authority so as to compete with the language of the narrator, and such competing authorities mirror the competing discourses of life on the bustling streets and within the bureaucratic systems of law and prison. Sam Weller's analogies and reading practices partake of the kind of authority that Grossman argues is vested in his father, Tony; despite his vernacular and Wellerisms that border on malapropisms, readers are inclined to credit Sam with sagacity and a knowledge of the world.

By making Sam's method of knowledge-making through analogy central to *The Pickwick Papers* and by rejecting the Enlightenment fantasy that the world can be known in its entirety, Dickens ironically opens up possibilities for a more democratic access to knowledge. Moving away from an Enlightenment model of knowing, Dickens affirms the empowering impulse that Griffiths attributes to comparative historicism. By working through analogies rather than hierarchical systems, and by making analogical reasoning central to historical thought, Griffiths argues that analogy "gave comparative historicism a method for disclosing new patterns and unsettling historical convention, for excavating perspectives, voices, and connections that were ignored by standard accounts."[72] Analogical reasoning—and by inference, comparative methods—helps to creatively bring to the fore diversity of perspectives and give voice to alterity that could be silenced by grand narratives. It also highlights what is real or true for a particular individual, no matter what his or her subject position is, and affirms the relative conditions of reading and knowing. Aside from the general hilarity promoted by *The Pickwick Papers,* perhaps such empowering models of reading and knowing contributed to the popularity of the novel for various classes of readers from street urchins to educated gentlefolk—for everyone, it seems, aside from Miss Jenkyns.[73]

5

The "Prae-railroadite" and the Railway Generation

Sharing Memories in Thackeray's *Vanity Fair*

During the railway boom of the 1840s, stage and mail coaches enter into competition with railways as media metaphors and take on the additional burden of signifying the implications of technological change—a trend made clear in the works of William Makepeace Thackeray. Focusing on Thackeray's use of transport metaphors to express concerns about the obsolescence of stagecoaches and what it means for the future of novels as a genre, this chapter explores how Thackeray theorizes the effects of technological change on personal and collective memory in *Vanity Fair* (1848). While railways contributed to Britain's modernization in important ways, Thackeray worries over how younger generations have limited access to the memory of a stagecoaching past. The images and experiences of coaching days become crystallized in the memory of older generations, Thackeray asserts, but younger generations will only know a railway present. Thackeray casts this problem of historical and technological change as a problem of memory; in so doing, he challenges the aspiration of historical novels to accurately represent history and instead attempts to build upon the workings of memory to establish his narrative realism. Conceptualizing memory's mediating role in forging connections among people both in person and in print, Thackeray thematizes the importance of communicating memory, especially across generations, both in his narrative commentary and in the narrative of *Vanity Fair*. Thackeray bypasses this communicative challenge across generations posed by the lack of a shared referent—such as the stagecoaching past—by relying on readers' own memories, including personal memories generated through reading.

Thackeray's nostalgia for stagecoaches—and the technologically deterministic outlook on history that comes with it—is heavily intertwined with the resigned, melancholic narrative voice that is so characteristic of Thackeray's novels. Ruth Livesey suggests that the sense of rupture between the age of stagecoaches and that of railways that Thackeray articulates makes him an exception rather than the rule among nineteenth-century writers.[1] But the exceptional nature of Thackeray's statement helps draw attention to the nuances of Thackeray's voice and the underpinning logic that leads to his sense of historical rupture. David Kurnick helpfully characterizes Thackeray's voice as "melancholic," and argues that "saturated with disappointment, regret, resentment, bitterness, insecurity, sarcasm, sentimentality and rancorous antisentimentality, accusation and self-accusation, Thackeray's voice is the bearer of an insistent affective surplus."[2] For Kurnick, this "affective surplus" derives from the diminution of theatrical space and the public, social energies that came with it. Implicit here is a sense of loss, which presumes a gap—a gap between the ideal and the real, what was and what is, the past and the present. Thackeray's acute sense of loss makes him participate in what Peter Fritzsche has called the "melancholy of history" that emerged in Western culture in the aftermath of the French Revolution, when people started to "consume and produce historical texts as a way to connect their personal ordeals with larger social narratives," particularly narratives of loss.[3] Like the French Revolutionary emigres that Fritzsche so vividly describes, Thackeray attempts to make sense of how his personal memory of past coaching days connects to larger narratives of social—and technological—change.

Thackeray's melancholy, however, impacts more than his narrative voice; it also influences Thackeray's sense of past genres and their continued relevance. Often considered a seminal novel in the Victorian realist tradition, *Vanity Fair* nevertheless resists generic categorization because it mobilizes an overabundance of generic tropes on the one hand, and because it persistently defines itself against its predecessors on the other. The novel builds upon the allegory of Vanity Fair and the puppet show motif, even as it famously resists identification with existing novelistic conventions. For George Levine, the generic instability of *Vanity Fair* and the way in which it undermines conventions such as the comic form or romance speak to Thackeray's struggle to find a narrative form that does not distort secular reality. It is not that Thackeray rejected conventions of past novels, according

140 · LIMITED ACCESS

to Levine, but that "his novels become nostalgic commentaries on forms no longer possible."[4] Kathleen Tillotson makes explicit the difficulty of defining *Vanity Fair* by using a laundry list of negatives. She argues that it is a novel of neither low nor high life, and that "it is not a military novel, despite Waterloo, nor a domestic novel, despite the number of family scenes. It is not historical, although it is a novel about the past; the period in which it is set is robbed of its usual glamour, and the past is strangely interpenetrated by the present."[5] Recent scholarship extends these observations to insist on how Thackeray modifies, challenges, or adapts existing conventions of "forms no longer possible" by underscoring the gap between generic expectation and reality or by redefining historical experience itself.[6]

While Thackeray regards the obsolescence of everything from stage-coaches to genre with a tinge of melancholy, his historical stance makes memory a central feature of his narrative to generate an alternative model of reader engagement based on subjective experiences. Tillotson makes clear the association between Thackeray's historical stance and his reliance on memory when she claims that "Thackeray has often been called the novelist of memory; all his stories are seen retrospectively."[7] Commenting on Thackeray's attempt to capture the diversity and multiplicity of human experience, George Levine further highlights how Thackeray's historical stance differs from the previous generation of writers like Walter Scott so that "Scott can frame that variousness only with history; Thackeray tries it through memory."[8] While Tillotson and Levine use "memory" to characterize the subjective and affective nature of Thackeray's relationship with the past, Juliet McMaster argues that Thackeray's use of memory generates a unique energy that drives reader engagement in *Vanity Fair*, especially through active narrative commentary: "Chesterton called Thackeray the novelist of memory, and it was Thackeray's achievement so to interweave his fiction with our lives that we draw on our memories of his novels almost as we draw on the material of our own past experience."[9] By arguing that Thackeray uses narrative techniques not only to present his own memories but also to draw upon—and even to help create—readers' memories, McMaster helps to lay the groundwork for exploring how Thackeray theorizes narrative inclusivity for the new generation of readers unfamiliar with the stagecoaching past.

Thus, when Thackeray speculates that "stage-coaches will have become romances" for the next generation of writers in *Vanity Fair*, he articulates more than just a knee-jerk reaction to new technology.[10] He imagines what it means to represent people, places, and novels from the past when industrial technology was quickly changing the landscape—and the world—as he knew it. By acknowledging that younger generations may have limited access to the memory of a stagecoaching past, he also muddies the distinction between history, memory, and genre. In doing so, he imagines an alternative relationship between representation and changing historical reality that relies not so much on mimetic descriptions but on how individual experiences create memories of people, places, and things that people can share to establish a sense of connectedness. Thackeray's impulse is to tie such memories, and the sense of belonging that comes with them, to a physical experience of place. But he also opens up the possibility for imagining how such mediation could work more broadly. By repeatedly mobilizing the verb "to remember," Thackeray highlights the process of cognitive recall that is necessary to activate memory. He mobilizes this process not just among characters but also to engage his own readers, prompting them to remember not just previous characters and events in the narrative but also past experiences stored in their memories—including the memories of what they had read in the past.

History vs. Memory

In "De Juventute" (1860), a short piece originally published in *The Cornhill Magazine* towards the end of his career, Thackeray underscores how the dramatic change in transport technology will create a generational gap.[11] In doing so, he muddies the distinction between history and memory to suggest that this generational gap will even have consequences for the history of the novel. The text of "De Juventute" is staged as a message from the older narrator to Walter Juvenis, a young child beginning to explore the wonders of the world. The narrator begins by defining his position not only as a relic of the past age, but also as a storyteller: "We who lived before railways, and survive out of the ancient world, are like Father Noah and his family out of the Ark. The children will gather round and say to us patriarchs, 'Tell us, grandpapa, about the old world.' And we shall mumble our old stories; and we shall drop off one by one; and there will be fewer and fewer of us, and these very old and feeble. There will be but ten prae-railroadites left: then three—then two—then one—then o!" ("DJ," 83). Thackeray

142 · LIMITED ACCESS

represents the time before railways as "ancient" and emphasizes how a very recent past has become an absolute and irretrievable one by associating it with a period far back in history—as far back as the days of the Old Testament. Thackeray is concerned not just with the disappearance of the objects and characters that belong to the pre-railroad age, but also with the disappearance of "patriarchs" who preserve a faint glimmer of that past through the act of storytelling. In staging such a scene of oral storytelling, Thackeray attempts to conjure "the same kind of community supposedly once defined by face-to-face oral exchange" in a manner akin to the imaginary storytellers that exert their voice powerfully within Victorian fiction that Ivan Kreilkamp draws attention to.[12] The children who have no experience of the past age, Thackeray imagines, will experience the days before railroads only through the stories told by these patriarchs.

Thackeray gives us a glimpse of what these "old stories" narrated by the patriarchs might contain when he proceeds to describe for young Walter the various amusements of his "prae-railroadite" youth. The dancers and singers on stage, he tells us, were more beautiful than they are now, and certainly were not "ludicrously old, out of time, and out of tune" ("DJ," 87). The operas of his youth did not all sound the same so that "they send all rational creatures to sleep" ("DJ," 88). The state of cooking in general has improved, he admits, except the art of making pastries. Much of the amusements he engaged in as a child, he tells us, are pretty much the same "in old times as they are now," with the exception of cricket ("DJ," 90). Vauxhall is no more and gone are the coaches and the "jolly teams" that the rustic youth rode as he left school and London to enjoy home and the holidays ("DJ," 96). Perhaps these are the "old stories" that young Walter is interested in hearing, but it is difficult not to think that this "patriarch" is being indulgent and acting like "your old fogey who can see no good except in his own time," contrary to the narrator's assertion ("DJ," 89). The "old stories" that Thackeray recounts tend to be personal experiences of bygone days that need a bit of nostalgia as garnish. These stories and memories may be "as good as jokes" for the narrator, but the narrator also admits that the listener "mayn't quite perceive the point" ("DJ," 95). These stories, then, are not the kinds of stories that can be passed down from generation to generation so as to eventually become "history."[13] Instead, these scattered stories are presented in the same historiographic spirit that pervades Thackeray's lectures on *The English Humourists* and *The Four Georges;* it is not his intention to attempt "grave historical treatises," but merely to "peep here and there into that bygone world" and "to amuse for a few hours with talk about the old society."[14]

Thackeray distinguishes his own stories from "grave historical treatises" because the kinds of memory that Thackeray recounts nostalgically are rooted in intimate, personal experience rather than an objective, bird's-eye view of history. While his recollections in "De Juventute" may appear trivial and merely personal, Thackeray's attitude towards history resembles that of Chateaubriand and numerous other European contemporaries who, according to Peter Fritzsche, struggled to make meaning of their own experiences. Fritzsche argues that revolutionary upheaval—and the migrations and displacements that people experienced as a result—led to a sense that "although the virtues of the past are cherished and their passage is lamented, there is no doubt that they are no longer retrievable. There can be no nostalgia without this sense of irreversibility, which denies to the present the imagined wholeness of the past."[15] In such a context, memories are not just personal. Building on the arguments of Joan Scott and Maurice Halbwachs, Fritzsche argues that "even the most personal memories depend on exchange of memories held in common and on the shared value of such an exchange."[16] In other words, while the remembrance of past experiences may remain personal, individuals can only make meaning out of those memories in a social context. When Thackeray indicates that there are numerous "prae-railroadites" who might mumble their stories to young listeners, he suggests that what appear to be simple childhood experiences are memories that are shared and valued by a certain generation. When Thackeray imagines that there will be fewer and fewer "prae-railrodites" remaining to tell their stories, he articulates the sense that the past is receding further and further out of reach.

Thackeray's attitude towards history in "De Juventute"—and specifically how he collapses history into memory—becomes particularly clear by contrasting it to that of Scott. Sir Walter Scott, too, presents a "grandfather" telling stories to children, but his grandfather figure refuses to merely ponder personal experiences of his youth. In *Tales of a Grandfather,* first published in 1827, Scott presents a series of tales addressed for young readers that make "some attempt at a general view of Scottish history, with a selection of its more picturesque and prominent points."[17] Scott indicates in his preface that the *Tales* were initially written for the use of his grandchild, John Hugh Lockhart, and that it contains stories that he may have

144 · LIMITED ACCESS

"repeated twenty times over" had it been possible for the grandfather and grandchild to "remain near to each other."[18] Print, in this particular case, substitutes for oral narratives and thus reminds us of the image that Thackeray presents when he describes how "children will gather round and say to us patriarchs, 'Tell us, grandpapa, about the old world.'" But the "old world" that Scott attempts to capture is different from Thackeray's in both scope and method. While the *Tales* claim "to be only a collection of Tales, or Narratives from the Scottish Chronicles, will nevertheless be found to contain a general view of the History of that country, from the period when it begins to possess general interest."[19] Thus, while pretending to be a series of short narratives about the "old world," Scott's *Tales* also aims to provide a "general view" that helps readers gain an understanding not just of each individual tale, but the relationship between them. Scott's attempt to provide young readers with a history that is friendly, yet complex enough to challenge their understanding and encourage their curiosity, was so successful that the subsequent editions include additional prefatory notes indicating that the author has "carefully revised the present edition . . . to bring the little book nearer its proper character, of an abridged History of Scotland, for the use of young persons."[20] Ann Rigney argues that Scott's novels made him a "manufacturer of collective memory par excellence"; like his novels, his *Tales* presents a way of "imaginatively engaging with the past that was at once highly personal, historically informed, and thoroughly synthetic."[21]

The grandfather figures of Thackeray and Scott both possess a stock of stories about the "old world" that fascinate young listeners. But these two grandfathers tell their stories in ways that promote a very different understanding of and relationship to the "old world" in the minds of the young listeners. While Scott demonstrates confidence that what he communicates in present tense will transmit past legacies to future generations, Thackeray acknowledges the precarious relationship between synchronous communication and cultural-historical transmission since, as Régis Debray puts it, "human beings *communicate;* more rarely do they *transmit* lasting meanings."[22] Thus, in contrast with Scott's grandfather figure, Thackeray's patriarch begins with the assumption that he must communicate effectively by accommodating his stories to his listeners who belong to the new railroad era and therefore cannot relate to his memories of a "prae-railroadite" past. His historical stance also influences the narrative form he chooses to adopt. Scott's grandfather (or rather, Scott *as* grandfather) presents discreet events of history in the entertaining form of "tales," but does so in an attempt to provide a "general view," an "abridged History of Scotland" that instill into young minds the sense that they inherit this history. The youths who gather around Scott's grandfather figure are told that though they have never experienced the events in the stories, there is a connection between themselves and the historical figures they hear about. It is not just the stories that are transmitted to them through the voice of the grandfather figure, but also the cultural inheritance of the nation, and perhaps even the spirit and bravery of a William Wallace. Thackeray, however, demonstrates no intention of attempting such communication of history and cultural identity. The narrator of "De Juventute" shares his stories with young Walter, but not with the express intent to encourage young Walter to remember those stories and pass them on to others. He shares his stories and encourages young Walter, in turn, to share his personal interests. Thus, the conversation between grandpapa and the children, in Thackeray's account, merely juxtaposes the juvenile amusements of two separate generations.[23]

The same attitude characterizes Thackeray's discussion of the novels he enjoyed in his youth. "Ah! I trouble you to find such novels in the present day!" he exclaims, even though the very novels he mentions are still very much available for youths like Walter Juvenis ("DJ," 90). The narrator reminisces over novels such as *Mysteries of Udolpho* and *Roderick Random* as though they no longer exist. Yet these novels were not just available to readers of Thackeray's time but were available much more cheaply so that children like Walter were more likely to be able to afford them.[24] As I discussed in my third chapter, keeping novels in print and in circulation seemed to be a sure way to keep the genre's history fresh in the readers' minds for Scott—particularly if those novels are carefully collected, introduced, and annotated by editors like himself. Thackeray, however, seems to think that just because a literary work is available in print, does not mean that that work is historically significant, or that it will necessarily be transmitted to future generations. Indeed, the abundance of reproductions as well as new productions at increasingly affordable prices probably meant that it became less and less likely for readers to return to the same texts over and over and over again, thus practicing what historians of reading call "intensive" reading. In a reading culture that promotes "extensive reading" to avidly consume more and more texts, Thackeray suggests that readers cannot be made to inherit a preference for certain novels.[25] For Thackeray and the companions of his youth, it was Walter Scott whom they considered as "the constant benefactor of [their] youth" by providing them with works like *Ivanhoe* and *Quentin Durward* ("DJ," 90–91). But times are no longer the same, readers' preferences have changed, and he "meet[s] people now who don't care for Walter Scott, or the 'Arabian Nights.'" Rather than attempting to recommend Walter Scott's novels to such readers, Thackeray can only feel "sorry for them, unless they in their time have found their romancer—their charming Scheherazade." Thus, even though the "patriarch" enthusiastically recounts his experience with the novels of Walter Scott and Tobias Smollett and Laurence Sterne, he does not attempt to force these novels on young Walter. Instead, he simply requests Walter to "tell me who is the favourite novelist in the fourth form now?" ("DJ," 92).

Even though Thackeray seems skeptical that stories can be passed down straightforwardly from one generation to another, it does not mean that such transmission fails to take place entirely. Indeed, it is Thackeray's own cherished wish that his stories will be read by generations upon generations of readers: "If the gods would give me the desire of my heart, I should be able to write a story which boys would relish for the next few dozen of centuries. The boy-critic loves the story: grown up, he loves the author who wrote the story. Hence the kindly tie is established between writer and reader, and lasts pretty nearly for life" ("DJ," 92). It is possible, in Thackeray's view, for the same work to be "relish[ed]" by readers "for the next few dozen of centuries." But in order for this to happen, authors must establish rapport with each individual reader of each succeeding generation. The novel that will continue to be "relish[ed]" by readers, in Thackeray's view, will need to affect readers and capture their attention despite historical or technological change, and despite the possibly outdated people, things, and worldview it presents since the new generations will have limited access to the memories of this past age. Scott valued the strangeness and peculiarities of past novels because they provided insight into history, but those very historical qualities are what threaten to make these novels inaccessible to the young readers Thackeray has in mind. By emphasizing the individual reader's lifelong relationship with favorite authors, Thackeray suggests that literary transmission is the result of personal choice repeated over generations rather than the product of historical preservation or reproduction. In doing so, however, Thackeray privileges the affective relationship of readers with texts and downplays the prestige of established literary histories, thus raising the question of what it would take for an author like himself "to write a story which boys would relish for the next few dozen of centuries."

Memory and Technological Determinism

Thackeray's concern about how technological change creates a generational gap—a gap that jeopardizes the continuing relevance of old novels—also appears in the pages of *Vanity Fair*. Less than a decade after the publication of Dickens's first serial fiction, Thackeray already refers to *The Pickwick Papers* (1836–37) as a stagecoach novel in danger of becoming obsolete. Describing Becky Sharp's stagecoach ride to Queen's Crawley, the narrator laments the disappearance of stagecoaches and asks, "Where is the road now, and its merry incidents of life?" (*VF*, 73). Among the characters who inhabited the road and made it interesting is "old Weller"—that is, Tony Weller, Sam Weller's father and stagecoach driver who makes numerous appearances in *The Pickwick Papers*. For the narrator of *Vanity Fair*, the disappearance of stagecoaches is not just a matter of nostalgic longing within the novel; it is a phenomenon that makes such characters and incidents disappear not only from the road but from collective memory. The loss of stagecoaches may make readers wonder about the fate of old Weller and ask, "Where is he, and where is his generation?" Such questions make the narrator anticipate the future consequences of this loss: "To those great geniuses now in petticoats, who shall write novels for the beloved reader's children, these men and things will be as much legend and history as Nineveh, or Coeur de Lion, or Jack Sheppard. For them stage-coaches will have become romances—a team of four bays as fabulous as Bucephalus or Black Bess" (*VF*, 73). Thackeray suggests that the dramatic change in transportation technology impacts more than just how readers experience the world and what memories they create. It may also have dire consequences for the novel as a genre, because future authors' experience of travel will be so different from that of their ancestors. By grouping together figures from various historical periods, ranging from the days of the Old Testament and the crusades to the century—and even decade—immediately preceding his own, Thackeray emphasizes the radical shift that happens when people start traveling on railways instead of coaches. Indeed, he characterizes this change as so radical and so sudden that Tony Weller, a character from a work of fiction published hardly a decade before, becomes part of the generation of people and things destined to become "romances." For those "great geniuses now in petticoats," then, stagecoaches will belong to the world of romance rather than that of the realist novel.

Just as he characterizes himself as a "prae-railroadite" in "De Juventute," Thackeray manifests technological determinism in this brief passage of *Vanity Fair* by ruminating on his own memory of stagecoach journeys as belonging to a past in perfect tense. In doing so, he suggests that memories are like representations—tableaus of people and places set into an arrangement on a surface, whether canvas or page—that exist within one's mind. Thus, when Thackeray reminisces the whole world of people and places associated with stagecoaches, he recalls them almost as a kind of panorama.[26] It is not the remarkable incidents of a coach journey that the narrator considers "with a sweet and tender regret." Rather, it is the expected and mundane sequence of people, objects, and scenery that he remembers nostalgically. The narrator simply describes the coach's progress, "now, threading the dark lanes of Aldergate, anon clattering by the Blue Cupola of Paul's, jingling rapidly by the strangers' entry of Fleet Market," but this very process of tracing the route of the coach reminds him that Fleet Market, along "with Exeter 'Change, has now departed to the world of shadows." Alongside these lost places, familiar people and things have also disappeared, such as "the waiters, yea, and the inns at which they waited, and the cold rounds of beef inside, and the stunted ostler with his blue nose and clinking pail." These people and things will disappear when they no longer occupy a landscape that people experience as continuous, and therefore part of the same extended and connected society. The continuity that passengers used to experience, the narrator suggests, is now broken up so that "there is no Chelsea or Greenwich for the old honest pimple-nosed coachmen" and there is no "asthmatic gentleman, the prim lady, who declared upon her sacred honour she had never travelled in a public carriage before . . . , and the fat widow with the brandy-bottle" (*VF*, 73).

Thackeray's technological determinism is by no means unique amongst his contemporaries. "Old Weller" himself reappears in Dickens's periodical series *Master Humphrey's Clock* (1840–41) to assert the superiority of stagecoaches to railways. Towards the end of one episode, he is asked "whether he approved of railway communication."[27] It turns out, of course, that as a former stagecoach driver he does not approve at all, but Tony Weller's objection to railway travel can be summed up into one main point—it is inferior to stagecoach travel. Much of that inferiority rests on how the railway restricts passengers' movements and puts them in helpless positions; they are subjected to repetitive sameness—of scenery, of other passengers, of signs on platforms—and they cannot even scream for their own lives.[28] For old Weller, the accoutrements of a stagecoach journey such as "a public-house," and "a glass o' ale," or "a change" of horses provide change and variety, and variety, he assumes, is necessarily a good thing.[29] He even suggests that he could drive his coach at a pace competitive with the railway if he were paid an exorbitant sum in advance as the railway forced people to do. Weller is doing more than just comparing the old technology to the new in his complaint; he is also engaging in technological determinism to exaggerate what was good about the old technology, contrasting his memories of the good old coaching days with his ideas about the evils of the railway, real or imagined. When Tony Weller observes that the railway prevents passengers from experiencing meals at inns and other accoutrements of a coach journey, he is observing the noticeable changes brought about in traveling practices just as many of his contemporaries did.[30] When he asserts that those meals at inns are "comfortable," however, he does so on the grounds of personal memory rather than objective history.

Similarly, in "The English Mail-Coach" (1849), Thomas De Quincey echoes such technological determinism to emphasize that it is not just the comforts of traveling that are at stake when coaches are superseded by railways; it changes the process of communication.[31] While De Quincey's reflections are much less exaggerated than Tony Weller's, he, too, relies on his own personal memory of traveling back and forth to Oxford by mail coach to assert the superiority of the coach to the railway. Unlike the railroad, the mail coach has characteristics like "the glory of motion," "grand effects for the eye," "animal beauty and power," and "conscious presence of a central intellect" ("EMC," 183). The railroad "cannot compare with the mail-coach system in grandeur and power" because it lacks active human and animal agency that constitute the virtues of the mail coach ("EMC," 193). The railway may boast more speed, but that speed is "a fact of our lifeless knowledge" and therefore fails to produce the sublime effect of the mail coach. Trains, for De Quincey, are "blind insensate agencies, that [have] no sympathy to give." The vehicles that consist of "iron tubes and boilers" cannot convey animal sensations to the passenger but rather "disconnect man's heart from the ministers of his locomotion." Machines will not convey intangible things like feelings, sensations, or sympathy. In machines, one cannot even see how boilers and iron tubes communicate and produce motion. In contrast, De Quincey can visibly witness, in the movement of the mail coach, how motion and speed are results of communications between man and animal. He can see the "intervening link," "the heart of man . . . propagating its own tumults by motions and gestures to the sympathies, more or less dim, in his servant the horse" ("EMC," 194). By looking at the physical details of the animal (eyes, nostrils, muscles, hooves) De Quincey feels that the coachman and his horses communicate more than just motion; they also communicate sympathy. The visible and organic connections that make mail coaches work are also what make mail coaches a metaphor of how national sympathy works. Unlike the railway, the mail coach can work as the medium for unifying the nation in De Quincey's account because of its very form and function.[32]

In the nostalgic reflections of both Tony Weller and De Quincey, the stage and mail coaches take on "an *exclusively* mythological character" in a manner akin to the antique objects that Jean Baudrillard analyzes. Baudrillard claims that while antique objects seem to lie outside the system of objects that constitute the modern subject in relationship to one another, they in fact perform the very specific role of signifying time, specifically in the "perfect" tense. As something that belongs to a closed-off past, the antique or "mythological" object fulfills our desire to go back in time and to experience "definitive or fully realized being"—that is, to escape the state of flux and incompleteness that characterizes life in the present tense.[33] Glorifying coaches as objects enshrined in their memories, Tony Weller and De Quincey both highlight the affective nature of the loss of coaches in ways that encourage their identification with a mythological past. Coaches, in other words, become "perfect" now that they belong to a past that resides only in their memories—memories that appear "perfect" only in retrospect.[34]

Tony Weller and De Quincey dramatize how the history of technological change is mediated through memory in their minds and thus helps to highlight the extent to which Thackeray relies on technologically deterministic memory to reminisce the good-old coaching days. Their rewriting of coach travel as a glorious journey—as everything that a railway journey is not—rests on the relative position of coaches in relationship to railways. Despite potential accidents and other dangers, stage and mail coaches begin to look harmless, peaceful, and comfortable when juxtaposed with that embodiment of industrial technology, the steam locomotive (which they personally disapprove). But coaches themselves seemed strange, unnatural, and detrimental to existing modes of transportation by revising the past. John Taylor, the seventeenth-century Thames water-poet, testifies to the evils of newly available coaches for hire in his "The World Runs on Wheels"

(1623).[35] He calls the early hackney coaches "hyred [*sic*] Hackney hell-Carts" that put businesses such as saddlers and watermen in jeopardy. These obnoxious hirelings, however, seemed to be "strange Monster[s]" and "the sight of them put both horse and man into amazement" when coaches were initially brought into the country.[36] Raymond Williams famously characterizes the "Golden Age" as an ever-receding past, a past that seems just out of reach for poets of one generation as well as the previous one.[37] While Williams considers this process in the framework of materialist history, these advocates of the mail coach show how the process of technological change can create an accelerated sense of a receding past. An escalator effect thus marks the history of technology as well, where the introduction of a new technology makes the previous technology seem less "technological" and more "natural." Thus, the previous technological era becomes an object of nostalgic memory. Even as railways were becoming part of everyday life in ways that permeated the lived reality of Victorian men and women, mail and stagecoaches continued to function as media metaphors—enshrined in the memory of a certain generation in perfect tense—that still very much worked to inform how people understood the world around them. Like myths that continue to inform cultural identities and worldviews long after they cease to perform a functional role, coaches continued to hold sway in the cultural imagination during the expansion of railways.

Thackeray echoes—and extends—such technological determinism expressed by others to theorize the relationship between representation and reality. His lament captures how the coach as a media metaphor will no longer be relevant to the realities of future generations. In the brief passage lamenting the loss of coach journeys in *Vanity Fair*, Thackeray not only declares that "these men and things" will become "legend and history" for future writers, but also asserts that "stage-coaches will have become romances." Despite how the coach "stays close to the ground" and "you have the sense that you understand how you are getting to where you are going, or at least how you got there after the fact" when riding the coach,[38] Thackeray claims that stagecoaches will become "romances" because the worldview it stands for seems unfamiliar and unrealistic in an age of industrial transport. In a society where railways convey passengers swiftly from one platform to another, passing rapidly over the intervening landscape, it may seem fanciful, perhaps even quixotic, to attempt to trace the gradation from city to country and to interact with the various characters that inhabit various parts of the landscape. Stagecoach novels, of course, still present to readers a fictional world dictated by the laws of probability; carriages will obey the laws of physics and characters will obey the dictates of human nature. But, Thackeray fears, stagecoaches will become less relevant and less accessible to readers, once the vehicle that mediates the reader's interaction with the fictional world becomes obsolete through the intervention of what is newer, faster, and presumably better.

Thus, while *Vanity Fair* is staged as a "historical" novel that takes place during the years of the Napoleonic Wars, Thackeray displays significant lack of confidence in history as the basis for realistic representation. A noted eighteenth-century buff, Thackeray attempted to resuscitate not just the representational practices but also the material presence of the eighteenth-century novel in the first edition of *The History of Henry Esmond*. But his historical representations are often conflicted and tongue-in-cheek, undermining his own attempts to represent history.[39] Likewise, Thackeray often skirts history as his direct subject matter. The war provides a historically realistic backdrop to the novel as a whole and touches the lives of the characters—some economically, some emotionally, and some fatally. And yet *Vanity Fair* does not quite represent the whole of the historical drama as do Scott's novels; he "trivializes" and "miniaturizes" history, as Kurnick argues, to subsume history within domesticity.[40] Thus, the novel partakes of the worldview that I have identified in *The Pickwick Papers*, where no one individual, including the narrator, seems able to comprehensively view the chaos of the modern world. Georg Lukács accounts for such a transition—from a comprehensive view of society that characterizes Scott's historical novels to a past that appears "as a gigantic iridescent chaos" presented in the works of Flaubert and his successors—by attributing it to the falling apart of a hitherto stable class relationship that enabled the bourgeois to monopolize the right of historical representation.[41] But Thackeray himself seems to take a somewhat different view of the matter. He asserts that when technology such as the railway marks off the previous generation as an absolute past, that past becomes the proper object of memory.

Going Down Memory Lane

The descriptions of coach journeys in *Vanity Fair* provide insight into why the loss of coaches presents such a threat to Thackeray. For Thackeray, history alone does not connect people to each other; rather, people forge ties by sharing memories. He conceptualizes the relationship between experience and memory as paralleling the relationship between historical reality and representation—the closer the relationship between the two, the more they work as solid foundations for creating shared meaning. Thus, the repeated coach journeys of *Vanity Fair,* though they are only described very briefly, become opportunities for experiencing, communicating, and sharing a place-based memory that ties people together. The coach route that takes Becky from London to Queen's Crawley is retraced twice more in the course of the narrative. If the first journey shows Becky traveling to Queen's Crawley for the first time in the company of the miserly Sir Pitt, the second journey—described in the chapter ironically titled "In which Becky Revisits the Halls of her Ancestors"—shows Becky retracing the same route in company with her husband, Rawdon Crawley. The narrator emphasizes that this is a repeat of a former journey, telling us that "Colonel Crawley and his wife took a couple of places in the same old High-flyer coach by which Rebecca had travelled in the defunct Baronet's company, on her first journey into the world some nine years before." The description of the journey, unlike the former one, does not include observations of the scenery as the passengers see it but how Becky "remembered the Inn Yard, and the ostler to whom she refused money, and the insinuating Cambridge lad who wrapped her in his coat on the journey!" Rawdon, whose relationship to the stagecoach route differs from Becky's, "sat by the coachman and talked about horses and the road the whole way; and who kept the inns, and who horsed the coach by which he had travelled so many a time, when he and Pitt were boys going to Eton" (*VF,* 402). The descriptions of the second journey to Queen's Crawley are mediated through the memories of Becky and Rawdon to emphasize how traveling the same stagecoach route confirms both the passing of time and their own personal journeys.

The third and final journey to Queen's Crawley, in contrast, takes place in the company of their son and highlights how the stagecoach ride works as an occasion for communicating memory to form generational ties. While maintaining the third person point of view, the narrator shifts to adopt little Rawdon's perspective in this scene, calling Becky "his mother" and Rawdon "his father." This is little Rawdon's first journey to Queen's Crawley, when he "made his first journey to the place which his father still called home." The journey helps to affirm the ties between father and son by giving the father an opportunity to take the role of a commentator who enhances the pleasures of the journey for the son. The son finds "endless interest" in "the incidents of the road," and that interest is heightened by "his father answering to him all questions connected with it." It is not just the present incidents that capture his attention, however. The father's own personal memories of past journeys are communicated to the son while "telling him who lived in the great white house to the right, and whom the park belonged to" (*VF*, 433). Sharing his stock of knowledge and memories accumulated through past journeys, Rawdon's narratives invite his son to participate in an experience that generations of Crawleys have shared. While their specific experiences and hence their memories may differ from one generation to another and from one sibling to another, their individual memories are rooted in the shared stagecoach route and the shared views of people and places that come with it. Thackeray describes a process through which memory gets passed down from father to son and from generation to generation to initiate youths into the collective unit designated as a "family," and this process consists of multiple layers of mediation. First, there is the coach journey that mediates an individual's interaction with people and places; second, there is the communication of memory between individuals; and third, the memories that reside in individuals' minds—memories that are at once personal and shared—help to form ties among members of a social unit.[42]

Significantly, Becky is an outlier in this scene, and her position within the scene helps to underscore her role in the narrative as a whole—as a character who disrupts the workings of a memory-based community. While the two generations of Rawdons occupy the outside of the coach, the narrator describes Becky alone inside the coach: "His mother, inside the vehicle, with her maid and her furs, her wrappers, and her scent bottles, made such a to-do that you would have thought she never had been in a stage-coach before—much less, that she had been turned out of this very one to make room for a paying passenger on a certain journey performed some half-score years ago" (*VF*, 433). Becky distances herself from both father and son not just by occupying a different place inside the coach but also by rejecting the memory of her former journeys—or at least acting as though she did. As a mother who consistently refuses to communicate with her son to form any familial ties, Becky is featured as a character who challenges the moral order that the novel upholds. But Becky's lack of maternal responsibility is only part of the picture. Becky is staged throughout the novel as a character who plays fast and loose with memories—by hiding or forgetting them, by inventing them, and by recalling them only when doing so serves her end. In so doing, Becky challenges the relationship between experience and memory that Thackeray imagines as the basis for establishing communal ties; but by characterizing her as an outlier, Thackeray only affirms the moral order of the novel and the importance of experiences generated by shared stagecoach rides within that order.

Taking Thackeray's ideas about memory to their logical extreme, experience-based memories can work to mediate a sense of belonging among people who possess a shared sense of "home." In a modernizing world that puts people into motion, as Kevis Goodman and Ruth Livesey have argued, memory works as a crucial medium that creates an affective sense of belonging to—and longing for—place.[43] Especially for individuals displaced from home in the context of imperial expansion, the memory of home works as a key anchor that helps to maintain a sense of belonging. Thus, Thackeray evokes a landscape that makes England as a home recognizable when he describes Dobbin's return from India:

> How happy and green the country looked as the chaise whirled rapidly from mile-stone to mile-stone, through neat country towns where landlords came out to welcome him with smiles and bows; by pretty roadside inns, where the signs hung on the elms, and horses and waggoners were drinking under the chequered shadow of the trees; by old halls and parks; rustic hamlets clustered round ancient grey churches—and through the charming friendly English landscape. Is there any in the world like it? To a traveller returning home it looks so kind—it seems to shake hands with you as you pass through it. (*VF*, 559)

The narrator goes out of his way to describe this landscape, even as "Major Dobbin passed through all this from Southampton to London, and without noting much beyond the milestones along the road." The narrator creates a disjunction between Dobbin's actual behavior (he is too eager to see Amelia again to notice the landscape) and the theoretical idea that revisiting and reexperiencing the English landscape can confirm one's memory of home. Far from making this description ineffective, the very disjunction between Dobbin's observations and the narrator's highlights how such descriptions function as the kinds of "portable memory" that Livesey argues were so central to the affect of locality in Victorian fiction.[44]

The recurrent references to and representations of stagecoach journeys in *Vanity Fair* indicate more than the historical setting for the novel; stagecoaches hold symbolic value for Thackeray. Specifically, Thackeray attempts to establish stagecoaches as a "memory site," a term that Ann Rigney borrows from Pierre Nora and defines as "actual locations or symbolic points of reference that serve as dense repositories of historical meaning (a 'minimum of signs with a maximum amount of meaning,' as Nora put it) and hence as communal orientation points in negotiations about self-definitions."[45] Memory sites can be anything from texts and images to places and monuments, and become important points of reference for establishing cultural memory in specific societies at specific times. For Rigney, who traces the "afterlives" of Scott's novels in their dynamic and shifting relevance as memory sites, "these memory sites are not fixed entities or finished products, moreover, but rather imaginative resources for generating new meaning and contesting old ones."[46] Thus, while Thackeray mobilizes stagecoaches to represent characters on the move like many of his predecessors and contemporaries, he invests new meaning into stagecoaches. By showing characters using stagecoaches to return "home" in ways that assert their sense of communal belonging, Thackeray associates coach journeys with familial and communal rootedness rather than with individual mobility. At the same time, by emphasizing the loss of stagecoaches for his own readers, Thackeray attempts to underscore the futility of trying to regain a sense of home and of childhood that disappeared along with the stagecoaching past.

The extent to which Thackeray invests stagecoaches with symbolic meaning becomes clear by contrasting stagecoaches with other things that invoke memories for characters. For example, the miniature portrait of George Osborne repeatedly appears in the novel and is intricately tied to Amelia's memories of her dead husband. She "goes and sits upstairs with her miniature" when upset by her mother's reproaches (*VF*, 382), and the narrator imagines her taking "refuge in the miniature of her husband" after Dobbin departs from Pumpernickel (*VF*, 652). "The early dear, dear memories of that brief prime of love rushed back on her" when gazing upon the picture so vividly that Amelia even imagines the image of her dead husband reproaching her for imagining that he had been unfaithful to her (*VF*, 642). George's picture, for Amelia, becomes a way of keeping company with her dead husband. And while the miniature is a source of fond memory for Amelia, that memory is not shared by others. On the contrary, other characters like Mrs. Sedley and Becky fault Amelia for clinging to the miniature, especially since the George Osborne that Amelia so fondly remembers is an idealized image of the real George—far different from the selfish, conceited dandy that others remember. In addition, such memories prevent Amelia from forging connections with others around her. While some memories can be shared to create social ties in the social world that Thackeray describes, Amelia's memory of George—concentrated in his miniature figure—works to exclude social ties and thus functions "as a reminder of the unnaturalness of the domestic," as Kurnick puts it.[47] In *Vanity Fair*, Amelia's exaggerated turn towards an enclosed, private domestic space is just as problematic as Becky's excessive social energy and fluidity. In both cases, the problem lies in how these characters establish or prevent social ties using past remembrances.

While Thackeray suggests that overly personal memories can hinder social connections, he also affirms the healing and generative potential for memory to create a sense of connection and belonging. The need to remedy the lack of shared memory with his son, for example, prompts George's father to visit Brussels just to be able to tour the path of the regiment so that he can vicariously experience the last living moments of his son: "In the Sergeant's company, who was also just convalescent, Osborne made the journey of Waterloo and Quatre Bras, a journey which thousands of his countrymen were then taking. He took the Sergeant with him in his carriage, and went through both fields under his guidance" (*VF*, 344). The sergeant works as both narrator and guide, helping Osborne experience the battle after the fact. In visiting the fields of Waterloo, it is not history that he seeks but the memory of an event that connects him, posthumously, to his son. In addition, the narrator also implicitly ties Osborne with "thousands of his countrymen" who are making the same journey.[48] While the historical and affective significance of the events vary, Thackeray expresses the presence of a similar want when he laments the passing of stagecoaches and worries that "stage-coaches will have become romances" for the younger generations. The statement exemplifies Thackeray's concern about the younger generation's limited access to a shared memory that connects them to a larger collective. Lacking the experience of a coach journey through the English countryside, the younger generations will presumably have limited access to memories about people and places that characterize it, even as older generations continue to hold on to those memories. Those like Old Weller, De Quincey, and Thackeray will nevertheless rely on coaches as a media metaphor that helps them understand the world—with all its pleasures and pains, smooth journeys and accidents—in perfect tense.

Do You Remember?

Despite Thackeray's technological determinism, memory is mobilized throughout *Vanity Fair* as something that can create shared meaning and shared narratives among people—even when the referent (such as stage-coaches) remains absent. This is possible because of how the human mind works as a kind of storage device. Summarizing theories of cognition, Elaine Auyoung explains that "features of our empirical experiences become encoded in memory as multimodal 'traces' of the original experiences themselves, and these experiential traces can subsequently be retrieved and combined to form new mental representations."[49] I have already discussed how scholars of memory such as Peter Fritzsche and Ann Rigney emphasize the social nature of memory; recollections of the past are made meaningful to individuals through social contexts and exchanges that help to frame individual experiences. But these individual experiences must first be stored as experiential traces for them to be available later for retrieval. Thus, Auyoung credits readers with the effort involved in textual comprehension, arguing that they "assist with the writer's attempt to evoke fictional persons and places by drawing upon their own rich store of background knowledge, which they have in turn acquired from their everyday labor of perceiving and moving through the physical world."[50] Thackeray highlights this social and cognitive process, often by invoking the active verb "to remember." To remember is to retrieve a memory stored in one's mind, and to retrieve a memory in response to another person's prompt is to acknowledge how that memory is shared in ways that affirm an existing bond between the parties that facilitate shared meaning-making. Throughout the novel, memory becomes central to the process of establishing social relationships among characters and even between the narrator and readers. Indeed, *Vanity Fair* not only represents but also performs—in mediated form—the process of communal meaning-making by referring back to past events in the serial novel that both characters and readers remember. While Thackeray's laments about the loss of stagecoaches seem to close off the possibility of literary-historical continuity, the constant call to remember opens up an alternative possibility for communicating and sharing memories, including memories based on reading novels past and present.

The characters who inhabit Russell Square repeatedly prompt each other to remember something, especially in the early chapters of the novel, to affirm their shared history and familial ties. John Sedley asks Amelia, "Do you remember when you wrote to [George] to come on Twelfth-night, Emmy, and spelt twelfth without the f?" (*VF*, 35), and George asks Jos, "Do you remember, Sedley, what a fury you were in, when I cut off the tassels of your Hessian boots, and how Miss—hem!—how Amelia rescued me from a beating, by falling down on her knees and crying out to her brother Jos, not to beat little George?" (*VF*, 37). Such prompts to remember both affirm the continuity of the children with the young adults they have now become and situate that continuity within a shared family history. Remembering, though, can also affirm more recent ties. The Vauxhall incident—in which Jos embarrasses himself after drinking too much rack punch—becomes a constant point of remembrance between characters. When Becky tries to win over Jos and Amelia after reuniting with them in Pumpernickel, she constantly appeals to them to remember shared experiences and asserts that she cannot forget the happy times she had spent with them. The narrator emphasizes how remembering is tied to a sense of belonging when Dobbin arrives at Slaughter's Coffee House after years of absence and again sees "the faithful waiter, who knew and remembered every officer who used the house, and with whom ten years were but as yesterday, led the way up to Dobbin's old room, where" the furnishings remained "just as the Major recollected them in his youth" (*VF*, 560). Remembering and recalling old memories, especially in conjunction with a physical environment that affirms that memory, creates a sense of continuity, shared history, and membership in a particular culture.

The kind of remembering that promotes a sense of social connectedness, however, is not limited to the interaction among characters; it is also a crucial part of how the narrator of *Vanity Fair* engages readers as well. McMaster argues that Thackeray's commentary is crucial to the novel's vitality, generated "from the reader's own personal responses, elicited, though not determined by" the narrator's.[51] In one of the many kinds of narrative interjections that characterize *Vanity Fair*, the narrator constantly appeals to and attempts to create a shared store of memory that he constantly asks readers to revisit. The memories that mediate the narrator's communications with readers can take the form of what readers have experienced within the narrative itself, such as when the narrator states: "But my kind reader will please to remember that this history has 'Vanity Fair' for a title, and that Vanity Fair is a very vain, wicked, foolish place, full of all sorts of humbugs and falsenesses and pretensions" (*VF*, 80). The narrator consistently asks readers to remember characters who have dropped out of the narrative and to remember previous incidents of the narrative. But the narrator also asks readers to recall their own experiences outside the narrative. The public boats that the characters take on their journey to the continent is not simply a fictional representation, since "all old travellers in Flanders must remember [it] for the luxury and accommodation they afforded" (*VF,* 262). There are individual experiences that are common enough in society to work as a point of shared reference such as how "some men who have unmarried sisters or daughters even, may remember how uncommonly agreeable gentlemen are to the male relations when they are courting the females" (*VF,* 556). And, of course, there are memories of historical events shared by all of "us": "All of us have read of what occurred [at Waterloo]. The tale is in every Englishman's mouth; and you and I, who were children when the great battle was won and lost, are never tired of hearing and recounting the history of that famous action" (*VF,* 314). History becomes meaningful for "all of us" through reading and recounting, thus treading the same ground (figuratively) again and again to remember it and to keep it alive in our memories.[52] The narrator thus assumes that "we" all know what happened at Waterloo without the narrator's detailed descriptions.

Far from disrupting the mimetic illusion that characterizes realism, Thackeray's appeal to readers to remember engages readers in the act of connecting fictional representations to their own versions of empirical reality as they are stored in their memories. George Levine draws our attention to the way *Vanity Fair* sustains realistic representation while it undermines the illusion of reality it creates by drawing readers' attention to the hands of the puppet master. He asserts that "there is no novel more self-conscious about the fact of its illusionism, about the difference between the claims of art and the claims of plausibility, about the inadequacies of omniscient representation in the efforts towards authentic representations of the real, than *Vanity Fair* (1848)." For Levine, these narrative devices and asides threaten to make the narrative "unstable and inconsistent,"[53] but these destabilizing narrative elements work to engage readers in testing the novel's representation against what they remember so as to gauge the distance or proximity between representation and reality as they remember it. Through these narrative devices, in other words, Thackeray suggests that realism is not just a mode of representation, a matter that rests upon the technical and artistic proficiency of the writer; it is also a principle of reading that invites readers—even younger readers who have limited access to the memories of a stagecoach past—to bring their own memories to bear on the meaning-making process called reading.

Thackeray's appeal for readers to remember undermines existing assumptions about the mimetic work of realism, since he asks readers to remember not just what they have observed in reality but anything from historical events and local landmarks to the behavior of friends and what they have read. The very title of the novel, *Vanity Fair,* refers to three different kinds of worlds—the world of the novel, the abstract world of Bunyan's allegory, and the actual world to which that allegory refers—and the narrator asks readers to repeatedly remember things about each of these worlds to make sense of the narrative. Moving back and forth between these worlds, the narrator often blurs the boundaries between people and things that belong to different ontological registers so that it becomes unclear whether his references are fictional or historical, allegorical or real. This instability is particularly apparent in the passage where Thackeray laments that "stage-coaches will have become romances" for the next generation. By claiming that "stage-coaches will have become romances" and not that stagecoach *novels* will become romances, Thackeray blurs the distinction between history and genre, between observed reality and textual representation. Thackeray's word choice suggests that an actual historical object can take on a fictional quality, so that stagecoaches will become something that one only hears about or reads about in stories—namely, a romance. He refers to "old Weller" alongside the "old honest pimple-nosed coachmen" and the "prim lady, who declared upon her sacred honour she had never travelled in a public carriage before" (*VF,* 73). Whereas "old Weller" is clearly a fictional character, it is much less clear whether the "pimple-nosed coachmen" and "prim lady" are character types that appear in fiction or the kinds of people one would likely encounter in the course of a stagecoach journey. While some may recall that a lady who claims that she is not used to riding a public coach appears in Henry Fielding's *Joseph Andrews,*[54] the narrator also claims that "there is always such a lady in a coach" without explaining whether this is the case in real life or in fictional representations (*VF,* 73).

By muddying the distinction between the real and the fictional in addition to using the allegory of Vanity Fair as the framework for his novel, Thackeray undermines the assumption that realism represents a mimetic illusion of an actual world. Thackeray works both with and against the theory of realism advanced by John Ruskin by suggesting that realism relies on readers testing the validity of representation through the act of "remembering." Exploring *Modern Painters* (1843–60) and other texts, Caroline Levine argues that not only was Ruskin's brand of realism highly influential in articulating the principles of realism in British literature and art after 1850, but also how Ruskinian realism challenges critical conventions that define realism as, first and foremost, representational. Ruskin's realism refuses to take the illusionism of representation for granted and demands "experimental activity of both reader and artist" in confronting visual or textual images.[55] The goal of such experiments, Levine explains, was to test the validity of representation—does it truly represent the world, or does it merely reproduce conventional forms inherited by tradition? As Levine argues, such questioning would hopefully prompt the artist and workman to break from convention to strive for a truer representation of nature; and such questioning will also urge readers and viewers to liberate ourselves from "deathly convention" and to think for ourselves.[56] Trained under such principles, the reader might respond to the call that Levine articulates: "Thus the realist call to experimentation arises from the possibility that a given image, or a particular hypothesis, or an established convention *might not fit the world.* The realist experiment is not about putting our faith in representation. It is about putting mimesis to the test."[57] The thought process that Thackeray articulates partially resembles the principles of Ruskinian realism; in the passages above, Thackeray's narrator considers how a reader might "test" his representation to see if his representation resonates with their experience and memory. But by including fictional reading as part of readers' experience and memory of that world, Thackeray undermines Ruskin's attempt to liberate art from "deathly convention."

Imagining an audience of future readers who will have grown up in the age of the railway and who therefore do not share the memories of a stagecoach era, Thackeray envisions the limits of realistic representation by lamenting the disappearance of stagecoaches and the characters and scenes that came with them. This lament does not lead to any attempt to resuscitate such scenes in the form of historical representation or to present a series of picaresque adventures on the road, since to bring this history back to life for readers is not his aim. Instead, the narrator mentions them only to claim that they "need not be told here." It is not the details of the lost scenery, but the fact of their disappearance that the narrator emphasizes. Far from attempting to transport the reader to a different time and immersing them in a stagecoach past, the narrator emphasizes their distance from that technologically determined past by lamenting, "Alas! we shall never hear the horn sing at midnight, or see the pike-gates fly open any more." The pronoun "we" unites the reader and narrator to underscore their shared predicament—a predicament where such objects no longer exist in reality and can only be accessed through acts of remembering. The narrator quickly moves past this moment of past longing and moves on to ask: "Whither, however, is the light four-inside Trafalgar coach carrying us? Let us be set down at Queen's Crawley without further divagation, and see how Miss Rebecca Sharp speeds there" (*VF,* 73). Readers are thus invited to observe how Becky Sharp's life unfolds as she enters the unfamiliar scenes of aristocratic, country life. They are invited to focus on the human character and drama illustrated by the puppet master, and not allow their eyes to "divagate" towards the scenery, costumes, and other necessary accouterments that belong to the stage. By expressing a longing for lost stagecoaches while relying on readers' memory to supply the details of a stagecoach journey—or not—as they see fit, Thackeray opens up room for readers to fill in the blanks in their own way. By doing so, he (Thackeray) can set his novel in a stagecoach past that he remembers so fondly while we (readers of a future generation) can move on more quickly to follow the fates of our favorite characters.

Accessing Past Novels

In *Vanity Fair,* Thackeray conceptualizes memory—and the act of remembering necessary to access memories—as integral to a mediating process that binds people together. By grounding his interactions with readers upon the same foundation while imagining a generation of readers who have limited access to the memory of a stagecoach past, he historicizes readers based on the kinds of memory they can be expected to have. Thackeray negotiates his own need to present lengthy descriptions based on his own memory of a stagecoach past and the possible irrelevance of such descriptions for future generations of readers by creating narrative shortcuts that enable him to move forward with the plot, simply asking readers to "remember" in lieu of presenting his own descriptions. Such maneuvering gives readers the alternative to pause and reminisce or to skip the process and move on with the narrative depending on what memories they have stored in their minds. Scott, too, was conscious of his reader's needs and expectations. But Scott tends to focus on what needs to be told for the reader to fully understand the historical circumstances under which the protagonist is acting, while in *Vanity Fair*, Thackeray minimizes the need for detailed historical representation by identifying what "need not be told here." The historicity of his narrative presents for Scott a "disadvantage" that needs to be overcome by "throwing the force of my narrative upon the characters and passions of the actors;—those passions common to men in all stages of society."[58] Thackeray, on the other hand, seems to be able to brush off such "disadvantage" with ease. He can do so not only because he assumes that character-driven plot is the focal point of his narrative, but also because he relates to history differently. Scott labors to reconcile historical specificity with what is "common to men in all stages of society" because history, for him, is something to be preserved and transmitted[59]; Thackeray begins with a defeatist attitude and assumes that such efforts at preservation and transmission are useless now that a wide gulf separates readers of his time from a pretechnological past. The realistic approach, for Thackeray, is to rely on readers' memories gained from experience or from reading.

Thackeray's outlook on readers' relationship to narratives echoes Sam Weller's relationship to stories and to knowledge-making that I have described in the previous chapter—it is the subjective meaning-making that counts rather than an overarching view of the world. For Scott, novels gained literary value because they performed the role of transmitting a shared past to readers, both through historical representations in individual novels and in the form of anthologies and collections that consolidate the genre's history into tangible form. Thackeray, in contrast, suggests that such transmission is difficult now that the younger generation inhabits a completely different era that makes it difficult for them to see themselves as connected with the past. For novels to survive, they must make strong appeals to individual readers and their personal interests since they can no longer assume that readers will value novels for the sake of the history they represent.

But Thackeray also suggests that the very workings of memory can help to create conditions where "the boy-critic loves the story: grown up, he loves the author who wrote the story." Thackeray provides some glimpses of youthful reading in *Vanity Fair:* Dobbin reading his personal copy of *Arabian Nights* under a tree at Dr. Swishtail's academy (*VF,* 47); Rose Crawley reading Smollett's *Humphry Clinker* (rather than Smollett's history) under the tutelage of Becky (*VF,* 90); and Georgy presumably reading the copy of *Sandford and Merton* with the inscription of "George Osborne,

THE "PRAE-RAILROADITE" AND THE RAILWAY GENERATION · 165

A Christmas gift from his affectionate mother" in the fly-leaf (*VF,* 449). While Thackeray does not elaborate on these scenes of reading in the pages of *Vanity Fair,* he details in *The History of Pendennis* how memories of prior reading persist not just as isolated memories of what novels represent but as entangled memories that intertwine reading with the experiences and passions of youth. Describing Pen reviewing the manuscript of *Leaves from the Life-book of Walter Lorraine,* which he had written after his failure at Oxford, the narrator describes the composition as a reflection of what Pen experienced, learned, read, and felt: "This book, written under the influence of his youthful embarrassments, amatory and pecuniary, was of a very fierce, gloomy, and passionate sort,—the Byronic despair, the Wertherian despondency, the mocking bitterness of Mephistopheles of Faust, were all reproduced and developed in the character of the hero; for our youth had just been learning the German language, and imitated, as almost all clever lads do, his favourite poets and writers."[60]

The narrator's description of the book fuses together Pen's reading and feelings so that they become indistinguishable from each other. The literature Pen read becomes such an integral part of his affective experience that it simply becomes adjectives in the phrases "Byronic despair" and "Wertherian despondency" that describe both the hero of *Walter Lorraine* and Pen himself. While these books no longer trigger the same feelings, Pen simultaneously remembers the books and the feelings that together inspired the manuscript. Such descriptions appear repeatedly in coming-to-age narratives of the period: Jane Eyre's memory of *Rasselas* is associated with her memory of Helen Burns, and David Copperfield's memory of *Tom Jones* is associated with the churchyard that his bedroom window overlooks. Books are thus part of their personal memory, intertwined with the histories and memories of other people, places, and things. Representing past novels within their own pages, these Victorian novels help us imagine how novels themselves become emmeshed with personal history in readers' memories, awaiting recall for the next occasion when a friend or narrator asks, "Do you remember?"

CONCLUSION

George Eliot and Contingent Access to Literary History

Tracing how authors mobilize transport metaphors from Henry Fielding through William Makepeace Thackeray, each of the preceding chapters has attempted to challenge the idea that reading is like traveling. Instead, I argue that transport metaphors manifest authors' anxieties about how their novels are implicated in a process of mediation—a process that is both social and material, technological and cognitive, and that involves not only authors and readers but also the numerous other bodies that intervene. In hindsight, transport metaphors seem to express the promises of realist fiction as a site of communal meaning-making, representations that powerfully engage readers in the experience of immediacy where they can feel what characters feel and experience through a carefully crafted perspective. By temporarily suspending belief that reading is like traveling, each of the chapters has imagined authors confronting the possibility that some readers have limited access to the pleasures of reading their texts. In the process, these authors conceptualize the conditions of mediation and negotiate access for these readers by envisioning—and validating—alternative models of reading. Explicitly, this book has argued that the question of readers' inclusivity mattered to the history of the realist novel, but implicit throughout is the question of how to access literary history itself when that history is constantly being revisited and revised through the intervention of later writers and readers.

George Eliot helps us understand the problems of accessing literary history when she uses transport metaphors to conceptualize the difficulty of tracing the process of historical transmission—a process that transmits

167

ideas and information through time. While seemingly associating the stage-coach ride with the narrative immersion characteristic of realist texts in the introduction to *Felix Holt, the Radical* (1866), Eliot unsettles the stability of this metaphor by further imagining a past that cannot be accessed by stage-coaches. She imagines narrative in both a spatial and temporal context of transmission using a method akin to what Régis Debray calls "mediology."[1] For Debray, all mediating agents—transportation among them—play a role in how communities create shared meaning to negotiate what gets passed on to future generations. Eliot associates the act of reading with the act of seeing the landscape as an outside passenger of a stagecoach to suggest that narrative realism enables readers to effortlessly immerse themselves in the text, just as acts of communication that happen synchronously (like looking at the landscape or listening to the stagecoach driver) feel effort-less and intuitive. But she adds additional layers of history to contextualize such acts of communication in the larger process of historical transmis-sion. By worrying about how various agents—including people as well as technologies—create a particular milieu that hides past narratives in plain sight, Eliot suggests that narratives that seemed realistic at one point in time may no longer be realistic at another, and what feels accessible now may no longer be accessible in the future. Eliot's theory of mediation suggests that while realism enables readers to immerse themselves in a fictional world that unfolds in the pages of the novel, it does so only through a process of transmission that has weeded out what appeared less relevant, less realistic with the passing of time.

The Nature of Forgetting

Three years before the publication of *Felix Holt,* Eliot and her fellow Lon-doners witnessed an interesting development in the history of transpor-tation. On January 10, 1863, the Metropolitan Railway extending from Paddington Station to Farringdon began operation, instituting for practical use the first underground railway in Britain.[2] Passengers familiar with the London tube system would be familiar with this as the Metropolitan Line, though after years of use, renovations, and improvements, both the tun-nels and the trains look quite different from what passengers experienced during Eliot's time. A major difference involved the use of steam—not electricity—for locomotive power, and the problem of smoke-filled under-ground tunnels led engineers to revive and experiment with an alternative solution called the pneumatic railway. The idea of the pneumatic railway had been entertained on and off for almost as long as steam engines, though it never made it onto the big stage of industrial history. The pneumatic railway, also called the atmospheric railway, attempts to move railway carriages using the pressure of air instead of a locomotive that drags carriages behind it.[3] In 1864, Thomas Rammell constructed an experimental track near the Crystal Palace on Sydenham Hill. The pneumatic railway was about six hundred yards in length, and the passenger carriage was propelled through a tunnel using air pressure provided by a large fan. The curious could buy a ticket to take a ride on this contraption, and it seemed to have been in operation for at least some months. But it was closed down, nobody knows exactly when, and is now only an obscure relic in the history of industrial experiments.[4]

The pneumatic railway appears in the introduction to *Felix Holt* as a transport metaphor that helps Eliot conceptualize the fate of narrative in a changing context of mediation. Eliot contrasts the experience of a "tube-journey" to a stagecoach ride, detailing how each kind of journey makes passengers relate differently to the stories that exist scattered about the English landscape:

> You have not the best of it in all things, O youngsters! The elderly man has his enviable memories, and not the least of them is the memory of a long journey in mid-spring or autumn on the outside of a stagecoach. Posterity may be shot, like a bullet through a tube, by atmospheric pressure from Winchester to Newcastle: that is a fine result to have among our hopes; but the slow old-fashioned way of getting from one end of our country to the other is the better thing to have in the memory. The tube-journey can never lend much to picture and narrative; it is as barren as an exclamatory O! Whereas the happy outside passenger seated on the box from the dawn to the gloaming gathered enough stories of English life, enough of English labours in town and country, enough aspects of earth and sky, to make episodes for a modern Odyssey.[5]

Memory-making is here associated with narrative-making, and memories are made, the narrator claims, by experiencing a journey that takes time, thereby enabling the passenger to fully take in the landscape. By historicizing how modes of transportation mediate the relationship between people, landscape, and narrative, and by claiming, in particular, the stagecoach's comparatively superior powers of mediation, Eliot seems to suggest that the narrative space that has been carved out by novels over the past century and a half is being squeezed out from the reader-passenger's view by the increasingly efficient modes of travel brought about by industrialization. She claims, in short, that narratives of the English countryside have become inaccessible. For Eliot, the idea that "posterity may be shot, like a bullet through a tube" entailed a threat to the business of storytelling, because travelers who see nothing can remember nothing and so they can report nothing.

The pneumatic railway works as a case study for the problem of historical access; it works as a reminder that history is created not just through a process of recording, but also through that of forgetting—and a particular kind of remembering. The narrator of *Felix Holt* anticipates a new era of transport when landscape is literally blocked from the view of passengers in order to abbreviate travel time—a fear that really begins to make sense by understanding that the "tube" traveled inside an airtight tunnel and therefore had no visual access to the landscape. Eliot alerts readers to the vanishing experience of the stagecoach ride by referring to the tube journey as the fate of future passengers. But for twenty-first-century readers, the "tube" to which she refers is part of a forgotten history and fails to strike a chord; indeed, in hindsight, it is tempting to lump the "tube" together with the steam locomotive or the underground railway. Even during the nineteenth century, the atmospheric railway tended to remain in the shadow of the steam locomotive and piqued public interest only occasionally. But it was remembered and revived with interest as Eliot was writing *Felix Holt* because it just so happened that the underground railway was being developed. The pneumatic railway, in short, was remembered and retrieved from historical obscurity in the pages of *Felix Holt* only because it served present interests.

In response to the perceived threat that pneumatic railways posed for narrative transmission, Eliot mobilizes the stagecoach as a transport metaphor that helps to anchor her narrative in a specific place and time. The first line of the first chapter of the novel ("On the 1st of September, in the memorable year 1832, someone was expected at Transome Court") is littered with proper names and familiar objects in a manner that exemplifies Eliot's realism (*FH* 12). But Eliot also stages an extensive journey to get there, textually as well as geographically, through a lengthy introduction that mediates readers' access to this specific place in a specific time.

The narrator begins by orienting readers historically, to "five-and-thirty years ago [when] the glory had not yet departed from the old coach-roads" (*FH* 3). That was the time when "there were pocket boroughs, a Birmingham unrepresented in Parliament and compelled to make strong representations out of it, unrepealed corn-laws, three-and-sixpenny letters, a brawny and many-breeding pauperism, and other departed evils,"—the evils, in short, of those days before the First Reform Act of 1832 that radicals like the titular Felix Holt were to help address. Situating the narrative in a specific historical period, the narrator highlights "some pleasant things, too, which have also departed"—the foremost of which is the experience of a stagecoach ride that enabled outside passengers to apprehend the landscape from a privileged point of view.

By treading the same ground as her predecessors using a stagecoach journey, Eliot appeals to the established communal standard for judging what does or does not belong to the genre of the novel as it has been transmitted through generations, thus helping to naturalize transport metaphors as part of the novelistic genre. Eliot uses another transport metaphor to describe this process of transmission when she discusses how habitual practices come to seem naturalized through interactions with numerous mediating agents in *Scenes of Clerical Life* (1857). In the small country town of Knebley, yet unenlightened by "turnpike roads and public opinion," things happen repetitively within a small contracted circle so that "men's minds and wagons alike moved in the deepest of ruts, and the landlord was only grumbled at as a necessary and unalterable evil, like the weather, the weevils, and the turnip-fly" (*Scenes,* 83). For Eliot, forces of habit are just as strong as material realities and have the power to change what counts as "nature" for a particular community of people. Hence, it is possible to state that "the Knebley farmers would as soon have thought of criticizing the moon as their pastor. He belonged to the course of nature, like markets and toll-gates and dirty bank-notes" (*Scenes,* 81). It makes sense to confuse actual nature (the moon, the weather, and the turnip-fly), the people inhabiting the place (the pastor and the landlord), and economic structures (toll-gates and dirty bank-notes) only when we recognize that Eliot's "nature" indicates the highly local and communal standard for judging what does and does not belong to the order of things. Eliot's invocation of the stagecoach journey travels in the same "rut" as her novelistic predecessors; she adds to the series of transport metaphors that recur throughout the eighteenth and nineteenth centuries to associate her novel with the history of realist fiction.

CONCLUSION · 171

Ruth Livesey points out how the stagecoach "was such a familiar device to carry implied readers back into the history of the age of the first Reform act that it was hardening into cliché by the time it appears in *Felix Holt*."[6] In returning to the image of the stagecoach journey that was so frequently invoked by her predecessors (including, but not limited to, Dickens and Thackeray whose works I have discussed), Eliot affirms the generic affiliation of her text, whether consciously or unconsciously. Invoked frequently through habitual practice, transport metaphors become naturalized, as it were, for the novel as a genre.

However, Eliot undermines the transport metaphor she initially presents by drawing attention to how the stagecoach merely passes through the landscape without giving passengers access to "nature."[7] She highlights the illusion of historical access that the stagecoach journey presents by introducing yet another metaphor—that of plants—to suggest that the stagecoach journey is not "natural" enough as a metaphor for reading. While the introduction uses a transport metaphor to give readers access to a past mode of storytelling when people were moved by natural rather than industrial power, her second analogy between plants and intimate historical narratives indicates that stories are so embedded in their localities that they might not be accessible to the passer-by at all, no matter the vehicle. Eliot draws an analogy between the landscape narrated in Mr. Sampson's stories and the "dolorous enchanted forest in the under world" narrated by poets such as Dante and Virgil (FH 10). The narrator tells us that "the thornbushes there, and the thick-barked stems, have human histories hidden in them; the power of unuttered cries dwells in the passionless-seeming branches, and the red warm blood is darkly feeding the quivering nerves of a sleepless memory that watches through all dreams" (FH 10–11). By directly invoking Canto XIII of Dante's *Inferno* to compare human stories and vegetation, Eliot insists that these stories cannot be detached from the landscape at will and suggests, similarly, that her own stories cannot be detached from their own context within literary history either. Furthermore, the narrator adds commentary that provides a more in-depth view of Mr. Sampson's observations, suggesting that what the coachman considers "fine stories" are merely stories that skim the surface and that glean the "thorn-bushes" and the "thick-barked stems" without penetrating the "human histories hidden in them." The plants are so firmly rooted in the soil that the only way to see them is to visit them in their own habitations—a visit that neither the coachman nor the passenger ever makes.

Mr. Sampson—and by association, the outside passenger—has limited access to narratives that are naturalized within a local community or landscape because their access to such stories is contingent on their perspective. Eliot illustrates how perspective and habits of the mind intersect when she discusses the different meaning of the word "railways" for different people. In "the mind of a man who is not highly locomotive," a railway guide, a nearby train station, and the vague image of a railway track would "represent his stock of concrete acquaintance with railways"—a much narrower view of the railway compared to various workers, travelers, and stakeholders who have more extensive experience with the railway.[8] While traveling extensively on a stagecoach, Mr. Sampson's perspective is confined to the parameters of the stagecoach route, thus leaving gaps in the range of narratives and knowledge available to him. His perspective contrasts with that of the German anthropologist Wilhelm Heinrich Riehl, whose pedestrianism enables him, according to Eliot, to apprehend the workings of communal transmission by joining close observations with detachment.[9] Riehl, whose "The Natural History of German Life" Eliot admired, is presented as a pedestrian-narrator resembling Wordsworth's "The Wanderer" in Eliot's review—much more so than Mr. Sampson the coachman.[10] Eliot believes "what [Riehl] tells us in his Preface . . . that years ago he began his wanderings over the hills and plains of Germany for the sake of obtaining, in immediate intercourse with the people, that completion of his historical, political, and economical studies which he was unable to find in books." The romantic view that "he was, first of all, a pedestrian, and only in the second place a political author" helps to sustain her belief in Riehl's disinterestedness and commitment to observing people and society as they are.[11]

Eliot's description of Riehl presents an important contrast to the stagecoach driver not only because of his pedestrianism but also because he makes clear the difficulty of gaining insight into the deep-seated nature of communal inheritance. Eliot explains that Riehl's observations of the European people provide a functional and accurate way of viewing society because he sees society not through grandiose theories or partial perspectives of party politics but through impartial observation of local details. Because Riehl is unprejudiced, he is able to see how the "external conditions which society has inherited from the past are but the manifestation of inherited internal conditions in the human beings who compose it; the internal conditions and the external are related to each other as the organism and its medium, and development can take place only by the gradual consentaneous development of both."[12] Eliot's emphasis on deep-rooted community—and the importance of such community for gradual, future change—has been thoroughly studied, especially in the context of nineteenth-century developments in the natural and social sciences.[13] Thus, when Eliot describes men's minds (internal conditions) and wagons (external conditions) as analogous things that run alike in a "rut," she echoes Riehl's terms to describe a condition of society brought about through communal inheritance that has sociological significance. When she refers to Dante's allegory to describe how "the thorn-bushes there, and the thick-barked stems, have human histories hidden in them," she continues to draw attention to the contrast between the external and internal but makes even more explicit what is at stake—the human histories, the narratives, and "un-uttered cries" that might remain hidden, especially when merely glimpsed from the top of a stagecoach.

Eliot associates the coach journey, then, with an experience more akin to skimming rather than close reading and cautions against taking Mr. Sampson as an authoritative agent of narrative transmission since the chatty coachman fails to really give readers access to those human narratives hidden in plain sight. Disconnected from local standards of transmission (like the "course of nature" as defined by the inhabitants of Knebley), the coachman sees the local only in the context of larger abstract concerns so that the stagecoach as a vehicle fails to penetrate human narratives embedded in a community. Instead, the stagecoach becomes a self-interested vehicle of nostalgia or prophesy. The signs of coming change turn Mr. Sampson into a prophet, like many others who are eager to catch at these signs as the messengers of coming and irreversible change. He can no longer feel that he holds "a position of easy, undisputed authority" ever since the "recent initiation of Railways had embittered him." His outlook on the landscape itself has become dismal so that "he now, as in a perpetual vision, saw the ruined country strewn with shattered limbs, and regarded Mr Huskisson's death as a proof of God's anger against Stephenson." William Huskisson famously died following an accident in 1830 during the opening ceremony of the Manchester Liverpool railway, and contemporaries (like Mr. Sampson) often referred to his tragic and widely publicized death in their invectives against the railway. The railroad is a sign of coming evil to Mr. Sampson. Thus, to his passengers, he would turn prophet and foretell the coming days: "'Why, every inn on the road would be shut up!' and at that word the coachman looked before him with the blank gaze of one who had driven his coach to the outermost edge of the universe, and saw his leaders plunging into the abyss." And yet these dismal and gloomy foretellings of the future do not seem sustainable, even for the coachman whose profession is threatened by the railway. Ultimately, "he would soon relapse from the high prophetic strain to the familiar one of narrative" and tell of things that were rather than things that are to be (FH 8). This abrupt transition from the future to the past in the coachman's narrative does not just tell us that "the high prophetic strain" is difficult to sustain. It indicates how Mr. Sampson is caught between the impulse to tell stories about the familiar past and prophetic future, just as the novel's main plot shows the lives of Harold Transome and Esther Lyon tossed between a hidden past and an unknown future.

Eliot's concern about problems of narrative transmission is enacted by the characters of *Felix Holt,* for many of whom the past is elusive because they do not have access to hidden, localized knowledge transmitted within a community. Eliot shows numerous glimpses in her narratives of revolutions that would seem to forever change the nature of things (such as the vision of Felix Holt, the radical), only to undermine such future-looking attitudes through reflections on how the hidden past determines or limits much of the characters' actions. As Livesey has argued, in *Felix Holt,* the "hope that the past might be a stable place of retreat and national unity is picked apart. But so, too, is the idea that any single uprising or reform . . . has an enduring effect on national life." It is not so much change itself, but the tension between forward-looking energy and the conditions created by the past that produces drama in her novels. Eliot highlights this difficulty of accessing the past in her novel by describing a peculiar environment of narrative transmission in which protagonists like Harold Transome and Esther Lyon remain ignorant of their own life stories (and their own biological progenitors) for long periods of time. If the eponymous Felix Holt presents an idealized but unrealized vision of a possible radical future, the characters who surround him remind us of the complex and involved circumstances inherited from the past that often prevent people from carving out their own futures.[14] Arguing that society can only move forward by building on past inheritances, Debray quips that a "society that no longer recognizes distant ancestors shoots its own future in the foot."[15] By literally describing such a predicament on the part of her characters, Eliot presents a mediological experiment in miniature where characters act out the drama of cultural transmission at the individual level.

CONCLUSION · 175

The narrative of *Felix Holt* further makes the problem of transmission concrete by focusing on the transmission of property. In one of the central plots of the novel that intertwines the histories of Esther Lyon and Harold Transome, the transmission—that is, inheritance—of the Transome family estate emerges as a key issue. Esther's birthright, as it turns out, entitles her not to the inheritance of Malthouse Yard, but to Transome Court because she is the daughter of Maurice Christian Bycliffe, the man who owns the rights to the Transome estates once the descendants of Thomas Transome expire. Forgotten and unacknowledged by the family at Transome Court, the last of Thomas Transome's descendants lurks about town, dismissed by many as poor, drunk, and "half-mad" (*FH*, 268). It is only when Tommy Trounsem is trampled to death in a riot that Harold learns about him and his key role in the transmission of the family estate. And yet, the importance of Tommy Trounsem's death is hardly acknowledged by those involved, and it is only the omniscient narrator who acknowledges his key role in the legal framework of the inheritance: "This second corpse was old Tommy Trounsem, the bill sticker—otherwise Thomas Transome, the last of a very old family-line" (*FH*, 321). Juxtaposing his commonly known status in the community with his unacknowledged importance within the larger plot, the omniscient narrator draws attention to how, despite his marginal status, Tommy Trounsem is nevertheless an important agent of transmission.

If we return to Eliot's introductory stagecoach metaphor in light of figures like Tommy Trounsem, the figure that stands out is not the coachman but "the shepherd" who makes way for the stagecoach to pass. While the outside passenger happily gleans stories from the English landscape, the shepherd has no access to the larger narrative frames that shape such stories. His sphere of life is much more contracted so that "his glance, accustomed to rest on things very near the earth, seemed to lift itself with difficulty to the coachman. Mail or stagecoach for him belonged to the mysterious distant system of things called 'Gover'ment,' which, whatever it might be, was no business of his" (*FH* 4). Realist narratives may appear natural enough and transparent enough to be apprehended as easily as the sight of a landscape from the top of a stagecoach. Not so, however, for the shepherd who is intent upon his own business in his very limited sphere of life—he is too busy working the land to be transported by the stories it might produce. The landscape that will make "episodes for a modern

Odyssey" for the stagecoach passenger remains inaccessible and unreal to the laboring shepherd. And yet, it is the shepherd—not the outside passenger of a stagecoach—who has ready access to the numerous plants that grow on native soil. An encounter with a "Wanderer" or a Riehl may be all it takes for the shepherd to play a key role in opening up the possibility of sharing their stories.

By conceptualizing the complex process of narrative transmission, Eliot not only articulates the challenges of novelistic representation but also the difficulty of parsing literary history itself. David Kurnick argues that Eliot's "ideal novelistic vision will cultivate a dauntingly diverse set of relations to the object of representation," focusing on the "representational demands" that Eliot draws attention to.[16] Eliot does indeed highlight the difficulty of reconciling a detached, abstract perspective with an intimate, local one. But she also articulates the problems of narrative transmission—a problem of how narratives get passed down from one agent to another to become habitual and "natural" or, alternately, forgotten. Eliot urges us to notice overlooked narratives as well as obscure, marginalized agents for transmitting such narratives, but this is difficult because there is no outside perspective that enables one to apprehend the process of transmission in its entirety.[17] By alternately highlighting the outside passenger, the stagecoachman, and the shepherd, Eliot shows the problems of narrative transmission for each; the stories that the outside passenger hears from the coachman merely skim the surface of the landscape, the coachman is not an authoritative storyteller occupying a privileged perspective but a "bad reader" of local stories hidden in plain sight, and the shepherd cannot access narratives that provide an abstract overview of the world he lives in, even as he holds the potential to communicate local narratives embedded in the land he occupies. Eliot suggests that we can strive to achieve a detached, all-encompassing perspective, but no matter what perspective we hold, we are all implicated in a process of transmission that we cannot see.

Agents of Literary Transmission

The chapters in this book focus on variously marginalized or wayward readers—like Eliot's shepherd—to trace mediological thinking in writers throughout the eighteenth and nineteenth centuries, showing how novels imagine readers in the context of mediation by taking into account how both historical and material conditions as well as literary history situate readers in a particular milieu. In doing so, they often respond to perceived threats to access—like Eliot's "tube"—that may no longer seem urgent in historical hindsight. Such threats register within narratives when narrators break the mimetic illusion to draw readers' attention to the act of story-telling, expectations of the reader, or the economic conditions of publishing. When Tristram Shandy exclaims "Dear Madam" or when Anthony Trollope apologizes to his readers for attempting to revive the epistolary form, fictional narrators refuse to maintain the illusion of virtual reality to communicate with readers. In doing so, texts often articulate the values that motivate which conventions they choose to inherit from earlier novels and which ones they choose to discard. Novels tend to negotiate their relationship to works that preceded them—and imagine those to follow—through various narrative commentaries and interjections. In a discourse of realism that privileges mimetic representation, such narrative interventions have often been considered as distractions or "noise." William Paulson provides a helpful definition of "noise" when he states that by "noise is meant not loud or obnoxious sounds but anything that gets mixed up with messages as they are sent."[18] This definition implies a hierarchy between "message" and "noise," where noise is that which we are supposed to ignore in order to focus on the message itself. But Kevis Goodman cautions otherwise in her eloquent discussion that associates Raymond Williams's famous concept, "the structure of feeling," with cognitive noise—noise that comes with "the difficulty of recording and recognizing history-on-the-move, or, . . . the difficulty of treating or recreating the historical process as a present participle . . . rather than as a past perfect."[19]

Paulson calls literature a "noisy transmission channel that assumes its noise so as to become something other than a transmission channel,"[20] but the problem with noise is that we can learn to tune it out. By focusing on transport metaphors, figures of readers inscribed within the text, and narrative commentaries across the long history of the novel, this book has tried to amplify a particular kind of noise that creates a refrain within that history—but with variations. Coachmen who remain invisible in Fielding's novels come to occupy center-stage in the novels of Dickens and Eliot, while sentimental manuscripts that are forever lost in Sterne's novelistic world are resuscitated through Scott's historicism. Such subtle commentaries provide insight into how communities of writers and readers continually reshape their cultural heritage by defining what counts as communication and what does not, what information has meaning and what is mere noise—thus constantly working to refine cultural ideas of a "realistic" novel in ways that prompt reading societies to repeatedly revise the very criteria for what counts as real. These novels variously illuminate the unstable nature of realism by showing how realism is not just a formal and historical concept, but also one that is contingent on readers' ability to make meaning out of a text in the here and now. Rather than attributing to realism the ability to produce a predictable response in each and every reader, the novels I read suggest that realism emerges through ongoing negotiations in fictional conventions as authors theorized the possibility of limited access for readers in their historical moments. For Henry Fielding, Tobias Smollett, and Laurence Sterne, realism is contingent on how readers experience temporality or the material environment. For Walter Scott, realism is contingent on one's ability to see the local, historical origins of a narrative. For Charles Dickens, William Makepeace Thackeray, and others, realism is contingent on how readers negotiate narrative forms and conventions with their everyday experiences and cognitive processes in an industrial society.

Realism thus emerges through ongoing negotiations that are integral to the process of cultural transmission—a process in which novels themselves participate as well as the numerous readers, teachers, scholars, and commentators of literature. Implicitly or explicitly, our books and articles define for future readers what is or is not worth transmitting to future generations. Implicitly or explicitly, our curricula and syllabi act as so many nodes in the project of cultural transmission. Thus, Debray can assert, "journalists communicate; professors transmit."[21] Like Eliot, we occupy an uneasy place, fondly preserving the literary history we have inherited while speculating about its future in an increasingly mediated age. Looking both backwards and forwards, we seek to give students access to the rich traditions of past ages that we have learned to love and cherish, often attempting to revive works that have been forgotten or obscured in the process of transmission, even as we fret over the possibilities and threats that the future holds in store. To acknowledge our own role as agents of transmission is to recognize that we have the power—albeit a circumscribed one—to facilitate or to withhold access, to create insiders and outsiders, and to define "us" and "them."[22] To make the texts and discussions in a literature classroom more accessible for an increasingly diverse student population, it may be helpful not only to embrace diverse literary traditions but also to acknowledge and validate alternative models of reading proposed by the writers I have discussed by acknowledging the contingent nature of realism. After all, we cannot achieve access without learning what stands in the way—that would not be realistic.

NOTES

Introduction

1. Fielding, *Tom Jones*, 808–9.

2. Scott, *Waverley*, 24.

3. Eliot, *Felix Holt*, 3.

4. Fielding, *Joseph Andrews*, 89–90.

5. Scott, *Waverley*, 24.

6. Eliot, *Felix Holt*, 8.

7. Sterne, *Sentimental Journey*, 13; Thackeray, *Vanity Fair*, 73.

8. Watt, *Rise of the Novel*.

9. McKeon, *Origins;* George Levine, *Realistic Imagination;* and Gallagher, *Nobody's Story*.

10. See, for example, Lynch, *Economy of Character;* Buzard, *Disorienting Fiction;* and Bender, *Ends of Enlightenment*.

11. Said, *Orientalism;* Eagleton, *Heathcliff and the Great Hunger*.

12. Scholars have pointed out how genres such as national tales as well as previous literary traditions including mythology become marginalized in a discourse that privileges realism. See, for example, Trumpener, *Bardic Nationalism* and Bonaparte, *Poetics of Poesis*. Realism has been a particularly problematic concept in eighteenth-century novel studies, where scholars have repeatedly critiqued assumptions about how the novel "rises" to achieve realism in the nineteenth century; this has led to a turn away from realism as a dominant, overarching category for eighteenth-century novel studies in works such as Nandrea, *Misfit Forms*.

13. See, for example, Srinivas Aravamudan's discussion of the intricate relationship between orientalist texts and the novelistic tradition in *Enlightenment Orientalism*. Mary Mullen discusses realism's role in the marginalization of texts from the novelistic canon in Mullen, *Novel Institutions*. Alternatively, Elaine Freedgood advocates for dispensing with realism as a critical framework, arguing that it limits the rich possibilities of literary history in Freedgood, *Worlds Enough*.

14. Leah Price combines book history and close reading to identify how anthologizing practices distinguish readers based on their different reading practices in Price, *Anthology and the Rise of the Novel*. Elaine Auyoung uses cognitive psychology to outline the complex cognitive process that accompanies reading in Auyoung, *When Fiction Feels Real*.

15. On normalcy itself as a socially constructed category, see Lennard Davis, *Enforcing Normalcy*, 2. Jason Farr defines disability in terms of access as "a social category in which people with impairments encounter institutional, social, or physical barriers that impede them from unfettered access to a given community or society" (*Novel Bodies*, 7).

16. For the purpose of this study, I focus on the pleasure of readerly immersion as one way that scholars have often defined the pleasures of reading realist fiction. For an in-depth history of professional and affective relationships to literature, see Lynch, *Loving Literature*.

17. Audrey Jaffee helps to explain the persistence of such fantasy by arguing that realist novels themselves produce what she calls "realist fantasy: a desire for the real that takes shape as a wish, dream, daydream, and, in its most exemplary form, the realist novel itself" (*Victorian Novel Dreams of the Real*, 10). Jaffee's conclusion, in particular, discusses in depth the idea that "surface reading," or the idea that we can "just" read what is on the page, is itself a "critical fantasy" (139–44).

18. Byerly, *Are We There Yet?*, 2, 5.

19. Byerly, *Are We There Yet?*, 10.

20. James Chandler analyzes references to various modes of transport in Walter Scott's *Waverley* and claims that "each vehicular medium is associated with a mode of probability, a style of world-making" ("Moving Accidents," 153). See also Chandler, *Archaeology of Sympathy*. For an in-depth exploration of the nuances of "transport," especially in relationship to the circulation of feeling in the literary and philosophical traditions of the Romantic period, see Burgess, "Transport," 229–60.

21. Menke, *Telegraphic Realism;* Grossman, *Charles Dickens's Networks.*

22. Livesey, *Writing the Stage Coach Nation;* Mathieson, *Mobility in the Victorian Novel.*

23. Langan. "Mobility Disability," 482. Using a disabilities studies approach, Langan argues that instead of taking mobility for granted, it would be more accurate "to say that people are born almost equally immobile" since infancy is a condition characterized by the lack of mobility. Langan's argument has further implications for this project; the terms "access" and "accessibility" are often mobilized in the discourse of democratic justice, but like mobility, it is possible to reframe "limited access" as the original condition that we all share. While this reframing applies to various forms of access, considering this in terms of access to textual meaning and pleasure should remind us that, very early in our lives, we all struggled to learn to read and that comprehension (not to mention the pleasures of reading) was out of our reach.

24. Stewart, *Dear Reader,* 16–17.

25. See Grossman, *Charles Dickens's Networks,* 7. Historically, communication and transportation technologies are so closely intertwined that the word "communication" can also mean "transport." Thus, Raymond Williams feels the need to clarify that "for describing the physical means of travelling and carrying, our other word, transport, is better than communications, but I suppose both will go on being used." Williams therefore defines communications in a way more closely aligned to a

popular understanding of media, as "institutions and forms in which ideas, information, and attitudes are transmitted and received" such as "steam printing, the electric telegraph, photography, wireless, film, television" and other forms of transmitting data (Williams, *Communications,* 17).

26. Debray, *Transmitting Culture,* 8, 7. See also Lisa Gitelman, whose definition of media deliberately includes the broader and messier process that I refer to as mediation, as "socially realized structures of communication, where structures include both technological forms and their associated protocols, and where communication is a cultural practice, a ritualized collection of different people on the same mental map, sharing or engaged with popular ontologies of representation" (Gitelman, *Always Already New,* 7).

27. Debray, *Transmitting Culture,* 8.

28. Brown, *Institutions of the English Novel,* 171–202.

29. See Brown, *Institutions of the English Novel,* 1–4, for a discussion of "institution" itself as a paradoxical term that reifies an action or process into noun form, thus effacing the very active process necessary for establishing and maintaining the legitimacy of something like a literary genre. Brown suggests that the "institution" of the novel is an ongoing process in which literary criticism participates.

30. According to *OED,* the word "metaphor" originates in French and Latin, which in turn derives from the ancient Greek word combining the prefix "meta-" with the root word indicating "to bear, carry" (Oxford English Dictionary, n. "metaphor"). The modern Greek word "metaphora (μεταφορα)" translates into English as "transport."

31. Boswell, *Life of Johnson,* 355.

32. Farquhar, *The Stagecoach.*

33. Hunt, "World of Books," 516–21.

34. By bringing together works from both the eighteenth and nineteenth centuries, this book sees realism as part of an ongoing project of theorizing access while also highlighting the contrasts between historical periods. In doing so, I build on Ted Underwood's contention that historical contrast is one of the prominent functions of periodization and that we may need to find ways to move beyond traditional literary periods to trace larger continuities. See Underwood, *Why Literary Periods Mattered.*

35. Livesey, *Writing the Stage Coach Nation,* 9.

36. Byerly, *Are We There Yet?,* 13.

37. Ewers, *Mobility in the English Novel.* For early discussions on the prominence and significance of transportation in eighteenth-century fiction, see Adams, "Coach Motif," and Dussinger, "'Glory of Motion.'"

38. Postman, *Teaching as a Conserving Activity,* 39.

39. Lupton, *Knowing Books,* 10.

40. Lupton, *Knowing Books,* 2.

41. For discussions of canals in relationship to literary works, see Burgess, "Transporting Frankenstein," 247–65, as well as Ellis, *Politics of Sensibility,* 129–59. On maritime and air travel, see Baker, *Written on the Water;* Carroll, *Empire of Air and Water;*

and Keen, *Literature, Commerce, and the Spectacle of Modernity.* On reading English fiction, especially in the context of global travel, see Flint, "Travelling Readers."

42. Bagwell's study of the transport revolution extends well into the twentieth century and includes studies of water transport (such as canals) in addition to road transport. Despite the date in his title, Bagwell begins the account of "Road Transport before the Railway Age" in the early eighteenth century, demonstrating how the impact of older laws regulating wheeled transport and road maintenance failed to keep up with increased traffic on the road (Bagwell, *Transport Revolution,* 35–41). It is also important to note that Bagwell includes discussions of inland water transport in the form of canals.

43. On advances in road transport, see Dyos and Aldcroft, *British Transport,* 62–79.

44. For an overview on the dazzling growth of the railway during the Victorian period, see Freeman, *Railways and the Victorian Imagination,* 1–6, as well as Schivelbusch, *Railway Journey.*

45. Livesey, *Writing the Stage Coach Nation,* 18.

46. Livesey, *Writing the Stage Coach Nation,* 19.

47. See, for example, Chris Ewers's discussion of mobility in Jane Austen's fiction, in which he vividly illustrates the gendered experience of travel for women as well as the impact of mobility on Austen's fictional form (*Mobility in the English Novel,* 161–89).

48. In outlining the various affordances of transport, I am influenced by Caroline Levine's discussion of various forms and their affordances in *Forms,* 6–11. For an extensive analysis of transport as a network in relationship to the portrayal of a networked society in Charles Dickens's novels, see Grossman, *Charles Dickens's Networks.*

49. Otis, *Networking.*

50. Griffiths, *Age of Analogy,* 2–3.

51. Otis, *Networking,* 3.

52. Guillory, "Genesis," 321–62.

53. Siskin and Warner, *This Is Enlightenment;* McLuhan, *Understanding Media,* 85–90.

54. See Burgess's discussion of Ricoeur in "On Being Moved," 295.

55. Freedgood, *Ideas in Things,* 10.

56. Freedgood, *Ideas in Things,* 11. See also Celeste Langan's discussion of the difference between analogy and metaphor, where analogy "subverts" the subordination imposed by metaphor (*Romantic Vagrancy,* 1–3).

57. My approach resembles that of Jesse Oak Taylor, who considers metaphors as central to the work of how novels "model" climate change. See Taylor, *Sky of Our Manufacture,* 14.

58. Johnson, *Dictionary,* s.v. "transport."

59. My interpretation of the term "transport" mirrors John Durham Peters's point that the idea of "communication" is dualistic and asserts itself as "at once bridge and chasm," bringing others closer often through technological means while underscoring

the distance between persons by highlighting the existence of a medium. See Peters, *Speaking into the Air,* 5.

60. Bolter and Grusin, *Remediation,* 5.

61. This project builds on arguments about the novel's self-reflexivity made by Lupton as well as Caroline Levine, *Serious Pleasures of Suspense.*

62. Byerly builds on the arguments of Buzard, George Levine, and Amanda Anderson's *Powers of Distance* and uses the word "effort" to describe how realism strives to create an immersive experience (Byerly, *Are We There Yet?,* 6). Anderson uses the word "striving" to describe how Victorian novels attempt to reach beyond a partial perspective (*Powers of Distance,* 31).

63. Stewart, *Dear Reader,* 53.

64. Stewart, *Dear Reader,* 8.

65. Stewart, *Dear Reader,* 82.

66. On engagement as a principle of virtual presence, see Byerly, *Are We There Yet?,* 20.

67. Best and Marcus. "Surface Reading," 1–21.

68. Eliot, *Felix Holt,* 3.

69. Using psychoanalytic theory, Burgess argues that "displacement, and so metaphor, are not so much symptomatic of anxiety as they are constitutive of it" ("On Being Moved," 296).

70. Lynch, *Economy of Character,* 11. See also Lupton, *Knowing Books,* 2–3.

71. Guillory, "Genesis," 357.

72. See Guillory, *Cultural Capital.*

73. Guillory, "Genesis," 356, 357.

74. Goodman, *Georgic Modernity,* 8; emphasis in the original. Goodman is interested in these moments when communication breaks down and when the smooth surface of the georgic verse is interrupted because they are "moments of excess and dissonance" that work "as records of an otherwise unknowable history" (9).

75. Debray, *Transmitting Culture,* 7.

76. Debray, *Transmitting Culture,* 5.

77. Debray, *Transmitting Culture.*

78. Latour, *We Have Never Been Modern,* 5–8.

79. Brown, *Institutions of the English Novel;* Siskin, *Work of Writing;* and St. Clair, *Reading Nation.*

80. Gitelman, *Always Already New,* 6. Gitelman further argues that "comparing and contrasting new media thus stand to offer a view of negotiability in itself—a view, that is, of the contested relations of force that determine the pathways by which new media may eventually become old hat" (6). My argument about how nineteenth-century writers' negotiations with eighteenth-century novelistic forms confirms the generic identity of realist fiction follows Gitelman's argument to assert that it is through negotiations that previous generations of fiction become "old hat."

81. Ayelet Ben-Yishai explores the intersection between legal precedents and narrative realism, suggesting that precedential reasoning creates the possibility of

a gradual change that maintains continuity and commonality that also informs the history of realism in Ben-Yishai, *Common Precedents*.

1. Delivering Narrative to Consumer-Readers

1. Fielding, *Tom Jones*, 132, 181. Hereafter indicated as *TJ*, followed by page numbers in parenthetical format.

2. Fielding's tightly knit plot and the emphasis it places on distancing and objectivity have been discussed most prominently in Crane, "Concept of Plot," 119–39, and Watt, *Rise of the Novel*, 260–89. Scholars who focus on the uncertainty that underpins Fielding's representations include Dobranski, "What Fielding Doesn't Say," and Sandra Sherman, "Reading at Arm's Length." For a discussion of how "history" interferes in Fielding's representation, see Mack, *Literary Historicity*, 73.

3. Wolfgang Iser famously builds his argument of the implied reader and how Fielding's representations shape reader response in *Implied Reader*. Scholars since Iser have identified a variety of readers. See Dobranski and Sandra Sherman as well as Hudson, "Fielding's Hierarchy of Dialogue."

4. Benedict Anderson, *Imagined Communities*, and Jürgen Habermas, *Structural Transformation of the Public Sphere*, both locate in the eighteenth century the emergence of a print-based community. However, numerous scholars provide a much less idealized view of a print-based community in the early eighteenth century and tend to depict a fragmented public. See, for example, Hunter, *Before Novels*, and Schmidgen, *Eighteenth-Century Fiction and the Law of Property*.

5. McKeon's *Origins of the English Novel* places Fielding in the context of the ideological and epistemological dialectic that underpinned the novel's emergence.

6. Anderson, *Imagined Communities*, 24–26.

7. Stewart Sherman argues that "clocks and watches, by rendering time palpable, audible, and visible, brought themselves to the center of temporal attention, established themselves as the new point of reference not only for measuring time but for talking and thinking about it" (*Telling Time*, 24).

8. While coaching and posting systems developed in the first half of the eighteenth century, the development of road systems was highly uneven and thus led to different experiences for travelers. Chris Ewers highlights this unevenness by analyzing how Jones travels not along coach routes but through country roads that followed the contours of the landscape (*Mobility in the English Novel*, 53–79).

9. Quoted in Black, *English Press in the Eighteenth Century*, 25.

10. See also Kevis Goodman's highly nuanced discussion of newspaper reading in the eighteenth century in relationship to mediation and a sense of history in *Georgic Modernity and British Romanticism*, 72–78.

11. Addison, *The Spectator* No. 10, in *The Spectator*, 1:32.

12. The newspaper—along with the novel—helps Anderson envision a print-based imagined community; the reading of newspapers is an activity that happens silently, in each reader's mind, and yet each reader knows that others, of whom she may know nothing, are simultaneously reading the same article, in the same paper, with the

same date printed on the upper right-hand corner. See Anderson, *Imagined Communities*, 24–25.

13. Anderson, *Imagined Communities*, 31.

14. Anderson, *Imagined Communities*, 32.

15. Anderson, *Imagined Communities*, 33.

16. For a discussion of how *The Tatler* and *The Spectator* complicate Habermas's idea of the public sphere, see Erin Mackie, *Market á la Mode*, 23–24.

17. Addison, *The Spectator* No. 452 in *The Spectator*, 3:397–98.

18. Fielding, *Joseph Andrews*, 119–21.

19. The narrator also draws the reader's attention to his use of calendrical time through reference to historical events. The narrator expects readers to infer the condition of the road, given the Jacobite rebellion of 1745 that was taking place simultaneously with the fictional events of the novel. "The reader will not wonder" that Jones could procure no horses, the narrator explains, "when he considers the hurry in which the whole nation, and especially this part of it, was at this time engaged, when expresses were passing and repassing every hour of the day and night" (*TJ*, 570). Thus, the novel asks readers to comprehend each character's actions as happening simultaneously, in a manner that overlaps with a broader historical event.

20. Ermarth, *Realism and Consensus*, 18.

21. Ermarth, *Realism and Consensus*, 25.

22. Ermarth, *Realism and Consensus*, 54.

23. My reading of the narrator in *Tom Jones* diverges from existing arguments. For instance, reading Fielding in the context of the eighteenth-century discourse of chance and probability, Jesse Molesworth makes the argument that "the narrator calls on the reader, through programmatic hints, to make a series of inductive inferences, which essentially amounts to an elementary system of risk analysis." In doing so, he builds on established arguments that uphold Fielding (or rather his narrator) as a figure who elevates novel reading into an instructive pastime by educating his readers. Molesworth, however, attributes skepticism over the possibilities of knowing to Fielding's later work, *Amelia*. See Molesworth, *Chance and the Eighteenth-Century Novel*, 162. For one of the most powerful arguments about how Fielding renders novel reading instructive, see William Warner, *Licensing Entertainment*, 273.

24. Welsh, *Strong Representations*, 12.

25. Welsh, *Strong Representations*, 17.

26. Welsh, *Strong Representations*, 67.

27. Schmidgen, *Eighteenth-Century Fiction and the Law of Property*. Like Schmidgen, Ruth Livesey also challenges Anderson's timeline and confirms the persistence of uneven, localized temporalities into the nineteenth century in *Writing the Stage Coach Nation*, 13–14.

28. Schmidgen, *Eighteenth-Century Fiction and the Law of Property*, 13.

29. Hunter, *Before Novels*, 129.

30. Hunter, *Before Novels*, 128.

31. Hunter, *Before Novels*, 158.

32. Hunter, *Before Novels*, 158.

33. Michel de Certeau reminds us to work against the view of reading constructed through Enlightenment pedagogy and reinforced through media empires in contemporary society. He asserts that though texts provide a limited range within which readers can range, readers are nevertheless independent to roam about the textual space in unpredictable and disorderly ways. See "Reading as Poaching" in *Practice of Everyday Life*, 165–76.

34. Shaftsbury, *Characteristics of Men, Manners, Opinions, Times*, 37.

35. Shaftsbury, *Characteristics of Men, Manners, Opinions, Times*, 51.

36. Hume, "Of the Original Contract," 476.

37. Hume, "Of the Standard of Taste," 232.

38. Hume, "Of the Standard of Taste," 233.

39. Hume, "Of the Standard of Taste," 232.

40. Hume, "Of the Standard of Taste," 237.

41. Hume, *Treatise of Human Nature*, 422; emphasis in the original.

42. For an overlapping yet alternative take on this scene that considers Partridge's response as a problem of reading character, see John E. Loftis, "Trials and the Shaping of Identity." For an in-depth discussion of the role of Garrick in the mid-eighteenth-century interpretive economy of character (including that presented in *Tom Jones*), see Deidre Lynch, *The Economy of Character*, 80–84.

43. J. Paul Hunter remarks that "what is unusual about *Tom Jones* is not the fact of Fielding's use of models or even that he uses more than one, but that he mixes ancient and modern models in a particular way." Hunter sketches his portrait of Fielding as a writer who ended up establishing a "new province," not because he intentionally set out to do so, but because the old province—namely the Augustan world of Pope and Swift that continued to hold up the universality of ancient literary standards—failed to accommodate him. Fielding arrived on the literary scene a bit too late for that, Hunter suggests, and had to accommodate himself and his work to a culture that was starting to see the universal ideals of the past generation with skepticism. Thus, Hunter summarizes, "Fielding mediated between the few and the many, and he developed a mediating method that meant, at its base, not only to amuse and instruct at the same time but also to maintain delicate balances among readers of many social classes, educational levels, and moral and cultural persuasions" (Hunter, *Occasional Form*, 137–38).

44. Hilary Teynor also discusses how contrasting communal circumstances force alternative perspectives upon characters in "A Partridge in the Family Tree," 349–72.

2. Noisy Vehicles and Oversensitive Readers

1. With the exception of Samuel Richardson's epistolary fiction, the body of work currently considered novels of sentiment tends to be excluded from canonical accounts of the novel's history. As a case in point, Sterne, whose *A Sentimental Journey* I discuss at length in this chapter, has been a problematic figure in the history of the novel—so much so that Thomas Keymer's influential *Sterne, the Moderns, and*

the Novel is dedicated to the project of arguing that Sterne should, indeed, be included in the history of the English novel.

2. The metaphors of harmony and contagion in the discourse of sensibility, critics argue, suggest the potential of affect to permeate the entire society. See Barker-Benfield, *Culture of Sensibility;* Ellis, *Politics of Sensibility;* Mullan, *Sentiment and Sociability;* and Todd, *Sensibility.* On the other hand, other critics suggest that the physical and performative aspects of sentiment undermine its genuineness. See Benedict, *Framing Feeling;* Goring, *Rhetoric of Sensibility;* Flynn, "Running out of Matter"; Keymer, "*Sentimental Journey* and the Failure of Feeling"; and Van Sant, *Eighteenth-Century Sensibility and the Novel.*

3. See Watt, *Rise of the Novel,* 9–34. For a more in-depth critique of Watt's idea of formal realism and the epistemic assumptions it entails, see Lynch, *Economy of Character,* 4, 123–24.

4. Christina Lupton draws attention to the contradictory impulse of mid-eighteenth-century fiction where the reader's passive enjoyment of the text seems to go hand in hand with reflexive mediations of the text that emphasize its own status as media in *Knowing Books,* 13–17. Miranda Burgess also emphasizes the centrality of mediation, particularly in Adam Smith's *The Theory of Moral Sentiments,* but to different effect in "On Being Moved," 297–302. For Burgess, mediation works to negotiate communal affect and individual emotion so as to ultimately privilege the feeling self in the Romantic period. In her discussion of Shaftsbury and his successors, Nancy Yousef casts this negotiation in a different light—as that between the moral and the epistemological or between intersubjective feeling and subjective knowledge. See Yousef, "Feeling for Philosophy," 610–11. Many of these critical accounts work to highlight mediation as a central epistemic concern in the eighteenth century, thus following the "invitation" to reconceive the Enlightenment as a media episteme by Clifford Siskin and William Warner in "This Is Enlightenment: An Invitation in the Form of an Argument," in *This Is Enlightenment,* 1–33.

5. Lynch, "Novels in the World of Moving Goods," 121–43.

6. See Bobker, "Carriages, Conversation, and *A Sentimental Journey,*" 243–66; Burgess, "On Being Moved," 308–15; Chandler, "Moving Accidents," 137–70; and Lupton, *Knowing Books,* 35–41.

7. Tucker, *Light of Nature Pursued.* Tucker's work was published posthumously under the pseudonym Ned Search. His work combines flights of fancy with a synthesized view of associationist psychology, moral philosophy, and metaphysics, and ranges over five unwieldy volumes. William Hazlitt, who later abridged the work, lamented that Tucker's work extended to seven volumes and included numerous digressions and repetitions, since this likely created an obstacle to a wider readership. Hazlitt explains that little is known about Tucker's private life except that he was a private gentleman and amateur philosopher. See Hazlitt, "Preface to an Abridgment of *The Light of Nature Pursued,*" 121–35. Despite Hazlitt's concern, Tucker is remembered (alongside figures like Joseph Priestley and Erasmus Darwin) as one of the notable proponents of associationist psychology after Locke, Hartley, and Hume, according to Warren, *History of the Association Psychology,* 65–67. Among Tucker's

contemporaries, William Paley dedicates an entire paragraph in the introduction of his work to extoll the influence Tucker had on his argument in *Principle of Moral and Political Philosophy*, xiii–xiv. *The Light of Nature Pursued* continued to be reissued into the nineteenth century, perhaps because, as Catharine Macaulay argued in her educational treatise from 1790, it "gives the best insight into the mechanism of the human mind, and the nature and progress of the passions, of any book yet extant" in *Letters on Education*, 135. Most interesting for my argument is the way the work theorizes metempsychosis, or the preservation of the spirit after death. James Chandler situates Tucker's fantasy of the vehicular state in the seventeenth-century post-mechanistic tradition stemming from Henry More's idea of the sensorium. See Chandler, "Languages of Sentiment," 21–39, as well as his "Politics of Sentiment," 553–75. Without mentioning Tucker in particular, Miranda Burgess traces the tradition of metempsychosis from Pythagoras to Erasmus Darwin and discusses its continued pervasiveness in the late eighteenth century (Burgess, "On Being Moved," 315). Tucker explicitly adds a physiological element to metempsychosis by arguing that the spirit carries with it part of bodily matter—a necessary apparatus to maintain the sensing, feeling self.

8. Tucker, *Light of Nature Pursued*, 4:135–36.

9. Hays, *Memoirs of Emma Courtney*, 120.

10. Peters, *Speaking into the Air*, 285.

11. Peters, *Speaking into the Air*, 80.

12. Peters, *Speaking into the Air*, 81.

13. My purpose here is not to discount the force of language. Indeed, this ambiguous attitude towards words can help to account for the renewed interest in rhetoric during the mid-eighteenth century described by Adam Potkay in *Fate of Eloquence*. John Guillory also helps to highlight the concern over words getting in the way of communication by discussing how Adam Smith dismisses the flourishes of ancient rhetoric to establish a more modern conception of rhetoric by arguing for brevity and elimination of noise in "Memo and Modernity," 123.

14. Peters, *Speaking into the Air*, 81.

15. Locke, *Essay Concerning Human Understanding*, 286.

16. Chandler, "Moving Accidents," 152.

17. Cheyne, *English Malady*, 4–5.

18. Sterne, *Sentimental Journey*, 110. Hereafter indicated as *SJ*, followed by page numbers in parenthetical format.

19. Hume, *Treatise of Human Nature*, 576.

20. Cheyne, *English Malady*, 5, 21.

21. Cheyne, *English Malady*, 64.

22. Cheyne, *English Malady*, 68.

23. Tucker, *Light of Nature Pursued*, 4:12.

24. Tucker, *Light of Nature Pursued*, 4:13–14.

25. Tucker, *Light of Nature Pursued*, 4:179.

26. Flynn, "Running out of Matter," 154.

27. Barker-Benfield, *Culture of Sensibility*, 8–9.

28. Barker-Benfield, *Culture of Sensibility*, 15–19.

29. Pinch, *Strange Fits of Passion*, 3.

30. Starr, *Lyric Generations*, 11.

31. Paulson, *Noise of Culture*, 67.

32. The consumption of luxury goods that John Sekora catalogs extensively, for instance, literally intervenes to prevent sociable feeling (*Luxury*). Pleased with his own generous sentiments after drinking to the king of France's health upon his first arrival at Calais, Yorick becomes conscious of a physical response within his body: "I felt every vessel in my frame dilate—the arteries beat all chearily together, and every power which sustained life, perform'd it with so little friction, that 'twould have confounded the most *physical precieuse* in France" (*SJ,* 6). As with the self-observations of his nervous system, Yorick does not allow easy answers regarding the cause of such sentiments. He peppers his sentimental effusion with the language of mechanism so that it becomes impossible to distinguish the physical and the spiritual (see Battestin, "Sterne among the Philosophes," 36). The toast, he writes, leads him to feel "a suffusion of a finer kind upon my cheek—more warm and friendly to man, than what Burgundy (at least of two livres a bottle, which was such as I had been drinking) could have produced" (*SJ,* 6). The wine, not the sentiment, causes Yorick's vessels to dilate, and Burgundy has the power to create friendly feelings. Cheyne supports this understanding of the relationship between feeling and commerce by arguing that modern luxury brought about by extensive commerce causes nervous disorders in humans by saturating them with food and drink, providing conveniences that hinder exercise, and sanctioning debauch and late hours. According to Cheyne, the nerves that are so central to Tucker's vision of spiritual communication cannot exist without the complementary functions of the cardiovascular system. Fluids like "blood and juices" function as a sort of climate control by creating an ideal environment where solids can thrive, while solids such as fibers and nerves help the fluids circulate (*English Malady,* 14). Cheyne makes it clear that although solids are what mainly cause nervous symptoms, fluids are more susceptible to influences from outside the body. The evils of modern life are imported into the body through various forms of consumption and circulate through the bloodstream, corrupting nerves and other solids in the process. Thus, Yorick's "suffusion" of finer feeling fails to extend beyond his own body, even in the mediated form of charitable giving. The very body that blocks the communication of feeling also allows foreign substances like wine to impact Yorick's affect.

33. Nagle, "Sterne, Shelley, and Sensibility's Pleasures of Proximity," 824–25.

34. Battestin points to this passage as one among many examples of how Sterne's religious faith takes on characteristics similar to the naturalism of the French *philosophes.* See Battestin, "Sterne among the Philosophes," 35. It is also worth noting that the term "sensorium" continues to be relevant in discussions about media and communications. See, for example, Walter Ong, "Shifting Sensorium," 47–60.

35. Laura Otis argues that nerves became a metaphor for understanding electronic transmission such as the telegraph in the early nineteenth century. But Otis's historical outlook also warns us not to apply this idea to the eighteenth century, when

no telegraph wires existed to suggest the possibility of lines connecting individuals (*Networking,* 120–46). For further insight into the epistemic conditions regarding bodies in the eighteenth century, see Allison Muri, *Enlightenment Cyborg.*

36. Smith, *Theory of Moral Sentiments,* 3.

37. Jonathan Lamb appropriately characterizes Smith's solution to sympathy as "conjectural," emphasizing the speculative nature of imaginative mediation in "Imagination, Conjecture, and Disorder," 53–69. Likewise, Burgess describes Smithian sympathy as a series of metaphorical "displacements" that work to distance the feeling self from the knowing self ("On Being Moved," 300–303). These critics underscore how Smith (unlike Shaftsbury or David Hume) delineates the process of transmission only to expose the impossibility of any real connection.

38. Samuel Johnson, "To Mrs Thrale, Lichfield, October 27, 1777," in *Rasselas, Poems, and Selected Prose,* 25.

39. Richardson, *Pamela,* 31.

40. Favret, *Romantic Correspondence,* 19–24.

41. While Smollett does not make a regular appearance in the critical catalog of sentimental fiction, he tends to emerge as a figure engaging issues of sensibility in specific contexts. One of these is when touching issues of physical sensing and corporeality as in Aileen Douglas, *Uneasy Sensations,* and Alex Wetmore, *Men of Feeling.* In addition, Evan Gottlieb, in *Feeling British,* discusses Smollett's engagement with feeling in the context of English-Scottish relationships.

42. Lynch, "Moving Goods," 123.

43. Smollett, *Expedition of Humphry Clinker,* 134. Hereafter indicated as *HC,* followed by page numbers in parenthetical format.

44. Bramble's and Jery's letters are silent about the method of delivering these letters. We might infer, therefore, that their very ability to ignore such concerns shows their privileged position within the public sphere.

45. A circumstance that troubles Yorick almost the moment he sets foot in France is that his property can be taken away from him upon his decease through *droits d'aubaine,* which gave the French monarch the right to confiscate the property of foreign visitors (*SJ,* 5).

46. Christensen, *Practicing Enlightenment,* 184.

47. Christensen, *Practicing Enlightenment,* 187.

48. On the problem of commercial proliferation and the problem of waste in relationship to mediation, see Annika Mann, *Reading Contagion,* 85–90.

49. Aileen Douglas asserts that the "novel implicitly justifies this [gender] disparity by representing the women as feeble correspondents" (*Uneasy Sensations,* 166). Janet Sorensen places less emphasis on gender and demonstrates how Bramble, Jery, and Lydia provide examples of "standard prose which effaces the writers' particular regional location," and thus models the distinction between "'good' language as 'disembodied' standard English and 'bad' language as a lewd corporeal Celtic dialect" (*Grammar of Empire,* 126).

50. Johnson, *The Rambler* No. 4. In *Selected Essays,* 12.

51. See Mark Blackwell's overview of it-narratives in *Secret Life of Things,* 10–11.

52. Mackenzie, *Man of Feeling*, 2.

53. Richardson particularly emphasizes the accessibility of feeling in epistolary form in the introduction to *Pamela*, 31. For a more thorough account of the history and fiction of privacy in correspondence during the eighteenth century, see Favret, *Romantic Correspondence*, 12–24.

54. Price, *Anthology and the Rise of the Novel*, 49.

55. Critics such as Danielle Bobker and James Chandler have argued that Yorick's subsequent choice of a carriage validates his genre and makes possible the subsequent movements that characterize his journey. Bobker suggests that the chaise in which Yorick flirts with Madame de L, which is the chaise he ultimately purchases, defines his subsequent adventures and their representation, producing "a more fluid relationship to communication and thus to form" ("Carriages, Conversation, and *A Sentimental Journey*," 256). Similarly, Chandler identifies this move as "the paradox of sentimental fiction, whereby the dynamics of the face-to-face encounter come to govern a cultural form (the novel) that is defined by action at a distance in Britain's literary public sphere" ("Accidents," 147). These critics argue that Yorick's subsequent adventures succeed in moving readers through his choice of an appropriate vehicle for his sentimental representations.

56. Lupton, *Knowing Books*, 10–17.

57. Jonathan Kramnick provides an intriguing insight when he discusses the idea of "presence." Kramnick argues that there is a substrain of theory of perception in the eighteenth century, one often overlooked in the visual bias of empiricist traditions. He outlines how writers like Bishop Berkeley, Thomas Reid, and Lord Kames tried to think about how representations (or what Locke called ideas) are not just objective images but something that needs to be continually assessed through touch; it is an active process that takes into account a creature in motion rather than a single point. See Kramnick, "Aesthetics and Ecology of Presence," 315–27.

58. Mackenzie, *Julia de Roubigné*, 4.

59. Elizabeth Carter, one of Sterne's contemporaries, commented that "merely to be struck by a sudden impulse of compassion at the view of an object of distress, is no more benevolence than it is a fit of the gout, and indeed has a nearer relation to the last than the first," in "Extract of a Letter to Mrs. Elizabeth Vesey, 19 April 1768," in Howes, *Sterne: The Critical Heritage*, 203. Her critique captures what would become one of the most enduring criticisms of sentimental literature as a whole. As sentimental literature celebrated excessive feeling in its heroes and heroines, so it also encouraged passivity and inaction. Carter's use of passive voice ("to be struck by") appropriately insinuates that sentimentalists are helpless in the same way that gout patients are helpless because they are both governed by their own physical and emotional conditions.

60. On the full scope of imitators who modeled their writings after *A Sentimental Journey*, see Newbould, *Adaptations of Laurence Sterne's Fiction*, 35–74.

61. Keate, *Sketches from Nature*, 1.

62. Pratt, *Travels for the Heart*, 1–16.

63. Thompson, *A Sentimental Tour*, 7.

3. Local History for Distant Readers

1. Scott, *Heart of Midlothian*, 13. Hereafter indicated as *H,* followed by page numbers in parenthetical format.

2. On the crucial role of periodicals in the literary and political milieu of the Romantic period, I have consulted Klancher, *Making of English Reading Audiences,* and Gilmartin, *Print Politics.*

3. Anderson, *Imagined Communities,* 35. I am also influenced by James Chandler's discussions about how historical consciousness was heightened during the Romantic period in *England in 1819,* especially 42–46. Timothy Campbell also presents a highly compelling account of how Scott's historicism emerges through interactions with contemporary commercial culture in *Historical Style,* 203–37.

4. See Mary Favret's discussion of the role of mail coaches in Romantic infrastructures of communication in *Romantic Correspondence,* 16–17.

5. For details about the development of mail coaches, particularly with a focus on the unevenness of their implementation in Scotland and Wales, see Livesey, *Writing the Stage Coach Nation,* especially 51–55.

6. Ferris, *Achievement of Literary Authority,* 137–60. See also Schor, "Scott's Hebraic Historicism," 105–20.

7. These accusations are not necessarily antagonistic but have been repeated frequently since the publication of Scott's novels. In 1825, William Hazlitt praises the Waverley Novels and characterizes them as cultural imports that are "brought us in ship-loads from the neighbourhood of Abbt's-ford" (Hayden, *Scott: The Critical Heritage,* 283). More recently, James Buzard states that Scott "appears to have known himself to be fabricating to suit the touristic interests of English readers" (Buzard, *Disorienting Fiction,* 63–64). Harry Shaw articulates this question head-on and frames it from an orientalist perspective in *Narrating Reality,* 168–75. See also an explicit rebuttal of this argument in McCracken-Flesher, *Possible Scotlands.* Ian Duncan, too, opts for a positive take on Scott's nationalism, arguing that Scott's realism influenced his Scottish contemporaries to cultivate the Scottish novel in *Scott's Shadow.*

8. The debate I describe here about the authenticity of Scott's historical representation is distinct from yet another critical tradition that situates Scott within the tradition of nineteenth century developments in novelistic realism. See, for example, Levine, *Realistic Imagination,* especially 81–128. See also Ann Rigney's wonderfully nuanced discussion of how Scott weaves history into fictional narrative in *Imperfect Histories,* 13–58.

9. For recent discussions of Scott's antiquarianism, see Ferris, "Printing the Past," 143–60, and Rigney, "Things and the Archive," 13–34. On the "imperfect" nature of Scott's historical fiction and how it prompts the need for supplementary history, see Rigney, *Imperfect Histories,* 13–58. On how antiquarianism and Scott's representation of it in *The Antiquary* troubles nationalism through emphasis on the hyperlocal, see Yoon Sun Lee, *Nationalism and Irony,* 74–104.

10. Lee argues that "it is a taste for obsolescence that makes antiquarians uneasy sharers in the celebrations of a purportedly timelsss patriotic ideology. Rather than

continuity, transmission, identity, and wholeness (the touchstones of traditionalism), obsolescence, scarcity, strangeness, and fragmentation (the formal expressions of irony) are the conditions of antiquarian value" (Lee, *Nationalism and Irony*, 104). Livesey argues that Scott is central to a literary tradition of novels that depict the recent past that make national imagining and belonging possible by making local affect portable through representations of interrupted coach journeys (*Writing the Stage Coach Nation*, 27–55).

11. Livesey, *Writing the Stage Coach Nation*, 42.

12. Livesey, *Writing the Stage Coach Nation*, 44. See also Duncan, *Modern Romance*, 1–6.

13. Scott, *Old Mortality*, 5, 6. Hereafter indicated as *O*, followed by page numbers in parenthetical format.

14. On the term "fictions of social circulation," see Lynch, *Economy of Character*, 135–38.

15. Fielding, *Tom Jones*, 648–49.

16. Scott, *Waverley*, 5.

17. Scott, *Waverley*.

18. Livesey, *Writing the Stage Coach Nation*, 42. While Livesey reads these layers of mediation as disrupting a coherent sense of the nation to reassert the power of the local, I argue that Scott draws attention to a broader structure of mediation that attempts to trace the continuity between the local and national, albeit in troubled ways.

19. Wordsworth, *The Prelude of 1805*, book 1, lines 174, 170, 172, 175–76.

20. My reading of this sequence emphasizes the proximity of history, while James Kerr argues that it helps place history at a safe distance. See Kerr, *Fiction against History*, 40–44.

21. Peters, *Speaking into the Air*, 138. Peters contrasts "time-binding media" made of lasting material like stone with "space-binding media" such as paper and electricity that can travel quickly to cover wide geographical areas. Peters inherits this contrast from Harold Innis, who argues that empires sustain their dominion by creating a balance between the two kinds of media (*Empire and Communications*).

22. Everett Zimmerman claims that Old Mortality's reliance on rhetoric lessens his value as a historical witness (*Boundaries of Fiction*, 218). I contend that Old Mortality is not so much a historical witness as he is an agent of transmission.

23. Debray, *Transmitting Culture*, 4.

24. Ferris details how the publication of *Old Mortality* triggered a paper war between Scott and contemporary Covenanters such as Thomas McCrie and John Wilson Croker. They accused Scott of adopting a perspective that is partial to the persecutors who sided with the English government and of representing Covenanters unjustly by caricaturing their use of biblical language. Ferris focuses on how participants in this debate contend over the authority to represent the history of a particular religious group, while Schor provides detailed analysis of how Scott's representation of the Covenanters is inflected by an anti-semitic rhetorical tradition. See Ferris, *Achievement of Literary Authority*, 137–60, and Schor, "Scott's Hebraic Historicism," 105–20.

25. Stewart, *On Longing,* 152.

26. Stewart, *On Longing.*

27. Stewart, *On Longing.*

28. Buzard, *Disorienting Fiction,* 64.

29. Buzard, *Disorienting Fiction.*

30. In his autobiographical fragment, Scott unfavorably compares the types of novels exemplified by Eliza Haywood's *The History of Jemmy and Jenny Jessamy* with those by Henry Mackenzie, the author of *Julia de Roubigné:* "The whole Jemmy and Jenny Jessamy tribe I abhorred, and it required the art of Burney, or the feeling of Mackenzie, to fix my attention on a domestic tale." See Lockhart, *Memoirs of Sir Walter Scott,* 1:35.

31. St. Clair, *Reading Nation,* 242. For further detail on circulating libraries, see Benedict, "Sensibility by the Numbers," 63–86.

32. St. Clair, *Reading Nation,* 244–45.

33. On the nation as a body, see, for instance, Hobbes, *Leviathan,* 300. Evan Gottlieb also considers the word "heart" as having a deceptively unstable significance in the novel in "'To be at Once Another and the Same.'"

34. Favret, *Romantic Correspondence,* 203.

35. See Habermas, *Structural Transformation of the Public Sphere,* 31–43.

36. See Peters, *Speaking into the Air,* 5–6.

37. Andrea Henderson claims that this scene exemplifies how the novel uses "an image of birth to render reproductive an energy that might otherwise be disruptive" in *Romantic Identities,* 134. While I agree that this scene shows how disruption can be turned productive, my reading emphasizes how the novel strives to dissociate itself from acts of reproduction.

38. Ayelet Ben-Yishai explores the intersection between legal precedents and narrative realism in *Common Precedents.* While Ben-Yishai's argument illustrates how Victorian fiction draws upon reasoning by precedent, Scott here suggests the constraining effect of precedential reasoning.

39. On the use of sympathy in *The Heart of Midlothian* as well as its limitations, see Gottlieb, *Feeling British,* 189–98.

40. Southey, *Essays, Moral and Political,* I:135, quoted in Gilmartin, *Print Politics,* 26.

41. On the power of periodical publications to represent and to convene crowds, see Plotz, *Crowd.*

42. Livesey, *Writing the Stage Coach Nation,* 41.

43. Livesey uses the terms "stage-manages" and "curatorial presentation" to describe the duke's role in this scene (*Writing the Stage Coach Nation,* 40).

44. Ian Duncan argues that the figure of the Duke of Argyle can be considered an analogy for Scott's role as literary mediator for the careers of other Scottish writers like James Hogg. See Duncan, *Scott's Shadow,* 167.

45. Benjamin, "Work of Art," 221.

46. Benjamin, "Work of Art," 220.

47. Benjamin, "Work of Art," 221.

48. St. Clair, *Reading Nation*, 221.

49. *Scott: The Critical Heritage*, 67.

50. *Scott: The Critical Heritage*, 215.

51. *Oxford English Dictionary*, s.v. "best" (first example of "best seller" 1889 in *Kansas Times & Star*).

52. For a brief history of the best-seller list as well as the main critical issues surrounding it, see Miller, "Best-Seller List," 286–304.

53. Miller, 286–87.

54. *Scott: The Critical Heritage*, 215.

55. *Scott: The Critical Heritage*.

56. *Scott: The Critical Heritage*.

57. Addison, *The Spectator* No. 529, in *The Spectator*, 4:168.

58. Crabbe, "Library," lines 127–34.

59. Crabbe, "Library," lines 157, 157–58, 179.

60. Crabbe, "Library," lines 189, 190.

61. Crabbe, "Library," line 191.

62. Crabbe, "Library," line 192.

63. Crabbe, "Newspaper," lines 219–20, 221.

64. Addison, *The Spectator* No. 529, in *The Spectator*, 4:168.

65. Johnson, *The Rambler* No. 106. In *Selected Essays*, 168.

66. Johnson, *The Idler* No. 327. In *Selected Essays*, 327.

67. Johnson, *The Rambler* No. 106, In *Selected Essays*, 168.

68. See St. Clair, *Reading Nation*, 534–37; Brown, *Institutions of the English Novel*, 179–85.

69. Scott claims that Johnstone is only interesting "as the author of what has been termed the Scandalous Chronicle of the time" and gives little merit to his work. But he also allows that "the time in which he lived called for such an unsparing and uncompromising censor" (Williams, *Sir Walter Scott on Novelists and Fiction*, 131, 132).

70. Brown, *Institutions of the English Novel*, 183.

71. Ann Rigney discusses how the novel becomes the source for historical accounts of Helen Walker and argues that the novel works as a peculiar vehicle for transmitting cultural memory in *Afterlives of Walter Scott*, 17–50.

72. Walter Scott's influence on Scottish tourism has been well explored by scholars. See, for example, Westover, *Necromanticism*, 142–73; Watson, *The Literary Tourist*, 93–105, 150–62; and Brown, *Literary Tourism*.

4. Information Overload in Industrial Print Culture

1. Gina Marlene Dorré also identifies this disjunction between the transportation technology the novel represents and the historical condition of travel at the time and suggests that the opening chapter of *The Pickwick Papers* "implies that a mysterious force was disrupting traditional means and deposing 'natural' sources of locomotion" ("Handling the 'Iron Horse,'" 1).

2. Grossman, *Charles Dickens's Networks,* 12; Livesey, *Writing the Stage Coach Nation,* 91–92.

3. The name of "Pickwick" famously derives from a Bath stagecoach proprietor, Moses Pickwick, who is briefly mentioned in the novel when Sam notices that the name "Pickwick" is painted onto the panel of the carriage (*Pickwick Papers,* 462). See Livesey, *Writing the Stage Coach Nation,* 94.

4. On the increased influence of John Loudon McAdam's method of road construction in the 1810s, see Bagwell, *Transport Revolution,* 40. On the temporality of *The Pickwick Papers,* including its setting in the 1820s, see Grossman, *Charles Dickens's Networks,* 10–12.

5. Chittick, "*Pickwick Papers* and the *Sun,*" 328–35.

6. For detailed discussion of Cockneyism in *The Pickwick Papers,* see Livesey, *Writing the Stage Coach Nation,* 93–96.

7. Grossman, *Charles Dickens's Networks,* 13.

8. Livsey, *Writing the Stage Coach Nation,* 90.

9. Gaskell, *Cranford.*

10. Gaskell, *Cranford,* 8.

11. See Christina Lupton's discussion of how Miss Jenkyns "can impute little more than texture" to Johnson's prose ("Theorizing Surfaces and Depths," 235–54, 239).

12. Gaskell, *Cranford,* 9.

13. On the focus on things in *Cranford,* see Lupton, "Theorizing Surfaces and Depths," 236–37. On the complex use of temporalities in *Cranford,* see Jewusiak, "The End of the Novel."

14. Menke, *Telegraphic Realism,* 253–54.

15. Gaskell, *Cranford,* 4.

16. Gaskell, *Cranford,* 17.

17. For example, chapter 8 bears the title "Strongly Illustrative of the Position, that the Course of True Love is not a Railway," thus suggesting that the word "railway" was becoming a common cultural reference. Dickens, *The Posthumous Papers of the Pickwick Club,* 91. Hereafter indicated as *PP,* followed by page numbers in parenthetical format.

18. Helen Small also discusses how Dickens is indebted to Fielding, but her discussion focuses mostly on the state of the literary profession and the Victorian rejection of the debauchery in many of Fielding's protagonists. See Small's "The Debt to Society," 14–40.

19. Deidre Lynch uses the term "fictions of social circulation" to characterize the "numerous mid-[eighteenth-century] fictions that treat the education of a gentleman who eventually becomes worthy of the station assigned him" by "sampl[ing] the world's variety and familiariz[ing] himself with a range of social conditions and degrees." See *Economy of Character,* 81.

20. See Lynch, *Economy of Character,* 81–86.

21. See Ackroyd, *Dickens,* 44–47, 1090.

22. On the "old canon," see St. Clair, *Reading Nation,* especially 130.

23. The term "equal wide survey" appears significantly as the subtitle of John Barrell's *English Literature in History* in which he demonstrates how various literary genres attempt to capture the nation as a rapidly expanding and diversifying economic unit. Barrell claims that the novel *Roderick Random* in particular is able to show readers both the diversity of British citizens and how they relate to one another.

24. On what was then a unique publication format of *The Pickwick Papers,* see Patten, *Charles Dickens and His Publishers,* 45.

25. For an overview of the sporting print genre as an important predecessor to *The Pickwick Papers,* see Livesey, *Writing the Stage Coach Nation,* 98–100.

26. Feltes, "Moment of *Pickwick,*" 203–18.

27. On Dicken's negotiations over format in the early stages of serialization, see Patten, *Charles Dickens and "Boz,"* 103–4.

28. Keymer, "Reading Time in Serial Fiction," 34–45.

29. Keymer, "Reading Time in Serial Fiction," 36.

30. Chittick, "*Pickwick Papers* and the *Sun,*" 328–35.

31. "What finally may have made *Pickwick* a novel," Chittick speculates, "was not only the continuing presence of Mr. Pickwick and Sam Weller as characters, [. . .] but the introduction by Dickens of pathetic elements into their comic strip progress." Chittick, however, seems ambiguous about the extent to which Dickens's foray into the pathetic adds novelistic characteristics to the text (Chittick, "*Pickwick Papers* and the *Sun,*" 335).

32. Chittick, "*Pickwick Papers* and the *Sun.*"

33. John Sekora details how numerous sections of Tobias Smollett's *Humphry Clinker,* mostly those that focus on "facts and opinions," were excerpted and reprinted in periodical publications with "such titles as 'The Present State of Bath,' 'The Present State of London,' 'Description of Harrigate,' 'A Description of Edinburgh,' 'Some Observations on Glasgow and Lachlomond' and 'Considerations on the Union by . . . Dr. Smollett'" (*Luxury,* 12).

34. My emphasis on the miscellaneous nature of the narratives contrasts with Robert Patten's point that these "interpolated tales" are in fact thematically in unison with the entire novel. See Patten, "Art of *Pickwick*'s Interpolated Tales," 349–66.

35. Menke, *Telegraphic Realism,* 26.

36. Feltes, "Moment of *Pickwick,*" 204.

37. Feltes, "Moment of *Pickwick,*" 208.

38. Brantlinger, *Reading Lesson,* 13.

39. See Patten, *Charles Dickens and "Boz,"* 106.

40. On Richard Edgeworth and others who made early speculations about how railways may be implemented for popular use, see Schivelbusch, *Railway Journey,* 24–26.

41. Livesey, *Writing the Stage Coach Nation,* 118.

42. This disjunction between the vehicle and infrastructure demonstrates how "forgotten questions about whether and how media do the job can bubble to the surface" when media is defamiliarized, and thus offers an instance of how media provides a glimpse into "negotiability" as Lisa Gitelman argues in *Always Already New,* 7.

43. Unlike Grossman, who reads the scenes of Pickwick's imprisonment as Pickwick's isolation from a networked society, I read this scene as an example of how the effect of information overload is heightened by situating it within a small compass. On how the Newgate scene isolates Pickwick from the transport network, see Grossman, *Charles Dickens's Networks*, 51–52.

44. Siskin and Warner, "This Is Enlightenment," 19. Siskin and Warner situate saturation in the context of late Enlightenment and considers it a part of the dynamic whereby the Enlightenment brought itself to a close: "saturation is signaled by the paradox of access. On the one hand, saturation means that more people have more access to the technology; on the other, it indicates that, strangely enough, direct access is not required—that even those lacking or refusing access are transformed by the ubiquitous presence of the technology" (19).

45. Menke, *Telegraphic Realism*, 17.

46. Rauch, *Useful Knowledge*, 2.

47. Menke, *Telegraphic Realism*, 18.

48. Livesey, *Writing the Stage Coach Nation*, 108.

49. Brown and Duguid, *Social Life of Information*, 119–20.

50. Fielding, *Tom Jones*, 409.

51. Fielding, *Tom Jones*, 420.

52. This contrast has also been pointed out by Barry Therauld in "Form as Process," 145–58. The tendency for villains to go unpunished may be attributed to the secular rather than the providential worldview of realist novels as George Levine discusses in "Literary Realism Reconsidered," 25–30.

53. Siskin, "Mediated Enlightenment," 164–72.

54. See Siskin and Warner, "This Is Enlightenment," 20. On the relationship between social status and the ability to see society as coherent in the eighteenth-century context, see Barrell, *English Literature in History*, 176–79.

55. Patten, *Charles Dickens and "Boz,"* 96.

56. Patten observes that Dickens wrote "so much in chapter 2 that the conclusion stretched onto a twenty-fifth page. Seeing no other solution, the printers added a leaf, beginning chapter 3 up to the start of 'The Stroller's Tale.' *Pickwick* Part I filled twenty-six rather than the stipulated twenty-four pages" (Patten, *Charles Dickens and "Boz,"* 98).

57. Patten, *Charles Dickens and "Boz,"* 97

58. Grossman, *Charles Dickens's Networks*, 68.

59. Grossman, *Charles Dickens's Networks*, 68.

60. Stagecoachmen are an important exception as Grossman points out and as I will discuss later.

61. Fiss, "'Out with It,'" 229.

62. On analogical reasoning and its history within the philosophical tradition, I have consulted Bartha, *By Parallel Reasoning*.

63. Griffiths, *Age of Analogy*, 18.

64. Ermarth, *Realism and Consensus*, 35.

65. Ermarth, *Realism and Consensus*, 21–22.

66. Fiss, "'Out with It,'" 229.

67. Ermarth, *Realism and Consensus*, 35.

68. In her analysis of Dickens's fictions, Ermarth claims that "in Dickens it is the world entire that is intelligible, not merely individual character," and that his representations as a whole confirm the "unitary" nature of that world (*Realism and Consensus*, 182). While Ermarth makes a claim about Dickens's fictional world in its entirety, I am arguing that Mr. Pickwick as a character cannot acknowledge the world he belongs to is "unitary" because his ideas about what is "unitary" or "intelligible" are outdated. This is precisely what makes him quixotic.

69. Ermarth, *Realism and Consensus*, 21.

70. Ermarth, *Realism and Consensus*, 21.

71. Grossman, *Charles Dickens's Networks*, 84, 85.

72. Griffiths, *Age of Analogy*, 20.

73. The popularity of *The Pickwick Papers* is well-documented. One of the most famous observations is by Mary Mitford, who wrote that "All the boys and girls talk his fun—the boys in the streets; and yet those who are of the highest taste like it the most. Sir Benjamin Brodie [a leading surgeon] takes it to read in his carriage, between patient and patient; and Lord Denman [Lord Chief Justice] studies *Pickwick* on the bench while the jury are deliberating." L'Estrange, *Life of Mary Russell Mitford*, III:78, quoted in Patten, *Charles Dickens and "Boz,"* 162.

5. The "Prae-railroadite" and the Railway Generation

1. Livesey, *Writing the Stage Coach Nation*, 2–3.

2. Kurnick, *Empty Houses*, 31.

3. Fritzsche, *Stranded in the Present*, 8.

4. George Levine, *Realistic Imagination*, 134.

5. Tillotson, *Novels of the Eighteen-Forties*, 235.

6. Kurnick, for instance, echoes Tillotson's negative definition to suggest that *Vanity Fair* is neither a historical novel nor a domestic one because history is "trivialized" and domestic space is rendered "grotesque" through the use of puppets and other theatrical figures (*Empty Houses*, 37, 40). Christina Griffin, in contrast, argues explicitly that *Vanity Fair* is indeed a historical novel, but she makes clear that the novel does not attempt to accurately represent historical events in the tradition of Walter Scott's historical novels. Instead, it nevertheless presents history as a lived experience, according to Griffin, by portraying how characters relive the Napoleonic Wars through events and performances in Pumpernickel ("Experiencing History and Encountering Fiction").

7. Tillotson, *Novels of the Eighteen-Forties*, 235.

8. George Levine, *Realistic Imagination*, 135.

9. McMaster, *Thackeray*, 1. While lacking the "sharper set of tools" derived from cognitive psychology that Elaine Auyoung utilizes, McMaster anticipates Auyoung's claim that "novelists strategically select verbal cues that are maximally effective at activating their readers' existing experiential traces" (*When Fiction Feels Real*, 2, 13).

10. Thackeray, *Vanity Fair,* 73. Hereafter indicated as *VF,* followed by page numbers in parenthetical format.

11. Thackeray, "De Juventute," 83. Hereafter indicated as "DJ," followed by page numbers in parenthetical format. "De Juventute" was originally published in 1860 in *The Cornhill Magazine* as part of an essay series titled *Roundabout Papers.* By then, as Adams argues, Thackeray was disillusioned with history writing after his failed aspirations to write an epic. See Adams, *Liberal Epic,* 154–55.

12. Kreilkamp, *Voice and the Victorian Storyteller,* 3.

13. On Thackeray's conflicted ideas over historical representation, see Adams, *Liberal Epic;* Gilmore, "Difficulty of Historical Work," 29–57; and Hack, *Material Interests of the Victorian Novel,* 11–36.

14. Thackeray, "George The First," 4. On the relationship of Thackeray's historiography to that of contemporary historians, see Barnaby, "Thackeray as Metahistorian," 33–55.

15. Fritzsche, *Stranded in the Present,* 65.

16. Fritzsche, *Stranded in the Present,* 63.

17. Scott, *Tales of a Grandfather,* i.

18. Scott, *Tales of a Grandfather,* vii.

19. Scott, *Tales of a Grandfather,* i.

20. Scott, *Tales of a Grandfather,* ii–iii.

21. Rigney, *Afterlives of Walter Scott,* 7, 7–8.

22. Debray, *Transmitting Culture,* 4.

23. Thackeray's strategy of creating a stark contrast between two periods is similar to the historiographic strategy employed by Frederic Kittler when he juxtaposes the two media cultures of 1800 and 1900 in *Discourse Networks 1800/1900.*

24. Most of the novels Thackeray mentions in this passage (with the exception of Sir Walter Scott's novels) would have been part of what William St. Clair characterizes as the "old canon" that started to be reproduced repeatedly after 1774, when the British courts imposed a limit on the practice of holding perpetual copyrights. According to St. Clair, "the old canon of prose fiction consisted of a long list of mainly eighteenth-century novels, especially *Robinson Crusoe, Gulliver's Travels,* the many works of Richardson, Fielding, and Smollett, Goldsmith's *The Vicar of Wakefield,* Johnson's *Rasselas* and Sterne's *Tristram Shandy,* and included many translations from French, Spanish and German" such as *Don Quixote* and *Gil Blas.* See St. Clair, *Reading Nation,* 119–21, 130.

25. Guglielmo Cavallo and Roger Chartier explain that traditionally, historians of reading have asserted that the industrialization of printing towards the end of the eighteenth century brought about a "revolution in reading." The "intensive" reader of earlier days "had access to a limited, closed corpus of books which were read and reread, memorized and recited, deeply understood and possessed, and transmitted from one generation to another." But with access to cheaper, mass-produced books, more and more people became "extensive" readers, who "devoured a large number and a wide variety of ephemeral print matter" ("Introduction," 24–25). Cavallo and Chartier caution us not to consider this as an absolute historical shift—while there

were many "extensive" readers in an otherwise "intensive" reading culture, there were also many instances of "intensive" readers in a predominantly "extensive" reading culture—but they also acknowledge that the shift is indicative of general trends in reading practices. See also Leah Price's cogent discussion of how old and new models of reading play out in the British print public sphere as anthologists waged battle against extensive reading in *Anthology and the Rise of the Novel,* especially 3–5.

26. On the prevalence of panoramic representations during the period, see Byerly, *Are We There Yet?,* 35–41.

27. Dickens, *Master Humphrey's Clock,* 79.

28. Michel de Certeau describes the railway carriage as a space that restricts passengers' movements in *Practice of Everyday Life,* 111–14.

29. Dickens, *Master Humphrey's Clock,* 79.

30. Victorian fiction abounds with images of inns and public houses whose business has declined because of nearby railway tracks. See, for example, the description of how an old inn became deserted in Wilkie Collins, *Woman in White,* 452.

31. De Quincey, "The English Mail-Coach," 183–233. Hereafter indicated as "EMC," followed by page numbers in parenthetical format.

32. John Plotz associates De Quincey's representation of the railroad with telegraphs and newspapers—that is, other channels of communication in Victorian England—to suggest that the contrasting models of communication provide De Quincey with a way to reenvision literary participation in an increasingly modernizing public sphere. See Plotz, *Crowd,* 101–26.

33. Baudrillard, *System of Objects,* 74–75; emphasis in the original.

34. By bringing together wildly different images into "confluence," De Quincey demonstrates how the mail coach is not just a nostalgic object that invokes visions of Miss Fanny, but also an object of latent horror. De Quincey's text does not just establish the mail coach as a "mythological" object that idealizes the past; it also exemplifies how, like mythological creatures, the mail coach as a media metaphor that symbolizes a communicative network of the past is able to reconcile a threatening "duality" ("English Mail Coach," 201).

35. Taylor, *World Runnes on Wheeles.*

36. Taylor, *World Runnes on Wheeles,* no page number.

37. Raymond Williams explains the escalator-like effect of looking back to a pastoral age in *Country and the City,* 9–12. Williams explains that such retrospectives function not only as critiques of the present, but also work towards an "idealization of a 'natural' or 'moral' economy" (*Country and the City,* 27). Williams invokes the word "natural" here to indicate an economic structure based on subsistence rather than extensive manufacture and marketing, but we might argue that this idealization of what is "natural" took on double meaning with the advent of technology in the industrial era.

38. Chandler, "Moving Accidents," 154.

39. See Gilmore, "Difficulty of Historical Work," 29–57; and Hack, *Material Interests,* 11–36.

40. Kurnick, *Empty Houses,* 37.

41. Lukács, *Historical Novel,* 182.

42. I suggest that Thackeray strives to create an effect that resembles that which Rae Greiner attributes to the less affective version of sympathy prominent in Victorian realist fiction—to generate communal and historical meaning (in this particular case, the shared historical meaning of the loss of stagecoaches). As Greiner puts it: "More so than 'It'-narratives, which track the adventures of things, or even sentimental novels, in which elaborately staged emotional displays force readers to emote on the other's behalf, the realist novel lays claim to the imaginative social affectivity through which human communities generate the meanings they hold dear. In so doing, it depicts the sympathetic consciousness as the basis for reality itself" (*Sympathetic Realism,* 10).

43. Livesey, *Writing the Stage Coach Nation,* 6–7. On the significance of the description of the "green" countryside described by Thackeray in the medical and literary history of nostalgia—a disease associated with bodies forced into motion in an imperial context—before 1900, see Goodman, "'Uncertain Disease,'" 197–227.

44. Livesey, *Writing the Stage Coach Nation,* 7.

45. Rigney, *Afterlives of Walter Scott,* 18.

46. Rigney, *Afterlives of Walter Scott,* 19.

47. Kurnick, *Empty Houses,* 40.

48. For an alternative take on visiting (and revisiting) historical sites in *Vanity Fair,* see Griffin, "Experiencing History and Encountering Fiction," 412–35.

49. Auyoung, *When Fiction Feels Real,* 12.

50. Auyoung, *When Fiction Feels Real,* 13.

51. McMaster, *Thackeray,* 2.

52. Mary Favret's observations provide a helpful reminder of the centrality of media to the experience of wartime affect: "by calling up questions of epistemology, of certainties and doubts, a mediated war evokes . . . the unsettled terrain of wartime affect. Within such conditions of mediated knowledge, feeling responds not only to the war itself but to one's privileged experience of it—the privilege of knowing war at a distance" (*War at a Distance,* 13).

53. Levine, "Literary Realism Reconsidered," 20.

54. Fielding, *Joseph Andrews,* 147.

55. Levine, *Serious Pleasures of Suspense,* 30.

56. Levine, *Serious Pleasures of Suspense,* 36.

57. Levine, *Serious Pleasures of Suspense,* 12.

58. Scott, *Waverley,* 5.

59. Scott, *Waverley.*

60. Thackeray, *History of Pendennis,* 399.

Conclusion

1. Debray, *Transmitting Culture,* 8, 7.

2. On the history of the London underground, see Wolmar, *Subterranean Railway.*

3. For details on the history of the pneumatic railway, see Hadfield, *Atmospheric Railways*.

4. In addition to Hadfield's discussion of the Chrystal Palace pneumatic railway, Hermoine Hobhouse explains the relationship between the railway experiment and the Great Exhibition in *Crystal Palace and the Great Exhibition*, 185.

5. Eliot, *Felix Holt*, 3. Hereafter indicated as *FH*, followed by page numbers in parenthetical format.

6. Livesey, *Writing the Stage Coach Nation*, 182.

7. Eliot also destabilizes the coach metaphor through her use of the subjunctive mood while describing the coach journey. See Livesey, *Writing the Stage Coach Nation*, 181–82.

8. Eliot, "Natural History," 107.

9. On Eliot's simultaneous embrace of railways and pedestrianism in her review of Riehl, see Kurnick, "Felix Holt," 143–44.

10. See Celeste Langan's discussion of pedestrianism in Wordsworth, in which she identifies the pedestrian as a liberal subject, and especially her discussion of the Wanderer (*Romantic Vagrancy*, 237–62).

11. Eliot, "Natural History," 125.

12. Eliot, "Natural History," 127. James Buzard argues that, through Riehl, Eliot describes an autoethnographic perspective (*Disorienting Fiction*, 291).

13. See, for instance, Graver, *George Eliot and Community*, 33–35; Shuttleworth, *George Eliot and Nineteenth-Century Science*, 8.

14. On the implication of the plot of *Felix Holt* for Eliot's vision of radicalism, see Livesey, *Writing the Stage Coach Nation*, 183.

15. Debray, *Transmitting Culture*, 70.

16. See also David Kurnick's discussion of this opening passage, encompassing everything from the tubes to the "dolorous enchanted forest" ("Felix Holt," 144).

17. Amanda Anderson views the Victorian aspirations towards detachment as "complex and ongoing self-critical practices," even while acknowledging that "valorized forms of detachment within Victorian culture are often allotted to those empowered by virtue of their gender, their race, their nationality, or their social position." Crucially, Anderson lists realism as one of the practices implicated in this Victorian project to cultivate detachment. See Anderson, *Powers of Distance*, 6, 5.

18. Paulson, *Noise of Culture*, ix.

19. Goodman, *Georgic Modernity*, 3.

20. Paulson, *Noise of Culture*, ix.

21. Debray, *Transmitting Culture*, 6.

22. Debray characterizes transmission as a politicized process through which "a collective organization is immunized against disorder and aggression, a protector of the coherence of an *us,* it ensures the group's survival by apportioning what individuals hold in common" (*Transmitting Culture*, 6). See Mary Mullen's spirited discussion of how modern institutionalism creates a single future outcome out of various possible ones, often suppressing marginalized voices in the process (*Novel Institutions*).

BIBLIOGRAPHY

Ackroyd, Peter. *Dickens.* New York: Harper Collins, 1990.

Adams, Edward. *Liberal Epic: The Victorian Practice of History from Gibbon to Churchill.* Charlottesville: University of Virginia Press, 2011.

Adams, Percy G. "The Coach Motif in Eighteenth-Century Fiction." *Modern Language Studies* 8, no. 2 (1978): 17–26.

Addison, Joseph, and Richard Steele. *The Spectator.* 4 Vols. London: J. M. Dent & Sons Ltd., 1946.

Anderson, Amanda. *The Powers of Distance: Cosmopolitanism and the Cultivation of Detachment.* Princeton: Princeton University Press, 2001.

Anderson, Benedict. *Imagined Communities: Reflections on the Origin and Spread of Nationalism.* London: Verso, 1991.

Aravamudan, Srinivas. *Enlightenment Orientalism: Resisting the Rise of the Novel.* Chicago: University of Chicago Press, 2012.

Auyoung, Elaine. *When Fiction Feels Real: Representation and the Reading Mind.* Oxford: Oxford University Press, 2018.

Bagwell, Philip S. *The Transport Revolution from 1770.* New York: Barnes and Noble, 1974.

Baker, Samuel. *Written on the Water: British Romanticism and the Maritime Empire of Culture.* Charlottesville: University of Virginia Press, 2010.

Barker-Benfield, G. J. *The Culture of Sensibility: Sex and Society in Eighteenth-Century Britain.* Chicago: University of Chicago Press, 1996.

Barnaby, Edward T. "Thackeray as Metahistorian, or the Realist via Media." *CLIO: A Journal of Literature, History, and the Philosophy of History* 31, no. 1 (2001): 33–55.

Barrell, John. *English Literature in History, 1730–80: An Equal Wide Survey.* London: Hutchinson, 1983.

Bartha, Paul. *By Parallel Reasoning: The Construction and Evaluation of Analogical Arguments.* Oxford: Oxford University Press, 2010.

Battestin, Martin C. "Sterne among the Philosophes: Body and Soul in *A Sentimental Journey.*" *Eighteenth-Century Fiction* 7, no. 1 (1994): 17–36.

Baudrillard, Jean. *The System of Objects.* Translated by James Benedict. London: Verso, 1996.

Ben-Yishai, Ayelet. *Common Precedents: The Presentness of the Past in Victorian Law and Fiction.* Oxford: Oxford University Press, 2013.

Bender, John. *Ends of Enlightenment.* Stanford: Stanford University Press, 2012.

Benedict, Barbara M. *Framing Feeling: Sentiment and Style in English Prose Fiction, 1745–1800.* New York: AMS Press, 1993.

———. "Sensibility by the Numbers: Austen's Work as Regency Popular Fiction." In *Janeites: Austen's Disciples and Devotees,* edited by Deidre Lynch, 63–86. Princeton: Princeton University Press, 2000.

Benjamin, Walter. "The Work of Art in the Age of Mechanical Reproduction." In *Illuminations,* edited by Hannah Arendt and translated by Harry Zohn, 217–51. New York: Harcourt Brace Jovanovich, 1968.

Best, Stephen, and Sharon Marcus. "Surface Reading: An Introduction." *Representations* 108, no. 1 (2009): 1–21.

Black, Jeremy. *The English Press in the Eighteenth Century.* Philadelphia: University of Pennsylvania Press, 1987.

Blackwell, Mark. *The Secret Life of Things: Animals, Objects, and It-Narratives in Eighteenth-Century England.* Lewisburg, PA: Bucknell University Press, 2007.

Bobker, Danielle. "Carriages, Conversation, and *A Sentimental Journey.*" *Studies in Eighteenth Century Culture* 35 (2006): 243–66.

Bolter, Jay David, and Richard Grusin. *Remediation: Understanding New Media.* Cambridge: MIT Press, 2000.

Bonaparte, Felicia, *The Poetics of Poesis: The Making of Nineteenth-Century English Fiction.* Charlottesville: University of Virginia Press, 2015.

Boswell, James. *Life of Johnson.* Edited by R. W. Chapman. Oxford: Oxford University Press, 1970.

Brantlinger, Patrick. *The Reading Lesson: The Threat of Mass Literacy in Nineteenth-Century British Fiction.* Bloomington: Indiana University Press, 1998.

Brown, Homer Obed. *Institutions of the English Novel: From Defoe to Scott.* Philadelphia: University of Pennsylvania Press, 1997.

Brown, Ian, ed. *Literary Tourism, the Trossachs, and Walter Scott.* Glasgow: Scottish Literature International, 2012.

Brown, John Seely, and Paul Duguid. *The Social Life of Information.* Harvard, MA: Harvard Business Press, 2002.

Burgess, Miranda. "On Being Moved: Sympathy, Mobility, and Narrative Form." *Poetics Today* 32, no. 2 (2011): 289–321.

———. "Transport: Mobility, Anxiety, and the Romantic Poetics of Feeling." *Studies in Romanticism* 49, no. 2 (2010): 229–60.

———. "Transporting Frankenstein: Mary Shelley's Mobile Figures." *European Romantic Review* 25, no. 3 (2014): 247–65.

Buzard, James. *Disorienting Fiction: The Autoethnographic Work of Nineteenth-Century British Novels.* Princeton: Princeton University Press, 2005.

Byerly, Alison. *Are We There Yet? Virtual Travel and Victorian Realism.* Ann Arbor: University of Michigan Press, 2013.

Campbell, Timothy. *Historical Style: Fashion and the New Mode of History, 1740–1830.* Philadelphia: University of Pennsylvania Press, 2016.

Carroll, Siobhan. *An Empire of Air and Water: Uncolonizable Space in the British Imagination, 1750–1850.* Philadelphia: University of Pennsylvania Press, 2015.

Cavallo, Guglielmo, and Roger Chartier. *A History of Reading in the West.* Amherst: University of Massachusetts Press, 2003.

Certeau, Michel de. *The Practice of Everyday Life.* Translated by Steven Rendall. Berkeley: University of California Press, 1984.

Chandler, James. *Archaeology of Sympathy: The Sentimental Mode in Literature and Cinema.* University of Chicago Press, 2013.

———. *England in 1819: The Politics of Literary Culture and the Case of Romantic Historicism.* Chicago: University of Chicago Press, 1999.

———. "The Languages of Sentiment." *Textual Practice* 22, no. 1 (2008): 21–39.

———. "Moving Accidents: The Emergence of Sentimental Probability." In *The Age of Cultural Revolutions: Britain and France, 1750–1820,* edited by Colin Jones and Dror Wahrman, 137–70. Berkeley: University of California Press, 2002.

———. "The Politics of Sentiment: Notes toward a New Account." *Studies in Romanticism* 49, no. 4 (2010): 553–75.

Cheyne, George. *The English Malady: Or, a Treatise of Nervous Diseases of All Kinds, as Spleen, Vapours, Lowness of Spirits, Hypochondriacal, and Hysterical.* London, 1733.

Chittick, Kathryn. "*Pickwick Papers* and the *Sun,* 1833–1836." *Nineteenth-Century Fiction* 39, no. 3 (1984): 328–35.

Christensen, Jerome. *Practicing Enlightenment: Hume and the Formation of a Literary Career.* Madison: University of Wisconsin Press, 1987.

Collins, Wilkie. *Woman in White.* Edited by Matthew Sweet. London: Penguin, 2003.

Crabbe, George. "The Library." In *Poems, Vol. 1 of 3,* edited by Adolphus William Ward, 100–118. Cambridge: Cambridge University Press, 1905.

———. "The Newspaper." In *Poems, Vol. 1 of 3,* edited by Adolphus William Ward, 137–57. Cambridge: Cambridge University Press, 1905.

Crane, R. S. "The Concept of Plot and the Plot of *Tom Jones.*" In *The Novel: An Anthology of Criticism and Theory, 1900–2000,* edited by Dorothy J. Hale, 119–39. Malden, MA: Blackwell, 2006.

Davis, Lennard J. *Enforcing Normalcy: Disability, Deafness, and the Body.* London: Verso, 1995.

De Quincey, Thomas. "The English Mail-Coach." In *Confessions of an English Opium-Eater and Other Writings,* edited by Grevel Lindop. Oxford: Oxford University Press, 1998.

Debray, Régis. *Transmitting Culture.* Translated by Eric Rauth. New York: Columbia University Press, 2004.

Dickens, Charles. *Master Humphrey's Clock.* In *Oxford Illustrated Dickens,* Vol. 20. Oxford: Oxford University Press, 1987.

———. *The Posthumous Papers of the Pickwick Club.* New York: Random House, 2003.

Dobranski, Stephen B. "What Fielding Doesn't Say in *Tom Jones*." *Modern Philology* 107, no. 4 (2010): 632–53.

Dorré, Gina Marlene. "Handling the 'Iron Horse': Dickens, Travel, and Derailed Masculinity in *The Pickwick Papers*." *Nineteenth Century Studies* 16 (2002): 1–19.

Douglas, Aileen. *Uneasy Sensations: Smollett and the Body*. Chicago: University of Chicago Press, 1995.

Duncan, Ian. *Modern Romance and the Transformation of the Novel: The Gothic, Scott, Dickens*. Cambridge: Cambridge University Press, 1992.

———. *Scott's Shadow: The Novel in Romantic Edinburgh*. Princeton: Princeton University Press, 2007.

Dussinger, John. "'The Glory of Motion': Carriages and Consciousness in the Early Novel." *Eighteenth-Century Fiction* 1, no. 2 (1989): 133–46.

Dyos, H. J., and D. H. Aldcroft. *British Transport: An Economic Survey from the Seventeenth Century to the Twentieth*. Leicester: Leicester University Press, 1971.

Eagleton, Terry. *Heathcliff and the Great Hunger: Studies in Irish Culture*. London: Verso, 1995.

Eliot, George. *Felix Holt: The Radical*. Edited by Lynda Mugglestone. London: Penguin, 1995.

———. "The Natural History of German Life." In *Selected Essays, Poems, and Other Writing*, edited by A. S. Byatt and Nicholas Warren, 107–39. London: Penguin, 1990.

Ellis, Markman. *The Politics of Sensibility: Race, Gender and Commerce in the Sentimental Novel*. Cambridge: Cambridge University Press, 1996.

Ermarth, Elizabeth Deeds. *Realism and Consensus: Time, Space and Narrative*. Edinburgh: Edinburgh University Press, 1983.

Ewers, Chris. *Mobility in the English Novel from Defoe to Austen*. Woodbridge: Boydell, 2018.

Farquhar, George. *The Stagecoach, a Farce*. London: T. Lowndes, 1766.

Farr, Jason. *Novel Bodies: Disability and Sexuality in Eighteenth-Century British Literature*. Lewisburg, PA: Bucknell University Press, 2019.

Favret, Mary A. *Romantic Correspondence: Women, Politics, and the Fiction of Letters*. Cambridge: Cambridge University Press, 1993.

———. *War at a Distance: Romanticism and the Making of Modern Wartime*. Princeton: Princeton University Press, 2010.

Feltes, N. N. "The Moment of *Pickwick*, or the Production of a Commodity Text." *Literature and History* 10, no. 2 (1984): 203–18.

Ferris, Ina. *The Achievement of Literary Authority: Gender, History, and the Waverley Novels*. Ithaca, NY: Cornell University Press, 1991.

———. "Printing the Past: Walter Scott's Bannatyne Club and the Antiquarian Document." *Romanticism: The Journal of Romantic Culture and Criticism* 11, no. 2 (2005): 143–60.

Fielding, Henry. *Joseph Andrews and Shamela*. Edited by Judith Hawley. London: Penguin, 1999.

———. *Tom Jones.* Edited by John Bender and Simon Stern. Oxford: Oxford World's Classics, 1998.

Fiss, Laura Kasson. "'Out with It,' as the Subeditor Said to the Novel: Wellerisms and the Humor of Newspaper Excerpts." *Victorian Periodicals Review* 50, no. 1 (2017): 228–37.

Flint, Kate. "Travelling Readers." In *The Feeling of Reading: Affective Experience & Victorian Literature,* edited by Rachel Ablow, 27–46. Ann Arbor: University of Michigan Press, 2010.

Flynn, Carol Houlihan. "Running out of Matter: The Body Exercised in Eighteenth-Century Fiction." In *The Languages of Psyche: Mind and Body in Enlightenment Thought,* edited by G. S. Rousseau, 147–85. Berkeley: University of California Press, 1990.

Freedgood, Elaine. *The Ideas in Things: Fugitive Meaning in the Victorian Novel.* Chicago: University of Chicago Press, 2006.

———. *Worlds Enough: The Invention of Realism in the Victorian Novel.* Princeton: Princeton University Press, 2019.

Freeman, Michael. *Railways and the Victorian Imagination.* New Haven: Yale University Press, 1999.

Gallagher, Catherine. *Nobody's Story: The Vanishing Acts of Women Writers in the Marketplace, 1670–1820.* Berkeley: University of California Press, 1994.

Gaskell, Elizabeth. *Cranford.* Edited by Elizabeth Porges Watson. Oxford: Oxford University Press, 2008.

Gilmartin, Kevin. *Print Politics: The Press and Radical Opposition in Early Nineteenth-Century England.* Cambridge: Cambridge University Press, 2005.

Gilmore, Dehn. "The Difficulty of Historical Work in the Nineteenth-Century Museum and the Thackeray Novel." *Nineteenth-Century Literature* 67, no. 1 (2012): 29–57.

Gitelman, Lisa. *Always Already New: Media, History, and the Data of Culture.* Cambridge: MIT Press, 2006.

Goodman, Kevis. *Georgic Modernity and British Romanticism: Poetry and the Mediation of History.* Cambridge: Cambridge University Press, 2004.

———. "'Uncertain Disease': Nostalgia, Pathologies of Motion, Practices of Reading." *Studies in Romanticism* 49, no. 2 (2010): 197–227.

Goring, Paul. *The Rhetoric of Sensibility in Eighteenth-Century Culture.* Cambridge: Cambridge University Press, 2004.

Gottlieb, Evan. *Feeling British: Sympathy and National Identity in Scottish and English Writing, 1707–1832.* Lewisburg, PA: Bucknell University Press, 2007.

———. "'To be at Once Another and the Same': Walter Scott and the End(s) of Sympathetic Britishness." *Studies in Romanticism* 43, no. 2 (2004): 187–207.

Graver, Suzanne. *George Eliot and Community: A Study in Social Theory and Fictional Form.* Berkeley: University of California Press, 1984.

Greiner, Rae. *Sympathetic Realism in Nineteenth-Century British Fiction.* Baltimore: Johns Hopkins University Press, 2012.

Griffin, Christina Richieri. "Experiencing History and Encountering Fiction in *Vanity Fair*." *Victorian Studies* 58, no. 3 (2016): 412–35.

Griffiths, Devin. *The Age of Analogy: Science and Literature between the Darwins*. Baltimore: Johns Hopkins University Press, 2016.

Grossman, Jonathan. *Charles Dickens's Networks: Public Transport and the Novel*. Oxford: Oxford University Press, 2012.

Guillory, John. *Cultural Capital: The Problem of Literary Canon Formation*. Chicago: University of Chicago Press, 1993.

———. "Genesis of the Media Concept." *Critical Inquiry* 36, no. 2 (2010): 321–62.

———. "The Memo and Modernity." *Critical Inquiry* 31, no. 1 (2004): 108–32.

Habermas, Jürgen. *The Structural Transformation of the Public Sphere: An Inquiry into a Category of Bourgeois Society*. Cambridge: MIT Press, 1991.

Hack, Daniel. *The Material Interests of the Victorian Novel*. Charlottesville: University of Virginia Press, 2005.

Hadfield, Charles. *Atmospheric Railways—A Victorian Venture in Silent Speed*. 1st ed. Newton Abbott: David & Charles, 1967.

Hayden, John O., ed. *Scott: The Critical Heritage*. New York: Barnes and Noble, 1970.

Hays, Mary. *Memoirs of Emma Courtney*. Edited by Marilyn Brooks. Peterborough, ON: Broadview, 2000.

Hazlitt, William. "Preface to an Abridgment of *The Light of Nature Pursued*." In *The Complete Works of William Hazlitt, Vol. 1*, edited by P. P. Howe, 121–35. New York: AMS Press, 1967.

Henderson, Andrea. *Romantic Identities: Varieties of Subjectivity, 1774–1830*. Cambridge: Cambridge University Press, 2006.

Hobbes, Thomas. *Leviathan*. Edited by C. B. Macpherson. London: Penguin, 1985.

Hobhouse, Hermoine. *The Crystal Palace and the Great Exhibition: Art, Science, and Productive Industry: A History of the Royal Commission of the Exhibition of 1851*. New York: Continuum, 2004.

Howes, Alan B., ed. *Sterne: The Critical Heritage*. London: Routledge and Kegan Paul, 1974.

Hudson, Nicholas. "Fielding's Hierarchy of Dialogue: 'Meta-response' and the Reader of *Tom Jones*." *Philological Quarterly* 68 (1990): 177–94.

Hume, David. "Of the Original Contract." In *Essays Moral, Political, and Literary*, rev. ed., edited by Eugene Miller, 465–87. Indianapolis: Liberty Classics, 1985.

———. "Of the Standard of Taste." In *Essays Moral, Political, and Literary*, rev. ed., edited by Eugene Miller, 226–49. Indianapolis: Liberty Classics, 1985.

———. *A Treatise of Human Nature*. Oxford: Clarendon Press, 1978.

Hunt, Leigh. "The World of Books." In *Leigh Hunt as Poet and Essayist, Being the Choicest Passages from His Works Selected and Edited with a Biographical Information*, edited by Charles Kent, 516–21. London: Frederick Warne, 1889.

Hunter, J. Paul. *Before Novels: The Cultural Contexts of Eighteenth-Century Fiction*. New York: W. W. Norton, 1990.

———. *Occasional Form: Henry Fielding and the Chains of Circumstance*. Baltimore: Johns Hopkins University Press, 1975.

Innis, Harold. *Empire and Communications.* Oxford: Clarendon, 1950.

Iser, Wolfgang. *The Implied Reader: Patterns of Communication in Prose Fiction from Bunyan to Beckett.* Baltimore: Johns Hopkins University Press, 1974.

Jaffe, Audrey. *The Victorian Novel Dreams of the Real: Conventions and Ideology.* Oxford: Oxford University Press, 2016.

Jewusiak, Jacob. "The End of the Novel: Gender and Temporality in Elizabeth Gaskell's Cranford." *Nineteenth-Century Gender Studies* 7, no. 3 (2011).

Johnson, Samuel, ed. *A Dictionary of the English Language.* London, 1755.

———. *Rasselas, Poems, and Selected Prose.* 3rd ed. Edited by Bertrand H. Bronson. New York: Holt, Rinehart and Winston, 1971.

———. *Selected Essays from the* Rambler, Adventurer, *and* Idler. Edited by W. J. Bate. New Haven: Yale University Press, 1968.

Keate, George. *Sketches from Nature; Taken and Coloured, in a Journey to Margate. Published from the Original Designs. By George Keate, Esq.* Vol. 1. Dublin, 1779.

Keen, Paul. *Literature, Commerce, and the Spectacle of Modernity, 1750–1800.* Cambridge: Cambridge University Press, 2012.

Kerr, James. *Fiction against History: Scott as Storyteller.* Cambridge: Cambridge University Press, 1989.

Keymer, Thomas. "Reading Time in Serial Fiction before Dickens." *The Yearbook of English Studies* 30 (2000): 34–45.

———. "*A Sentimental Journey* and the Failure of Feeling." In *The Cambridge Companion to Laurence Sterne,* edited by Thomas Keymer, 79–94. Cambridge: Cambridge University Press, 2009.

———. *Sterne, the Moderns, and the Novel.* Oxford: Oxford University Press, 2002.

Kittler, Frederic. *Discourse Networks 1800/1900.* Translated by Michael Metteer with Chris Cullens. Stanford: Stanford University Press, 1990.

Klancher, Jon. *The Making of English Reading Audiences, 1790–1832.* Madison: University of Wisconsin Press, 1987.

Kramnick, Jonathan. "An Aesthetics and Ecology of Presence." *European Romantic Review* 26, no. 3 (2015): 315–27.

Kreilkamp, Ivan. *Voice and the Victorian Storyteller.* Cambridge: Cambridge University Press, 2005.

Kurnick, David. *Empty Houses: Theatrical Failure and the Novel.* Princeton: Princeton University Press, 2012.

———. "Felix Holt: Love in the Time of Politics." In *A Companion to George Eliot,* edited by Amanda Anderson and Harry E. Shaw, 141–52. Malden, MA: John Wiley & Sons, 2013.

Lamb, Jonathan. "Imagination, Conjecture, and Disorder." *Eighteenth-Century Studies* 45 no. 1 (2011): 53–69.

Langan, Celeste. "Mobility Disability." *Public Culture* 13, no. 3 (2001): 459–84.

———. *Romantic Vagrancy: Wordsworth and the Simulation of Freedom.* Cambridge: Cambridge University Press, 1995.

Latour, Bruno. *We Have Never Been Modern.* Translated by Catherine Porter. Cambridge, MA: Harvard University Press, 1993.

Lee, Yoon Sun. *Nationalism and Irony: Burke, Scott, Carlyle.* Oxford: Oxford University Press, 2004.

L'Estrange, A. G., ed. *Life of Mary Russell Mitford.* 3 vols. London: Richard Bentley, 1870.

Levine, Caroline. *Forms: Whole, Rhythm, Hierarchy, Network.* Princeton: Princeton University Press, 2015.

———. *The Serious Pleasures of Suspense: Victorian Realism and Narrative Doubt.* Charlottesville: University of Virginia Press, 2003.

Levine, George. "Literary Realism Reconsidered: 'The world in its length and breadth.'" In *Adventures in Realism,* edited by Matthew Beaumont, 13–32. Malden, MA: Blackwell Publishing, 2007.

———. *The Realistic Imagination: English Fiction from Frankenstein to Lady Chatterley.* Chicago: University of Chicago Press, 1981.

Livesey, Ruth. *Writing the Stage Coach Nation: Locality on the Move in Nineteenth-Century British Literature.* Oxford: Oxford University Press, 2016.

Locke, John. *An Essay Concerning Human Understanding.* London: Penguin, 1998.

Lockhart, J. G. *Memoirs of Sir Walter Scott.* Vol. 1. London: Macmillan, 1915.

Loftis, John E. "Trials and the Shaping of Identity in 'Tom Jones.'" *Studies in the Novel* 34, no. 1 (2002): 1–20.

Lukács, Georg. *The Historical Novel.* Translated by Hannah and Stanley Mitchell. Lincoln: University of Nebraska Press, 1983.

Lupton, Christina. *Knowing Books: The Consciousness of Mediation in Eighteenth-Century Britain.* Philadelphia: University of Pennsylvania Press, 2012.

———. "Theorizing Surfaces and Depths: Gaskell's *Cranford.*" *Criticism* 50, no. 2 (2008): 235–54.

Lynch, Deidre Shauna. *The Economy of Character: Novels, Market Culture, and the Business of Inner Meaning.* Chicago: University of Chicago Press, 1998.

———. *Loving Literature: A Cultural History.* Chicago: University of Chicago Press, 2014.

———. "Novels in the World of Moving Goods." In *A Concise Companion to the Restoration and Eighteenth Century,* edited by Cynthia Wall, 121–43. Oxford: Oxford University Press, 2004.

Macaulay, Catharine. *Letters on Education. With Observations on Religious and Metaphysical Subjects.* London, 1790.

Mack, Ruth. *Literary Historicity: Literature and Historical Experience in Eighteenth-Century Britain.* Stanford: Stanford University Press, 2009.

Mackie, Erin. *Market á la Mode: Fashion, Commodity, and Gender in* The Tatler *and* The Spectator. Baltimore: Johns Hopkins University Press, 1997.

Mann, Annika. *Reading Contagion: The Hazards of Reading in the Age of Print.* Charlottesville: University of Virginia Press, 2018.

Mathieson, Charlotte. *Mobility in the Victorian Novel: Placing the Nation.* London: Palgrave Macmillan, 2013.

McCracken-Flesher, Caroline. *Possible Scotlands: Walter Scott and the Story of Tomorrow.* Oxford: Oxford University Press, 2005.

Mackenzie, Henry. *Julia de Roubigné*. Edited by Susan Manning. East Lothian, Scotland: Tuckwell Press, 1999.

———. *The Man of Feeling*. New York: W. W. Norton, 1958.

McKeon, Michael. *The Origins of the English Novel, 1600–1740*. Baltimore: Johns Hopkins University Press, 1987.

McLuhan, Marshall. *Understanding Media: The Extensions of Man*. Edited by W. Terrence Gordon. Berkeley, CA: Gingko, 2011.

McMaster, Juliet. *Thackeray: The Major Novels*. Toronto: University of Toronto Press, 1971.

Menke, Richard. *Telegraphic Realism: Victorian Fiction and Other Information Systems*. Stanford: Stanford University Press, 2008.

Miller, Laura J. "The Best-Seller List as Marketing Tool and Historical Fiction." *Book History* 3 (2000): 286–304.

Molesworth, Jesse. *Chance and the Eighteenth-Century Novel: Realism, Probability, Magic*. Cambridge: Cambridge University Press, 2010.

Mullan, John. *Sentiment and Sociability: The Language of Feeling in the Eighteenth Century*. Oxford: Oxford University Press, 1988.

Mullen, Mary. *Novel Institutions: Realism, Anachronism, and Nineteenth-Century Realism*. Edinburgh: Edinburgh University Press, 2019.

Muri, Allison. *The Enlightenment Cyborg: A History of Communications and Control in the Human Machine, 1660–1830*. Toronto: University of Toronto Press, 2007.

Nagle, Christopher. "Sterne, Shelley, and Sensibility's Pleasures of Proximity." *ELH* 70, no. 3 (2003): 813–45.

Nandrea, Lorri G. *Misfit Forms: Paths not Taken by the British Novel*. New York: Fordham University Press, 2015.

Newbould, Mary-Céline. *Adaptations of Laurence Sterne's Fiction: Sterneana, 1760–1840*. Farnham, VT: Ashgate, 2013.

Ong, Walter. "The Shifting Sensorium." In *The Varieties of Sensory Experience*, edited by David Howes, 47–60. Toronto: University of Toronto Press, 1991.

Otis, Laura. *Networking: Communicating with Bodies and Machines in the Nineteenth Century*. Ann Arbor: University of Michigan Press, 2011.

Paley, William. *The Principle of Moral and Political Philosophy*. London, 1785.

Patten, Robert L. "The Art of *Pickwick*'s Interpolated Tales." *ELH* 34, no. 3 (1967): 349–66.

———. *Charles Dickens and "Boz": The Birth of the Industrial-Age Author*. Cambridge: Cambridge University Press, 2012.

———. *Charles Dickens and His Publishers*. Oxford: Oxford University Press, 1978.

Paulson, William R. *The Noise of Culture: Literary Texts in a World of Information*. Ithaca, NY: Cornell University Press, 1988.

Peters, John Durham. *Speaking into the Air: A History of the Idea of Communication*. Chicago: University of Chicago Press, 1999.

Pinch, Adela. *Strange Fits of Passion: Epistemologies of Emotion, Hume to Austen*. Stanford: Stanford University Press, 1996.

Plotz, John. *The Crowd: British Literature and Public Politics.* Berkeley: University of California Press, 2000.

Postman, Neil. *Teaching as a Conserving Activity.* New York: Delacorte, 1979.

Potkay, Adam. *The Fate of Eloquence in the Age of Hume.* Ithaca, NY: Cornell University Press, 1994.

Pratt, Samuel Jackson. *Travels for the Heart. Written in France, by Courtney Melmoth. In Two Volumes.* Vol. 1. Dublin, 1777.

Price, Leah. *The Anthology and the Rise of the Novel: From Richardson to George Eliot.* Cambridge: Cambridge University Press, 2000.

Rauch, Alan. *Useful Knowledge: The Victorians, Morality, and the March of Intellect.* Durham, NC: Duke University Press, 2001.

Richards, I. A. *The Philosophy of Rhetoric.* London: Oxford University Press, 1936.

Richardson, Samuel. *Pamela.* Edited by Peter Sabor. London: Penguin, 1985.

Ricoeur, Paul. *The Rule of Metaphor: The Creation of Meaning in Language.* Translated by Robert Czerny with Kathleen McLaughlin and John Costello. London: Routledge, 2003.

Rigney, Ann. *The Afterlives of Walter Scott: Memory on the Move.* Oxford: Oxford University Press, 2012.

———. *Imperfect Histories: The Elusive Past and the Legacy of Romantic Historicism.* Ithaca, NY: Cornell University Press, 2001.

———. "Things and the Archive: Scott's Materialist Legacy." *Scottish Literary Review* 7, no. 2 (2015): 13–34.

Said, Edward W. *Orientalism.* New York: Vintage Books, 1979.

Schivelbusch, Wolfgang. *The Railway Journey: The Industrialization of Time and Space in the 19th Century.* Berkeley: University of California Press, 1986.

Schmidgen, Wolfram. *Eighteenth-Century Fiction and the Law of Property.* Cambridge: Cambridge University Press, 2002.

Schor, Esther. "Scott's Hebraic Historicism." In *British Romanticism and the Jews: History, Culture, Literature,* edited by Sheila A. Spector, 105–20. London: Palgrave Macmillan, 2002.

Scott, Walter. "Charles Johnstone." In *Sir Walter Scott on Novelists and Fiction,* edited by Ioan Williams, 131–37. New York: Barnes and Noble, 1968.

———. *The Heart of Midlothian.* Edited by Claire Lamont. Oxford: Oxford University Press, 1999.

———. *Old Mortality.* Edited by Jane Stevenson and Peter Davidson. Oxford: Oxford University Press, 1999.

———. *Tales of a Grandfather,* I. In *The Prose Works of Sir Walter Scott, Bart.,* Vol. 22. Edinburgh: Adam and Charles Black, 1881.

———. *Waverley.* Edited by Claire Lamont. Oxford: Oxford University Press, 1986.

Sekora, John. *Luxury: The Concept in Western Thought, Eden to Smollett.* Baltimore: Johns Hopkins University Press, 1977.

Shaftsbury, 3rd Earl of, Anthony Ashley Cooper. *Characteristics of Men, Manners, Opinions, Times.* Edited by Lawrence Klein. Cambridge: Cambridge University Press, 1999.

Shaw, Harry. *Narrating Reality: Austen, Scott, Eliot.* Ithaca, NY: Cornell University Press, 1999.

Sherman, Sandra. "Reading at Arm's Length: Fielding's Contract with the Reader in 'Tom Jones.'" *Studies in the Novel* 30, no. 2 (1998): 232–45.

Sherman, Stewart. *Telling Time: Clocks, Diaries, and English Diurnal Form, 1660–1785.* 1st ed. Chicago: University of Chicago Press, 1997.

Shuttleworth, Sally. *George Eliot and Nineteenth-Century Science: The Make-Believe of a Beginning.* Cambridge: Cambridge University Press, 1984.

Siskin, Clifford, and William Warner, eds. *This Is Enlightenment.* Chicago: University of Chicago Press, 2010.

———. "This Is Enlightenment: An Invitation in the Form of an Argument." In *This Is Enlightenment,* edited by Clifford Siskin and William Warner, 1–33. Chicago: University of Chicago Press, 2010.

Siskin, Clifford. "Mediated Enlightenment: The System of the World." In *This Is Enlightenment,* edited by Clifford Siskin and William Warner, 164–72. Chicago: University of Chicago Press, 2010.

———. *The Work of Writing: Literature and Social Change in Britain, 1700–1830.* Baltimore: Johns Hopkins University Press, 1998.

Small, Helen. "The Debt to Society: Dickens, Fielding, and the Genealogy of Independence." In *The Victorians and the Eighteenth Century: Reassessing the Tradition,* edited by Frank O'Gorman and Katherine Turner, 14–40. Aldershot: Ashgate, 2004.

Smith, Adam. *The Theory of Moral Sentiments.* Amherst, NY: Prometheus Books, 2000.

Smollett, Tobias. *The Expedition of Humphry Clinker.* Edited with an introduction and notes by Lewis M. Knapp and revised by Paul-Gabriel Boucé. Oxford: Oxford University Press, 2009.

Sorensen, Janet. *The Grammar of Empire in Eighteenth-Century British Writing.* Cambridge: Cambridge University Press, 2000.

Southey, Robert. *Essays, Moral and Political.* 2 vols. London: John Murray, 1832.

St. Clair, William. *The Reading Nation in the Romantic Period.* Cambridge: Cambridge University Press, 2004.

Starr, G. Gabrielle. *Lyric Generations: Poetry and the Novel in the Long Eighteenth Century.* Baltimore: Johns Hopkins University Press, 2004.

Sterne, Laurence. *A Sentimental Journey through France and Italy.* Edited by Paul Goring. London: Penguin, 2001.

Stewart, Garrett. *Dear Reader: The Conscripted Audience in Nineteenth-Century British Fiction.* Baltimore: Johns Hopkins University Press, 1996.

Stewart, Susan. *On Longing: Narratives of the Miniature, the Gigantic, the Souvenir, the Collection.* Durham, NC: Duke University Press, 1993.

Takanashi, Kyoko. "Circulation, Monuments, and the Politics of Transmission in Sir Walter Scott's *The Tales of My Landlord.*" *ELH* 79, no. 2 (2012) 289–314.

———. "Mediation, Reading, and Yorick's Sentimental Vehicle." *Novel* 49, no. 3 (2016): 486–503.

Taylor, Jesse Oak. *The Sky of Our Manufacture: The London Fog in British Fiction from Dickens to Woolf.* Charlottesville: University of Virginia Press, 2016.

Taylor, John. *The World Runnes on Wheeles, or, Oddes Betwixt Carts and Coaches.* London: Henry Gosson, 1623.

Teynor, Hilary. "A Partridge in the Family Tree: Fixity, Mobility, and Community in *Tom Jones.*" *Eighteenth-Century Fiction* 17, no. 3 (2005): 349–72.

Thackeray, William Makepeace. "De Juventute." In *The Works of William Makepeace Thackeray,* Cornhill Edition, Vol. 22, 77–97. New York: Charles Scribner's Sons, 1911.

———. "George The First." In *The Works of William Makepeace Thackeray,* Cornhill Edition, Vol. 21, 3–37. New York: Charles Scribner's Sons, 1911.

———. *The History of Pendennis: His Fortunes and Misfortunes, His Friends and His Greatest Enemy.* New York: Harper & Brothers, 1898.

———. *Vanity Fair.* Edited by Geoffrey and Kathleen Tillotson. Boston: Houghton Mifflin, 1963.

Therauld, Barry. "Form as Process in *The Pickwick Papers:* The Structure of Ethical Discovery." *Dickens Quarterly* 24, no. 3 (2007): 145–58.

Thompson, George. *A Sentimental Tour, Collected from a Variety of Occurrences, from Newbiggin, Near Penrith, Cumberland, to London, By Way of Cambridge; and from London, to Newbiggin, By Way of Oxford. &c.* Penrith, 1798.

Tillotson, Kathleen. *Novels of the Eighteen-Forties.* Oxford: Clarendon, 1956.

Todd, Janet. *Sensibility: An Introduction.* London: Methuen, 1986.

Trumpener, Katie. *Bardic Nationalism: The Romantic Novel and British Empire.* Princeton: Princeton University Press, 1997.

Tucker, Abraham. *The Light of Nature Pursued By Edward Search, Esq., 5 Vols.* London, 1768.

Underwood, Ted. *Why Literary Periods Mattered: Historical Contrast and the Prestige of English Studies.* Stanford: Stanford University Press, 2013.

Van Sant, Ann Jessie. *Eighteenth-Century Sensibility and the Novel: The Senses in Social Context.* Cambridge: Cambridge University Press, 1993.

Warner, William. *Licensing Entertainment: The Elevation of Novel Reading in Britain, 1684–1750.* Berkeley: University of California Press, 1998.

Warren, Howard C. *History of the Association Psychology.* New York: Charles Scribner's Sons, 1921.

Watson, Nicola. *The Literary Tourist: Readers and Places in Romantic and Victorian Britain.* New York: Palgrave, 2006.

Watt, Ian. *The Rise of the Novel: Studies in Defoe, Richardson and Fielding.* Berkeley: University of California Press, 1957.

Welsh, Alexander. *Strong Representations: Narrative and Circumstantial Evidence in England.* Baltimore: Johns Hopkins University Press, 1992.

Westover, Paul. *Necromanticism: Travelling to Meet the Dead, 1750–1860.* London: Palgrave, 2012.

Wetmore, Alex. *Men of Feeling in Eighteenth-Century British Literature: Touching Literature.* Basingstoke: Palgrave, 2013.

Williams, Raymond. *Communications.* London: Penguin, 1968.

——. *The Country and the City.* Oxford: Oxford University Press, 1975.

Wolmar, Christian. *The Subterranean Railway: How the London Underground Was Built and How It Changed the City Forever.* New Ed. London: Atlantic Books, 2005.

Wordsworth, William. *The Prelude of 1805 in Thirteen Books.* In *The Prelude 1799, 1805, 1850,* edited by Jonathan Wordsworth, M. H. Abrams, and Stephen Gill. New York: W. W. Norton, 1979.

Yousef, Nancy. "Feeling for Philosophy: Shaftesbury and the Limits of Sentimental Certainty." *ELH* 78, no. 3 (2011): 609–32.

Zimmerman, Everett. *The Boundaries of Fiction: History and the Eighteenth-Century British Novel.* Ithaca, NY: Cornell University Press, 1996.

INDEX

access of readers. *See* readers' access to texts

Ackroyd, Peter, 117

Adams, Edward, 202n11

Addison, Joseph, 107–9. See also *Spectator, The*

affordability: of delivery of correspondence, 70; of novels, 146; of serials, 120; of travel, 12

analogies: harmonic analogies, 135; history of analogical reasoning, 135, 200n62; metaphors vs., 13, 184n56; Priestley's use of, 135; "Wellerisms" as in Dickens's *The Pickwick Papers,* 112, 114, 134–38

Anderson, Amanda, 185n62, 205n17

Anderson, Benedict, 29, 32–33, 38, 83, 94, 186n4, 186–87n12, 187n27

anthologies of novels, 8, 109–10, 117–18, 203n25

Arabian Nights, 147, 165

Aravamudan, Srinivas, 181n13

Aristotelian logic, 135

artwork: Ruskin on realism in, 163; viewer's taste in, 47–48

Augustan era, 188n43

Austen, Jane, 184n47; *Northanger Abbey,* 18

authenticity, 24–25, 82–85, 91–93, 98, 103–5, 110–11, 194n8

autoethnographic perspective, 92, 205n12

Auyoung, Elaine, 5, 159, 181n14, 201n9

Bagwell, Philip, 12, 184n42

Ballantyne's Novelist's Library, Scott's editorial role, 109–10

Barbauld, Anna Laetitia, 8

Barker-Benfield, G. J., 63

Barrell, John, 118, 199n23

barriers to mobility, 2, 12, 15

Battestin, Martin C., 191n34

Baudrillard, Jean, 151

belonging, sense of, 20; memory's ability to create, 156; Thackeray's use of stagecoach to return home and, 157. *See also* localized knowledge and history; shared meaning created by a community

Benjamin, Walter, 104–5

Ben-Yishai, Ayelet, 185–86n81, 196n38

Berkeley, George, 193n57

Berrow's Worcester Journal, 31–32

Best, Stephen, 18

best sellers and best-seller lists, 105–7, 109–10, 197n52

Black, Jeremy, 31

Bobker, Danielle, 193n55

body. *See* human body

Bolter, Jay, 16

Bookman, The (periodical): "Behind a Bookseller's Counter" (section), 106; "Monthly Report of the Wholesale Book Trade" (section), 106

Boswell, James, 9

Bothwell, battle of (1679), 86

Brantlinger, Patrick, 123

The British Critic on *Waverley*'s circulation, 105
Brontë, Charlotte: *Jane Eyre,* 166
Brown, Homer Obed, 9, 23, 110
Brown, John, 128
Burgess, Miranda, 6, 185n69, 189n4, 190n7, 192n37
Buzard, James, 92–93, 185n62, 194n7, 205n12
Byerly, Alison, 6, 9–10, 18, 185n62
Byron, Lord, 166

Campbell, Timothy, 194n3
Carter, Elizabeth, 193n59
Cavallo, Guglielmo, 202–3n25
Cave, Edward, 120
Certeau, Michel de, 188n33, 203n28
Cervantes, Miguel de: *Don Quixote,* 118, 202n24
Chandler, James, 6, 60, 182n20, 190n7, 193n55, 194n3
Chapman and Hall (publishers): Dickens's *The Pickwick Papers,* 119–20, 131, 199n27; *The Library of Fiction,* 131
Chartier, Roger, 202–3n25
Chateaubriand, François-René de, 144
Chesterton, G. K., 141
Cheyne, George, 60–63, 191n32
Chittick, Kathryn, 120–21, 124, 199n31
Christensen, Jerome, 71–72
Christianity: as mediated idea in our culture, 8. See also *specific sects*
circulating libraries, 19, 23, 94–95
circulation: heart's function of circulating blood used in analogies, 97, 196n33; national circulation of local, traditional stories, 88–93; national circulation of periodicals, 24–25, 98; social circulation, 85–86, 116–18, 198n19. See also economic circulation; generational transmission; mail coach as metaphor
circumstantial evidence, 36–37

class, educational levels, and cultural backgrounds: access to technologies of mobility and, 7; detachment in Victorian era and, 205n17; Dickens's *The Pickwick Papers* challenging class stereotypes, 112, 114, 118, 130, 132–33, 137–38; novel characters representing variety of, 4, 42, 52–53; readers coming from variety of, 24, 45, 138, 188n43; realism's inclusion/exclusion and, 4, 19, 167; relationship of social status and ability to see society as coherent, 200n54; in Scott's *The Heart of Midlothian,* 102–3; sentimental novels' characters from variety of, 69, 79, 192n49; societal shift from bourgeois monopoly of historical representation, 153; theater audiences from variety of, 44–45, 51
Cockneyism, 113, 130, 198n6
coherence. *See* shared meaning created by a community
commoditization. *See* economic circulation
common sense, 45–46
communication: affective communication in Sterne's *A Sentimental Journey,* 7, 10–12, 21, 55, 57, 59, 63–67, 74, 137, 191n32; anxiety associated with, 21, 30, 185n69; barriers to, 21–22, 27, 185n74; creation of cultural legacies via, 21–22; creation of culture that unites a body of people, 22, 90–91; definition of, 182–83n23; distinguished from transmission, 8, 90, 145; of feelings, 55, 64–65; gossip networks, 28, 39–42; mail coach increasing speed of, 83, 87, 88, 97–98; man-animal communication involved in mail coaches, 150–51; merged with transportation in concept of mediation, 8, 182–83n25, 184–85n59; noise associated with, 21–22, 65–66, 68, 77–78, 178–79; novels' delivery of, 22; reshaping

cultural heritage, 179, 183n26; spiritual communication in Tucker's *The Light of Nature Pursued,* 58–63. *See also* generational transmission

community. *See* imagined communities; localized knowledge and history; shared meaning created by a community

competing technologies of transport (coach vs. railway), 5, 12, 25, 139, 149–50, 197n1

Cooke's Pocket Library series, 117–18

Cooper, Anthony Ashley. *See* Shaftsbury, 3rd Earl of

Covenanters in Scott's *Old Mortality,* 83, 86, 89–90, 92, 97, 104, 195n24

Crabbe, George, 108, 110; *The Library* (poem), 108

cultural backgrounds. *See* class, educational levels, and cultural backgrounds

Dante, 172; *Inferno,* 172, 174

Darwin, Erasmus, 189–90n7

Day, Thomas: *Sandford and Merton,* 165–66

Debray, Régis: distinguishing between communication and transmission, 90, 145, 179, 205n22; on mediology, 8, 21–22, 168; on need to recognize the past to move forward, 175

Defoe, Daniel, 118; *Robinson Crusoe,* 40, 202n24; *A Tour Through the Whole Isle of Great Britain,* 126

De Quincey, Thomas: "The English Mail-Coach," 150–51, 158, 203n32, 203n34

Descartes, René, 62

Dickens, Charles: bureaucracy criticized by, 123; coachmen's role in, 178; on inferiority of railway travel to stagecoach, 149–50; mediation role of, 114, 128–33, 179; as *Morning Chronicle* reporter, 131; multiple

work engagements of, 131; networked society in, 7, 10, 132, 184n48; reader engagement as preoccupation of, 23, 123; transport network in, 7, 10, 132, 184n48

Dickens, Charles, works by: *Bleak House,* 122–23; *David Copperfield,* 166; *Little Dorrit,* 122–23; *Master Humphrey's Clock,* 149–50; *Sketches by Boz,* 119, 131. See also *Pickwick Papers, The* (Dickens)

disability studies, 5, 182n15, 182n23

Dorré, Gina Marlene, 197n1

Douglas, Aileen, 192n49

Duguid, Paul, 128

Duncan, Ian, 194n7, 196n44

Eagleton, Terry, 4

economic circulation: commoditization of letters and texts, 71–72, 79, 123, 126; Dickens's *The Pickwick Papers* marking transition to industrialized production of books, 123; feelings conveyed through, 55, 69; literary value in relation to, 104–9; repetitious plots of novels due to, 96; Scott's authentic local history requiring reconciliation with, 82, 104–9, 196n37; Smollett's *Humphry Clinker* joining bloated print market, 73; stagecoaches as network of, 24–25; Sterne's *A Sentimental Journey* facing communication problems due to, 77–78; "world of moving goods" (Lynch), 57. *See also* serialization

Edgeworth, Richard Lovell, 124, 199n40

Edinburgh Tolbooth, 97, 98

educational levels. *See* class, educational levels, and cultural backgrounds

Eliot, George: coachmen's role in, 178; mediation role of, 168–70, 175, 179; "nature" indicating local and communal standard for order of things, 171; as realist fiction writer, 171;

INDEX · 223

Eliot, George (*continued*)
recognition of literary history by, 25, 167–68, 171–72, 179; transport metaphors in, 5, 25, 167, 169–71, 205n7; works by: *Scenes of Clerical Life,* 171. See also *Felix Holt, the Radical*

Enlightenment era, 114, 130, 138

epistolary novels, 64, 68, 75–76, 78, 178, 188n1, 193n53

Ermarth, Elizabeth Deeds, 35–36, 44, 135–37, 201n68

Ewers, Chris, 10, 184n47, 186n8

exclusion and marginalization. *See* class, educational levels, and cultural backgrounds; readers' access to texts

Expedition of Humphry Clinker, The. See *Humphry Clinker* (Smollett)

Farquhar, George: *The Stagecoach,* 9

Farr, Jason, 182n15

Faust legend, 137

Favret, Mary, 68, 97, 194n4, 204n52

Felix Holt, the Radical (Eliot), 168–79; coachman Sampson's perspective in, 173–74; detachment in, 172–73, 177, 205n17; memory-making associated with narrative-making in, 169; narrative transmission's complexity acknowledged in, 177; nature of forgetting in, 170–77; outside passenger on stagecoach in, 1, 168, 173, 176–77; plants and plant metaphor in, 172, 177; pneumatic railway in, 169; property transmission in Transome family in, 176; radicalism in, 171, 175, 205n14; railways, meaning and effect of, 173–74; Riehl's pedestrianism admired in, 173, 205n9, 205n12; shepherd in, 13, 19, 176–77; stagecoach metaphor in, 170–71, 176, 205n7; stagecoach ride's superior mediation to other transport modes in, 168–71; warning of future travel without visual access to landscape, 170

Feltes, N. N., 119, 123, 124

Ferris, Ina, 83, 91, 195n24

Fielding, Henry: in anthologies of novels, 118; centrality to rise of realist fiction, 27, 37, 186n5; compared to Dickens's *The Pickwick Papers,* 116–18, 128–30, 134, 198n18; distinguishing novel writing from newspapers, 33, 37, 108; educational purpose of writings of, 187n23; imagined communities in print-based culture and, 28, 32, 37–38; invisibility of coachmen in, 178; judgment of his readers' failings, 18; mediation role of, 27–29, 39, 43, 53, 188n43; objectivity as component of realism in, 28–29, 53, 186n2; reader engagement in, 23, 27–28, 43–45, 48–52, 179; Scott's *Old Mortality* and, 86; Thackeray's *Vanity Fair* referencing, 162, 202n24; transport metaphors in, 1–2, 5, 9, 14, 16, 24, 27–28, 31, 54, 167; works by: *Amelia,* 187n23; *Joseph Andrews,* 1, 162. See also *Tom Jones* (Fielding)

First Reform Act (1832), 171–72

Fiss, Laura Kasson, 135

Flaubert, Gustave, 153

Freedgood, Elaine, 14, 181n13

Fritzsche, Peter, 140, 144, 159

future generations' knowledge of the past. *See* generational transmission

Gallagher, Catherine, 4

Garrick, David, 49, 188n42

Gaskell, Elizabeth: *Cranford,* 115–16, 198n13

gender: codes of conduct for traveling and, 12, 184n47; Gaskell's *Cranford* pitting aging female community against newfangled fiction, 115; letters of Richardson's heroines, 68; Smollett's *Humphry Clinker* marginalizing correspondence of women,

224 · INDEX

73; women as circulating libraries' main clientele, 19, 95; women as correspondents, 73, 192n49; women as newspaper readers, 32; women as travelers, 184n47

generational transmission: change in technologies of mobility creating generational gap, 142, 148; creation of cultural legacies for, 21–22; Debray on, 168, 175, 179, 205n22; novels' circulation in posterity, 110; as politicized process creating coherence and marginalization in, 205n22; Scott's confidence in, 90, 145–46; teachers' role in, 179–80; Thackeray's inclusion of new generation of readers, 141; Thackeray's skepticism of transmission of stories, 146–47, 158; in Thackeray's *Vanity Fair* memories of stagecoach rides passed to next generations, 154–55

Gitelman, Lisa, 23, 183n26, 185n80, 199n42

Glorious Revolution (1688), 86

Goethe, Johann Wolfgang von: *Faust,* 166; *Werther,* 166

Goldsmith, Oliver: *The Vicar of Wakefield,* 118, 202n24

Goodman, Kevis, 21, 156, 178, 185n74, 186n10

gossip networks, 28, 39–42

Gothic fiction, 18

Gottlieb, Evan, 192n41, 196n33

Great Britain: creation of unified nationhood, 84, 93; expansion of national transportation system throughout, 2, 12, 82, 97, 194n5; feudal mentality of eighteenth-century Britons, 38

Greiner, Rae, 205n42

Griffin, Christina, 201n6

Griffiths, Devin, 13, 135, 138

Grossman, Jonathan: on coachman Tony Weller as deserving of respect in Dickens's *The Pickwick Papers,* 138; on Dickens's *The Pickwick Papers* illustrating condition of modernity, 113–14, 200n43; distinguishing between transportation and communication, 8; on serialization of Dickens's *The Pickwick Papers,* 132; on stagecoach metaphors in Dickens, 10, 113, 116; on transport as infrastructure to mediate networked society, 7, 132

Grusin, Richard, 16

Guillory, John, 13, 20–21, 190n13

Habermas, Jürgen, 32, 98, 186n4, 187n16

Halbwachs, Maurice, 144

Hays, Mary: *Memoirs of Emma Courtney,* 58–59, 68

Haywood, Eliza: *Jenny and Jemmy Jessamy,* 95, 196n30

Hazlitt, William, 189n7, 194n7

Heart of Midlothian, The (Scott), 95–99; 1830 preface for Magnum Opus edition, 110–11; carriage's accident requiring extraction of its insides by "Caesarean process of delivery" in, 98, 196n37; Cleishbotham as outsider claiming to tell narrative with impartiality, 92–93; compared to Scott's *Old Mortality,* 97; criminal biographies as model for Hardie's stories instead of novels, 96; Duke of Argyle as mediator for Jeanie's story in, 103–4, 196nn43–44; Effie portrayed as tragic heroine in keeping with romance novels, 100–101; Heart of Midlothian prison as place of confinement in parallel to boundaries of novel writing, 96–97; heart's function of circulating blood used in analogies, 97, 196n33; introduction as discussion between Pattieson and two Edinburgh lawyers, 96, 98;

Heart of Midlothian, The (Scott)
(*continued*)
  law's authority to create false
  narrative in, 99–100; localized
  knowledge and history in, 103–4,
  110–11; mediation in, 83–84, 103;
  narrative framework in, 84, 96, 99;
  Porteous Riot (Edinburgh, 1736)
  described in, 101–2; *The Quarterly
  Review*'s review of, 105; readers'
  sympathy temporarily aroused in,
  101, 196n39; as retroactive source for
  historical accounts of Helen Walker
  (Jeanie Deans's original), 111, 197n71;
  seclusion of Jeanie Deans in her
  local community, 102, 109; story of
  Jeanie Deans's journey to London to
  obtain criminal pardon for her sister,
  96, 99–104, 107, 111; "true" story
  prevailing over fiction in, 99–104.
  See also *Tales of My Landlord, The*
  series (Scott)
heart's function of circulating blood
  used in analogies, 97, 196n33
Henderson, Andrea, 196n37
historical novels: accessibility of, 25, 38;
  depicting intersection of temporal
  and spatial transmission, 87, 195n20;
  Scott compared to Thackeray, 141,
  144; Thackeray on challenge to
  represent history accurately in, 139,
  201n6, 202n13; Thackeray's *Vanity
  Fair* as, 153, 201n6. See also *specific
  works by Scott*
historical precedents, Hume's theory
  of, 46
historical sites, visiting and revisiting of,
  158, 204n48
historical thinking: analogies used
  in comparative historicism, 138;
  escalator-effect of looking back
  (Williams), 152, 203n37; "melancholy of history" in Western
  culture, 140; memories vs. history,

  25, 143–47, 161; Riehl collecting
  stories of communal history by
  talking and observing, 173; speed of
  receding past shown by materialist
  history of mail coaches, 152. *See also*
  memories/memory
History of Tom Jones, A Foundling, The.
  See *Tom Jones* (Fielding)
Hobhouse, Hermoine, 205n4
human body: heart's function of
  circulating blood used in analogies,
  97, 196n33; as problematic in culture
  of sentiment, 58–63, 74; as vehicle
  for soul, 55, 58–59. *See also* nervous
  system
Hume, David: compared to Smith,
  192n37; complaint against book trade
  for revealing private correspondence
  by, 71, 72; on formation of community, 27, 46; on individual's response
  as matter of taste, 46–47; "Of the
  Original Contract" (essay), 46; "Of
  the Standard of Taste" (essay), 46;
  on principles of "universal beauty,"
  47–48; sensory metaphor in, 61
Humphry Clinker (Smollett), 68–78;
  Bramble's and Jery's letters on
  newspapers' unreliability, 72–73;
  circulating in market of false and
  quality-less goods, 73–74; commoditization of letters and texts, 71–72,
  126; compared to Sterne's *A Sentimental Journey*, 69; Dustwich's violation of privacy in creating text from
  letters in, 71–72, 75, 193n53; Lydia's
  and Winifred's letters dependent on
  delivery methods, 69–71; marginalization of women as correspondents,
  73, 192n49; mediation problems in,
  57; mocking epistolary novels, 68, 78;
  narrative in form of letters, 69; problems with sentiment in, 73; sections
  extracted as independent sketches
  for later publication, 121, 199n33;

Thackeray's *Vanity Fair* referencing, 165; transport metaphor in, 24
Hunt, Leigh, 9
Hunter, J. Paul, 38–41, 43, 188n43
Huskisson, William, 174

imagination: as mediation for feelings toward others, 67
imagined communities: Anderson on, 32; Fielding's *Tom Jones* and, 28, 37–38; national imagined community of Scott, 84–85; newspapers, 186–87n12; sentimental fiction, 57
inclusiveness of novel as a genre: broader audience accessibility and, 3–5; realist novels and, 4, 167; Thackeray's inclusion of new generation of readers, 141; transport metaphor as way to address, 6–7, 10. *See also* class, educational levels, and cultural backgrounds
individualism, 56, 59–60
industrial society: Dickens's realism based on readers' mediation in, 179; publishing industry's industrialization, 123, 202n25; romances of stagecoaches in, 152, 158, 162; serial format's suitability to, 114; Thackeray's realism based on readers' mediation in, 179. *See also* railways
information and information overload: British overload of mail in Victorian era, 126–27; cognitive agency of individuals to handle, 132–33; contrasting Victorian information culture with Enlightenment era, 114, 130; culture's mediation in age of information overload, 121, 179; in Dickens's *The Pickwick Papers*, 112, 114, 121–28; information bias and, 132; overload of circulating information as recurring theme in literary history, 126; pointless information and texts generated by Mr. Pickwick, 122–23; readers'

processing of information in Dickens's *The Pickwick Papers*, 128–33; saturation and, 125, 132, 200n44; Victorian era understanding of "information" vs. "knowledge," 128. *See also* generational transmission
Innis, Harold, 195n21
institutionalization of novel: anthologies of novels, 8, 109–10, 117–18, 203n25; Brown on, 183n29; Gitelman on new media applicable to, 185n80; literary canon formation, 8, 20, 118, 202n24; Scott's role in, 8–9, 85, 95–96; serial fiction recognized as a novel, 113; Sterne as problematic figure in, 188n1; transport metaphors recurring in genre of novel, 22–23, 172. *See also* literary history
Iser, Wolfgang, 17, 28, 186n3

Jaffee, Audrey, 182n17
Johnson, Samuel: *A Dictionary of the English Language* on definition of "transport," 15; in Gaskell's *Cranford*, 115; *The Idler* (series), 109; on letters as reflection of human emotions, 67–68; on literary value of enduring classics, 109–10; on novels' power over human minds, 73–74, 75; *The Rambler* (series), 109, 116; *Rasselas*, 166, 202n24; transport metaphor used in conversation with Boswell, 9
Johnstone, Charles: *Chrysal*, 110, 197n69

Kames, Lord, 193n57
Keate, George: *Sketches from Nature*, 80
Kerr, James, 195n20
Keymer, Thomas, 120, 188–89n1
Kittler, Frederic, 202n23
knowledge and knowing: blurry boundaries of knowingness in Sterne's *A Sentimental Journey*, 78; in Dickens's *The Pickwick Papers*, 8, 112–14, 117,

INDEX · 227

knowledge and knowing (*continued*)
128–38, 201n68; "knowledge texts"
of Victorian era, 126; Society for
the Diffusion of Useful Knowledge
(SDUK), 126–28; Victorian era
understanding of "information" vs.
"knowledge," 128. *See also* localized
knowledge and history
Kramnick, Jonathan, 193n57
Kreilkamp, Ivan, 143
Kurnick, David, 140, 153, 158, 177,
201n6, 205n16

Lamb, Jonathan, 192n37
land transportation: as focus, 11–12;
vs. other types of transport,
183–84nn41–42. See also *specific types
of transport*
Langan, Celeste, 7, 182n23, 184n56,
205n10
Latour, Bruno, 22
Lee, Yoon Sun, 84, 194–95nn9–10
Lesage, Alain-René: *Gil Blas,* 118,
202n24
letters and delivery of correspondence:
British overload of mail in Victorian
era, 126–27; compared to music, 102;
feelings conveyed through, 55, 67–73;
marginalization of women as correspondents, 73, 192n49; method of
delivery to reach destination, 69–71,
192n44; as "personal substitute,"
40, 71; Richardson's readers writing
about his novels in their letters,
75; Smollett's *Humphry Clinker* as
example of violation of privacy of,
71–72, 75, 193n53. *See also* epistolary
novels; mail coaches
Levine, Caroline, 163, 184n48, 185n61
Levine, George, 4, 140–41, 161, 185n62,
194n8, 200n52
Lillo, George: *The London Merchant,* 137
literary history: Augustan era, 188n43;
"best sellers," development of

concept of, 104–7, 109–10; Eliot's
recognition of, 25, 167–68, 171–72,
179; industrialization of publishing
industry, 123, 202n25; legacy of
cumulative literary history, 23–24;
literary value, determination of,
104–10, 115; mediological thinking
traced in, 177–78; national tales
and mythology, marginalization of,
181n12; omission of sentimental novels, 56, 188n1; overload of circulating
information as recurring theme in,
126; periodization of, 183n34; realism
rejected as overarching category for
eighteenth-century novel studies,
181nn12–13; romances of stagecoaches in industrial age, 152, 158,
162. *See also* institutionalization of
novel; Romantic period; *specific genre*
Livesey, Ruth: Anderson's timeline
challenged by, 187n27; on Britain's
overload of information in Victorian
age, 126–27; on Dickens's *The Pickwick Papers* illustrating unevenness
of local time and experience, 113; on
Duke of Argyle's role in Scott's *The
Heart of Midlothian,* 196n43; on
Eliot's *Felix Holt*'s desire for stability
in national life, 175; on engagement
with place in fiction, 7, 156; on Jeanie
Deans's character in Scott's *The Heart
of Midlothian,* 103; on mail and
stagecoach system in modernizing
nation, 10, 12; on memory's ability
to create sense of belonging, 156; on
Scott's centrality to literary tradition
involving stagecoach metaphors,
195n10; on Scott's indeterminacy of
relating authentic history, 83–84,
195n18; on Scott's "serio-comic
thresholds" to narrative, 87; on
stagecoach metaphors becoming
cliché by time of Eliot, 172; on
stagecoach metaphors in Dickens,

113, 116; on Thackeray's foreboding caused by railways' emergence, 140; on transport metaphors in realist fiction, 7, 9–10

localized knowledge and history: economic circulation of Scott's stories of, 82, 104–9, 196n37; in Eliot's *Felix Holt*, 175; historical mediation of local narratives as distortion, 92; in Scott's editorial contributions to *Ballantyne's Novelist's Library*, 109–10; in Scott's *The Heart of Midlothian*, 103–4, 110–11; in Scott's *Old Mortality*, 88–93; Scott's realism focused on, 24–25, 179. See also *The Tales of My Landlord* series

Locke, John: on communication, 59, 193n57; possessive individualism and, 56, 59–60; on spirits' lack of bodies, 60; on spiritual communication, 59; in Tucker's *The Light of Nature Pursued*, 58–59, 62

Lockhart, John Hugh, 144–45

London booksellers' monopolization of book trade, 72

Loyalists, 86, 91–93

Lukács, Georg, 153

Lupton, Christina, 11, 19, 78, 185n61, 189n4, 198n11

Lynch, Deidre, 19, 57, 69, 117, 198n19

Macaulay, Catharine, 190n7

Mackenzie, Henry: *Julia de Roubigné*, 79, 95, 196n30; *The Man of Feeling*, 75, 79

mail coach as metaphor: national sympathy metaphor in De Quincey, 151; Scott's audience's familiarity with mail coach allowing for, 83; in Scott's historical fiction, 24–25, 82, 87, 98

mail coaches: De Quincey's recollection of, 150–51, 203n34; Edgeworth on creating coach-railway hybrid, 124; enabling speed of distribution, 83,

87, 88, 93, 97, 194n4; man-animal communication involved in, 150–51; uneven implementation of, 12, 82, 194n5

Marcus, Sharon, 18

Marxism, as mediated idea in our culture, 8

Marxist criticism, 4

Mathieson, Charlotte, 7

McAdam, John Loudon, 12, 198n4

McCracken-Flesher, Caroline, 194n7

McKeon, Michael, 4, 29, 186n5

McLuhan, Marshall, 13

McMaster, Juliet, 141, 160, 201n9

media: comparing and contrasting of new media, 185n80; definition of, 183n26; Gitelman on definition of media, 183n26; Guillory on media concept, 13; history of media theory's use of metaphor, 13; informed by Postman's "media metaphor," 10; monuments as, 88–90; problematic status of novels as, 74; Scott's works associating space-binding with time-binding media, 105, 195n21; Sterne's placement of readers and novels in same environment of, 78, 193n59; Williams's alignment of communication with, 182–83n25

mediation: authors' conceptualization of, 11, 27, 180; communication merged with transportation in concept of, 8, 182–83n25, 184–85n59; culture's mediation of information in age of information overload, 16, 121, 179; Debray on, 8, 21–22, 168; defined, 7, 183n26; Dickens's conceptualization of, 114, 128–33, 179; Eliot's conceptualization of, 168–70, 175, 179; failure of cultural critics to tackle, 21; Fielding's conceptualization of, 27–29, 39, 43, 53, 188n43; historical mediation of local narratives as distortion, 92;

INDEX · 229

mediation (*continued*)
imagination's role in, 67; long poems of eighteenth century and, 21, 185n74; nature of, 20, 189n4; network of, 2, 6–7, 63, 82; newspaper reading and, 186n10; readers' passive enjoyment of text and, 189n4; Scott's conceptualization of, 82–84, 103–9, 195n18; sentimental fiction and, 56–57; Smollett's conceptualization of, 53, 57, 78; Sterne's conceptualization of, 53, 78; Thackeray's conceptualization of, 155–56, 179; transport metaphors and, 3, 6, 12–14, 22, 24, 55, 167; transport's definition including emotional transport and, 15–16; unmediated communication encountering obstacles, 38, 59, 67. *See also* generational transmission; information and information overload

medical discourse: using transport metaphor for relationship between soul and its corporal vehicle, 14. *See also* human body; nervous system; scientific discourse

mediological imagination, 20–24

mediology, 8, 21–22, 168

memories/memory: cognitive recall necessary to activate, 142, 159, 201n9; collective memory created by Scott, 145–46; forgetting's effect on history, 170–77; history vs., 25, 143–47; "memory sites" in novels, 157; Mr. Pickwick's adventures to provide him with pleasant recollections for retirement years, 118–19; print replacing oral transmission of, 145; recall of Sam Weller as model of knowledge in Dickens's *The Pickwick Papers,* 133–34; Scott's confidence in survival of transmission to future generations, 90, 145–46; Scott's transmission of cultural inheritance of the nation, 146; shared meaning and narratives

through, 153–64; social nature of memory, 140, 144–45, 159–60; stagecoach era recalled in personal memory, 14, 21, 25, 139–42, 148–53; Thackeray as novelist of memory, 141, 143–47; Thackeray relying on readers' memories of past novels, 164–66

Menke, Richard, 7, 121, 126

metaphors: analogies vs., 13, 184n56; definition and origin of term, 183n30; as epistemological tools, 13; Freedgood on strong metonymic reading vs., 14; Richards's subordination of vehicles to "symbolic servitude," 14. *See also* mail coach as metaphor; stagecoach as metaphor; transport metaphors

metempsychosis, 190n7

Metropolitan Railway (London's first underground railway), 168

Millar, Andrew, 71

Miller, Laura, 106

mimesis, 19, 57, 161–63, 178

miscellany, principle of, in novel's development, 112, 121

Mitford, Mary, 201n73

modernization: disorientation of encroaching modernity in Dickens's *The Pickwick Papers,* 113–14, 124, 200n43; Livesey on mail and stagecoach system's role in, 10, 12; novel's innovation during era of, 4; railways' contribution to, 139; urban migration and, 38–39. *See also* technologies of mobility

Molesworth, Jesse, 187n23

monuments: as media, 88–90; novels included in *Ballantyne's Novelist's Library* deemed to be, 110; Scott's *The Heart of Midlothian* intended to serve as, 111

More, Henry, 190n7

Mullen, Mary, 181n13, 205n22

musical metaphors, 61

mythology: cultural imagination informed by, 152; national mythology, marginalization of, 181n12; stage and mail coaches becoming objects of, 151, 203n34

Nagle, Christopher, 66
national tales and mythology, marginalization of, 181n12
nationhood: creation of unified Great Britain, 84; traditional, local communities co-existing in, 83; transport shaping ideas of, 7
nervous system: Cheyne on, 60–62, 191n32; in eighteenth-century medical and philosophical treatises, 60, 62; feelings conveyed through, 55; as most sophisticated communication system known to humanity, 67; role in sentimental novels, 63, 77; in Sterne's *A Sentimental Journey* on, 65–66, 191n32; telegraph wires compared to, 13
networks: Dickens's representation of, 7, 10, 113–16, 132, 184n48; exclusions illustrated by transport modes in, 7; gossip networks, 28, 39–42; Grossman on transport as mediation agent for, 7; of mediation, 2, 6–7, 63, 82; stagecoaches and mail coaches as network of national circulation, 12, 24–25
neutral medium of conveyance: time and space as neutral media, 35, 43, 136, 186n2; Tucker and, 60
newspapers and periodicals: commercial interests as prime purpose of, 33; compared to novels, 33, 37, 54, 107; compared to stagecoaches, 30–32; literary value of, 108–9; mail coach delivery of, 93, 97–98; mediation and newspaper reading, 186n10; need to fill pages, 31; "old canon" of novels published in periodical format, 118;

radical periodicals able to incite a crowd, 102, 196n41; Scott's work in contrast to periodical journals and circulating libraries, 94; serial publications compared to, 120; temporality and, 30, 31, 37, 107; unreliability of, 72–73; virtual community of readers and, 38, 186–87n12; women as readers of, 32
Nicoll, William Robertson, 106
noise or distractions, 21–22, 65–66, 68, 77–78, 178–79
Nora, Pierre, 157
Novelist's Magazine, The, 118
novel's history. *See* literary history
novels of manners, 86–87

Old Mortality (Scott), 82–99; circulating library's reader's depiction in, 94–95; Cleishbotham as armchair traveler in, 85–86, 92; Cleishbotham's introduction disapproving of Pattieson's story in, 93; Cleishbotham's misunderstanding of historical novel genre in, 86–87; compared to Fielding, 86; compared to Scott's *The Heart of Midlothian,* 97; conveyer belt–like process of story transmission in, 93; criticism of, 83–84; distinguishing between communication and transmission in, 90; friction at each stage of narrative transmission, 91–93; locals preserving memory of Covenanters in, 83, 86–90, 92, 97; monuments as source of information in, 7, 88–90; narrative framework in, 84, 93; national circulation of local, traditional stories in, 7, 91–93, 126; Old Mortality's role as agent of transmission, 89–90, 107, 195n22; oral transmission process in, 82, 88, 195n22; Pattieson as actual author and preserver of history in, 87;

Old Mortality (Scott) (*continued*)
Pattieson's attempt to balance/
correct narrative of Old Mortality,
91, 92–93; rejection of novel genre's
conventions in, 94–95, 196n30;
Scottish culture viewed from "the
outside" in, 92–99; social circulation
typical of eighteenth-century novels
reversed in, 85–86. See also *Tales of
My Landlord, The* series (Scott)
Old Testament as historical references,
142–43
oral transmission: print substituting for,
145; in Scott's *Old Mortality,* 82, 88,
195n22; Thackeray on storytelling of
elders creating community of oral
exchange, 143
orientalist texts in relation to novelistic
tradition, 181n13, 194n7
Otis, Laura, 13, 191–92n35

Paley, William, 190n7
Palmer, Robert, 12
Patten, Robert, 119, 131, 199n34, 200n56
Paulson, William, 65, 178
pedestrianism, 173, 205nn9–10
penny post, 126
periodicals. *See* newspapers and
periodicals
periodization, need to broaden approach to, 183n34
Peters, John Durham, 59, 88, 184–85n59,
195n21
philosophers' reliance on metaphors, 13
Pickwick Papers, The (Dickens), 112–38;
alternative model of knowing represented by Sam Weller in, 8, 112, 114,
132–38; ambiguous genre later recognized as a novel, 120–21, 124, 199n31;
analogical thinking in, 112, 114,
134–38; Bath visit of Pickwickians in,
125; benevolence of Mr. Pickwick in,
118; coach journey in, 8, 25, 124–25;
coachman's role depicted by Tony

Weller in (and later in *Master Humphrey's Clock*), 134, 138, 148–50, 158;
Cockneyism in, 113, 130, 198n6; compared to Fielding's *Tom Jones,* 116–18,
128–30, 137; compared to Smollett's
Humphry Clinker, 116, 128; compared
to Smollett's *Roderick Random,* 130,
137; compared to Thackeray's *Vanity
Fair,* 153; consensus formed between
Sam Weller and his readers, 136–37;
contrasting Victorian information
culture with Enlightenment, 114,
130, 138; "The Convict's Return"
in, 121, 129; Dickens's difficulties in
adhering to schedule and quantity
for, 131–32, 200n56; disorientation of
encroaching modernity and series of
disjunctions in, 113–14, 124, 200n43;
Feltes characterizing as commodity
text, 123; Gaskell's association of railroad's emergence with, 116; Gaskell's
Cranford citing as example of fiction
without literary merit, 115–16; information overload of miscellany in, 112,
114, 121–28; Jingle's rapid production
of stories in, 121–22; knowledge
acquisition and knowing in, 8,
112–14, 117, 128–38, 201n68; literary
knowledge of Sam Weller superior to
other characters in, 137–38; Mr. Pickwick imprisoned as debtor in Fleet
Prison, 125, 200n43; naming titular
protagonist after Moses Pickwick, a
stagecoach proprietor, 113, 117, 198n3;
narrator's description of his role in
chain of knowledge production, 127;
Pickwickians' failure to mature and
learn in, 8, 128–29, 131, 136, 201n68;
pointless information and texts
generated by Mr. Pickwick, 122–23;
popularity of, 123, 138, 201n73;
preface acknowledging predecessor stagecoach novels, 117; priced
to encourage mass distribution,

120; publisher's negotiations with Dickens over format of, 119; readers' response to, 123, 128–33; realistic engagement of fictional world by Sam Weller in, 135–36; saturation depicted in, 125, 132; in serial form, 112–13, 115–20, 132, 199n24; stagecoach metaphors in, 112, 114, 138; in stagecoach novel tradition, but with different purpose, 8, 112–13, 117, 119, 124, 148; "The Story of Goblins Who Stole a Sexton" in, 129; "The Stroller's Tale" in, 121, 129; Thackeray referencing in *Vanity Fair,* 148; "The True Legend of Prince Bladud" in, 129

Pinch, Adela, 64

Plotz, John, 203n32

Pope, Alexander, 9, 188n43

Porteous Riot (Edinburgh, 1736), 101–2

Postman, Neil, 10

Potkay, Adam, 190n13

Pratt, Samuel: *Travels for the Heart,* 80

precedential reasoning, constraints of, 100, 196n38

predecessors' novels, nineteenth-century authors' reflection on, 9, 23, 24, 114–15, 120, 140

Prelatists. *See* Loyalists

Presbyterians, 88, 92. *See also* Covenanters

Price, Leah, 5, 75, 181n14, 203n25

Priestley, Joseph, 135, 189n7

print-based culture: all types of novels circulating in, 87; emergence of, 186n4; feelings conveyed through, 55; imagined communities in, 28, 32, 37–38; literary value created in, 104–9; public sphere and, 28; recycling narrative conventions in novels, 94–96; speed of print distribution enabled by mail coaches, 83, 87, 88, 97; in Victorian era, 114, 115. *See also* literary history

public sphere: of eighteenth-century print-based culture, 28; Habermas on, 32, 187n16; public opinion and sense of society as a whole, 45–46

Quakers, 93

Quarterly Review, The: review of Scott's novels, 105–7

Radcliffe, Ann: *Mysteries of Udolpho,* 146

radicalism. See *Felix Holt*

railways: competing technologies (coach vs. railway), 5, 12, 25, 139, 149–50, 197n1; De Quincey's comparison of railway to mail coach, 150–51; Dickens's *The Pickwick Papers* predating dominance of, 113; Edgeworth on creating coach-railway hybrid, 124, 199n40; Gaskell associating Dickens's *The Pickwick Papers* with emergence of, 115–16; landscape changes required for, 12; Manchester Liverpool railway, 174; negative effect on businesses of inns and public houses, 174, 203n30; pneumatic railway, 169–70, 205nn3–4; steam locomotives, 12, 168, 170; underground railway, 170; during Victorian era, 116, 152, 184n44, 198n17

Rammell, Thomas, 169

Rauch, Alan, 126

reader engagement, 15–20, 178–79; authors concerned about, 6–7, 10, 23; of bad readers, 19–20, 177; Certeau on, 188n33; "conscripted reader" of Stewart and, 17–18; Dickens's approach to, 123, 128–33; Fielding's approach to, 23, 27–28, 43–45, 48–52, 179; imagined readers and, 11, 17; Iser's "implied reader," 28, 186n3; locating readers inside vs. outside the text, 17; model of "how not to read" and, 18;

reader engagement (*continued*)
novel's self-reflexivity and, 11, 16, 185n61; range of readers' class, educational level, and cultural persuasion, 24, 45, 138, 188n43; Scott's approach to, 23, 82, 164–65; Smollett's approach to, 81, 179; Sterne's approach to, 23, 81, 179; surface reading and, 18, 174, 182n17; Thackeray's approach to, 23, 141–42, 145, 147, 159–62; transport metaphors and, 6, 24, 167–68; validation of readers of different types, 20, 43; virtual presence and, 185n66

readers' access to texts: "access" and "accessibility" as terms of democratic justice, 182n23; anthologies of earlier novels and, 109–10; assumptions about, 5; of authentic history of Scotland, 82, 93; authors' goal to overcome limited access, 24; best sellers and, 104–7, 109–10; broader audience accessibility in eighteenth and nineteenth centuries, 3–5; circulating libraries and, 19, 23, 94–95; generic form facilitating, 23; industrialization of printing, effect of, 202n25; limited access, 2–4, 6, 8, 19–20, 167, 179; mail coach's speed changing expectations of, 97–98; out of reach in early childhood, 182n23; teachers' role in students' access, 179–80; Thackeray relying on readers' memories of earlier novels, 164–66

reading as traveling, 1–3, 9, 14, 16, 19, 24, 27–28, 31, 54, 167. See also *various types of transport metaphors*

reading process: alternative model for sentimental novels, 24, 55, 81; Crabbe's reproach of modern readers for, 108; Dickens's *The Pickwick Papers* explaining how readers process information, 128–33; different kinds and complexity of, 5, 19–20, 22, 167, 180, 181n14; intensive reading vs. extensive reading, 146, 202–3n25; memories of readers as part of textual comprehension, 159–62; serial format's suitability to industrial society, 114; skimming, 20, 174

realism of British literature and art (Ruskin), 163

realist fiction: ability to create consensus among readers, 28; continual reshaping of cultural heritage in, 178–79, 185–86n81; Ermarth on "the horizon" in, 136; experimentation in, 4, 16, 20; Fielding contributing to new genre of, 27, 37; history of improving communication with readers, 23; immediacy vs. representational techniques in, 16; inclusion/exclusion of, 4, 19, 167; institutionalization of, 22–23, 185n80; legal precedents and, 185–86n81; literary critics taking pleasure in, 5; narrator's role in, 35–36; ongoing from eighteenth into nineteenth century, 183n34, 185–86n81; ordering of information circulation, 7; picaresque hero in eighteenth century in, 10; as problematic concept in eighteenth-century novel studies, 181nn12–13; readerly access to, 5–6, 17, 19, 179, 182n16; realist fantasy, 182n17; rise of, 3–4; Scott's place in tradition of, 194n8; self-reflexivity of, 11, 16, 185n61; sentimental fiction compared to, 57; Thackeray as writer of, 140, 153, 161–63, 165, 204n42; time and space as neutral media in, 35; transport metaphors in, 3–10, 23–24, 167; unstable nature requiring mediation, 179. See also transport metaphors

reception studies, 17

Reid, Thomas, 193n57

religious enthusiasm: in Sterne's *A Sentimental Journey*, 66–67, 191n34; transmission of historical narratives inspired by, in Scott's *Old Mortality*, 90–91

remediation, 16

rhetoric, 14, 17, 60, 67, 100, 102, 190n13

Richards, I. A., 14

Richardson, Samuel, 64, 68, 75, 120, 188n1, 193n53, 202n24; *Clarissa*, 68; *Pamela*, 68, 193n53

Ricoeur, Paul, 13

Riehl, Wilhelm Heinrich, 173, 177, 205n9, 205n12; "The Natural History of German Life," 173–74

Rigney, Ann, 145, 156–57, 159, 194nn8–9, 197n71

road systems, 12, 184nn42–43, 186n8, 187n19, 198n4

Romantic period: best seller concept institutionalized during, 110; history conceived of as ongoing in, 83, 194n3; literature and poetry's powers of preservation recognized in, 87; mediation of eighteenth century leading to self-perception in, 189n4; Scott as best seller of, 105; Scott's description of reading public in, 93; speed of print distribution in, 83, 87, 88, 194n4; transportation technologies intertwined with affective movement in, 6, 182n20. See also *specific authors*

Ruskin, John, 162–63; *Modern Painters*, 163

Said, Edward, 4

Schmidgen, Wolfram, 38

Schor, Esther, 195n24

scientific discourse: heart's function of circulating blood used in analogies, 97, 196n33; plants and plant metaphor in Eliot's *Felix Holt*, 172, 177; use of analogies and, 13

Scotland: mail and stagecoach's limited access in, 12, 82, 194n5; national transportation system connecting to, 97; public's limited access to authentic history of, 82; Scott's influence on contemporaries in, 194n7; Scott's influence on tourism in, 197n72; Scott using localized knowledge and history from, 7, 24–25, 83–84, 91–94, 97, 103–11, 126, 144–46, 179, 194n7

Scott, Joan, 144

Scott, Walter: antiquarianism of, 92, 194–95nn9–10; *Ballantyne's Novelist's Library*, Scott's role in, 109–10; as best seller of Romantic period, 105; Buzard on autoethnographic model of writing of, 92–93, 194n7; cherishing past novels for historical insights, 147; compared to Thackeray, 141, 144–47, 153, 164–65, 201n6; criticized for perpetuating English image of Scotland, 83, 194n7; institutionalization of novel by, 8–9, 85, 95–96; localized knowledge and history in, 7, 24–25, 83–84, 91–94, 97, 103–11, 126, 144–46, 179, 194n7; mediation role of, 82–84, 103–9, 195n18; "memory sites" in works of, 157; popularity vs. literary value of, 104–10, 115; reader engagement in, 23, 82, 164–65; Scottish contemporaries influenced by, 194n7; Scottish tourism influenced by, 197n72; Sterne and, 178; Thackeray's remembrance of reading in his youth, 146–47, 202n24; transport metaphors in, 1–2, 7, 81; willing to sacrifice authenticity for wider distribution of his works, 110

Scott, Walter, works by: *The Antiquary*, 194n9; *Bride of Lammermoor*, 105; *Ivanhoe*, 93, 105, 147; *Kenilworth*, 105; *Monastery*, 105; *Montrose*, 105; *Quentin Durward*, 147; *Rob Roy*, 105;

Scott, Walter, works by (*continued*)
Tales of a Grandfather, 144–46.
See also *Heart of Midlothian, The*
(Scott); *Old Mortality; Tales of
My Landlord, The* series (Scott);
Waverley
Sekora, John, 191n32, 199n33
sensibility: discourse of, 24, 189n2;
in Sterne's *A Sentimental Journey,*
66–67
Sentimental Journey, A (Sterne), 63–67,
73–81; blurry boundaries of knowingness in, 78; choice of vehicle
by Yorick in, 3, 65, 75, 77, 193n55;
compared to Smollett's *Humphry
Clinker,* 69; compared to Tucker's
sentient language, 65, 77–78; Dickens's *The Pickwick Papers* referencing,
137–38; erotosocial moments from
physical contact in, 65–66; inspiring
imitators, 80, 193n60; interference of
things and movements with feelings
in, 65; Lupton on, 11; material reality
of, 78–81; musical metaphor in, 61;
noise of culture and from Yorick's
body in, 66, 77–78; powerlessness of
readers and writers in, 11, 78, 193n59;
preface's purpose in, 75–77; public
circulation of text, effect on Yorick,
75–77, 126; reader engagement in,
81, 179; religious enthusiasm tied
to sensibility in, 66–67, 191n34;
sentimental travelogue billed as new
kind of "vehicle" in, 3, 73–75; vehicle
as transport metaphor in, 7, 24, 77,
81; Yorick as reader of fragment in,
74, 79; Yorick's bodily response to
affective communication, 7, 12, 55, 57,
63–67, 74, 137, 191n32; Yorick's imagined audience becoming narrative
characters in, 76
sentimental novels of mid- to late
eighteenth century, 55–57; criticism
of, 84, 193n59; daily life's sentimental

moments, highlighting importance
of, 79; interrupted communication
in, 55, 58; materiality of text in,
74–75, 78–80; nervous system's role
in, 63; Smollett's role in, 192n41;
travelers and transport as common
elements of, 80
serialization: compared to newspapers
and periodicals, 120; Dickens' *The
Pickwick Papers* employing publishing in numbers, 112–13, 115–20,
131–32, 199n24; Grossman on
Dickens's role in, 132; publishers
choosing as format for Dickens's *The
Pickwick Papers,* 119–20, 131, 199n27;
Smollett and Sterne experimenting
with, 120; suitable to industrial
society, 114
Seymour, Robert, 119
Shaftsbury, 3rd Earl of (Anthony Ashley
Cooper), 27, 45–46, 189n4, 192n37
Shakespeare, William: *Hamlet,* 49–50
shared meaning created by a community: Debray on transmission
to future generations and, 21, 168;
Dickens's *The Pickwick Papers'*
failure to see coherence, 130, 132,
135; in Eliot's *Felix Holt,* 174–75; in
Fielding's *Tom Jones,* 27–30, 43, 45,
48, 54; as politicized process creating
coherence and marginalization in,
205n22; relationship of social status
and ability to see society as coherent,
200n54; Scottish peasants maintaining memory of Covenanters as
example of, 22, 90–91; in Thackeray's
Vanity Fair, 143, 159–60. *See also*
generational transmission; localized
knowledge and history
Shaw, Harry, 194n7
Sherman, Stewart, 30, 186n7
Siskin, Clifford, 23, 125, 130; *This Is
Enlightenment* (with Warner), 13,
189n4, 200n44

Small, Helen, 198n18

Smith, Adam, 67, 189n4, 190n13, 192n37

Smollett, Tobias: in anthologies of novels, 118; compared to Dickens's *The Pickwick Papers*, 116, 128, 134, 137; experimenting with serial publication, 120; mediation role of, 53, 57, 78; narrator's concern about how to communicate with readers in, 23; reader engagement in, 81, 179; sentimental fiction and, 192n41; Thackeray's remembrance of reading in his youth, 147, 202n24; works by: *Peregrine Pickle*, "The Memoirs of a Lady of Quality" in, 121; *Roderick Random*, 118, 130, 137, 146, 199n23. See also *Humphry Clinker*

sociability, Shaftsbury's theory of, 45–46

social circulation, 85–86, 116–18, 198n19

Society for the Diffusion of Useful Knowledge (SDUK), 126–28

Sorensen, Janet, 192n49

Southey, Robert, 102

space. *See* time and space

Spectator, The: critiquing newsmongers, 42; gaining literary value when transformed into bound volumes, 107–8; public sphere and, 187n16; ritualized reading of, 32–33

stagecoach as metaphor: in *Berrow's Worcester Journal*, 32; communal interior of, 6, 30–38, 53; in Dickens's *The Pickwick Papers*, 112, 114, 138; in eighteenth- vs. nineteenth-century novel, 15; in Eliot's *Felix Holt*, 170, 172, 205n7; Fielding using as metaphor for reading, 1–2, 5, 9, 14, 16, 24, 27–28, 31, 54, 167; as generic trait of eighteenth-century novels, 25; in Scott's novels, 195n10; signification of, 5–6, 14

stagecoaches: compared to newspapers, 30–32; compared to realist narrative, 25; competing technologies (coach vs. railway), 5, 12, 25, 139, 149–50, 197n1; memories of stagecoach era, 14, 21, 25, 139–42, 148–53; as network of national circulation, 24–25; as primary form of long-distance travel (mid-eighteenth to mid-nineteenth century), 12; as romances in industrial age, 152, 158, 162; Thackeray's nostalgia for, 139–40, 144

stagecoach novels: Dickens and Thackeray's works contending with, 23; Dickens's *The Pickwick Papers* as, 112–13, 117, 148

Starr, G. Gabrielle, 64

St. Clair, William, 23, 95, 105, 118, 202n24

Sterne, Laurence: experimenting with serial publication, 120; mediation role of, 53, 78; problematic in history of novel, 188n1; reader engagement in, 23, 81, 179; Scott and, 178; Thackeray's remembrance of reading in his youth, 147; transport metaphors in, 5, 7, 10–11, 14; vehicles' ability to interfere with affective communication in, 7, 10–11, 21, 59; works by: *Tristram Shandy*, 178, 202n24. See also *Sentimental Journey, A*

Stewart, Garrett, 7, 17–19

Stewart, Susan, 92

Sun, The: on Dickens's *The Pickwick Papers*, 120

surface reading, 18, 182n17

Swift, Jonathan, 188n43; *Gulliver's Travels*, 202n24; *The Tale of a Tub*, 126

sympathy: readers' sympathy in *The Heart of Midlothian* (Scott), 101, 196n39; Smith's approach to, 67, 192n37; in Victorian realist fiction, 205n42. See also *Sentimental Journey, A*

Tales of My Landlord, The series (Scott), 85–111; as authentic original narratives vs. reproductions of conventional patterns, 82, 85, 96, 101, 104; continuity between local and national in, 84–85, 195n18; difficulty of telling local history, 84, 93; local Scottish tales collected in, 83; mediation prioritized over representation in, 93, 104–9; narrative framework used in, 82–84, 93, 96, 99. See also *Heart of Midlothian, The* (Scott); *Old Mortality* (Scott)

Tales of the Genii (in Cooke's Pocket Library series), 117

taste: Fielding allowing for variety of tastes in his readers, 48–52; Hume's theory of, 47–48

Taylor, Jesse Oak, 184n57

Taylor, John: "The World Runs on Wheels" (poem), 151–52

technologies of mobility: accelerated speed of replaced technology moving into distant past, 152; access to, 7; competing technologies (coach vs. railway), 5, 12, 25, 139, 149–50, 197n1; generational gap created by change in, 142, 148; minimization of time and space via, 15; nostalgia for previous technological era, 139–40, 144, 152; Thackeray on technological determinism, 139, 148–53; transport metaphors continuing despite changes in, 15, 152. *See also* transport metaphors; *specific types of transport*

telegraph wires compared to organic nervous system, 13

temporal duration of transport metaphors, 9, 13, 14–15, 25

temporality in eighteenth century: clocked time, effect of, 5, 30, 186n7; historical novels depicting intersection of temporal and spatial transmission, 87; localized nature

of, 187n27; newspaper publication and, 31; novels referencing historical events to create sense of time, 187n19; realism and, 179; stagecoach providing new way to measure, 30; subject to distortion by commercial forms like newspapers, 37

Teynor, Hilary, 188n44

Thackeray, William Makepeace: accommodating stories of the past to readers of new era, 145–47; coach metaphors in, 5, 139, 158, 167; compared to Kittler, 202n23; compared to Scott, 141, 144–47, 153, 164–65, 201n6; on effects of technological change in transport, 139–40; experiencing Fritzsche's "melancholy of history," 140; failed aspiration to write epic, 202n11; historiographic strategy of, 153, 202n14, 202n23; Kurnick's "affective surplus" of, 140; mediation role of, 155–56, 179; memories of popular novels of the past evoked by, 165–66; nostalgia for and personal memory of stagecoach era in, 14, 21, 25, 139–40, 144, 156–57; "old canon" of novels referenced by, 202n24; "prae-railroadites" in, 16–17, 142–45, 149; reader engagement in, 23, 141–42, 145, 147, 159–62; return home by stagecoach as way of asserting sense of communal belonging in, 157; Ruskinian realism and, 163; Scott, Smollett, and Sterne as authors favored by Thackeray in his youth, 147; skeptical of transmission of stories from one generation to another, 146–47, 158; on storytelling of past creating community of oral transmission in, 143

Thackeray, William Makepeace, works by: "De Juventute" (*The Cornhill Magazine* essay), 142–44, 146, 149, 202n11; *The English*

Humourists (lecture), 143–44; *The Four Georges* (lecture), 143–44; *The History of Henry Esmond,* 153; *The History of Pendennis,* 166. See also *Vanity Fair*

theory of affect, 11

Therauld, Barry, 200n52

Thompson, George: *A Sentimental Tour,* 80

Tillotson, Kathleen, 141, 201n6

time and space: as neutral media, 35, 43, 136, 186n2; Scott's works associating space-binding with time-binding media, 105, 195n21; transport's definition including emotional transport outside of, 15–16. *See also* temporality in eighteenth century

Tom Jones (Fielding), 27–54; accessing community in, 52–54; Allworthy's relationship to gossip network in, 40; circumstantial evidence in, 37; compared to Dickens's *The Pickwick Papers,* 118, 129–30, 137; consensus of community based on social gossip network in, 38–43; continuity of time in, 35–36; customary forms of presenting narrative in, 48–52; Dickens's *David Copperfield* referencing, 166; disavowal of commercial purposes in, 34; Enlightenment agency of Tom Jones in, 130; experimentation with genre in, 27; formal realism of, 29; "form follows substance" in, 34, 37, 44; historical events referenced to create sense of time, 187n19; "History of the Man of the Hill" in, 41, 121, 129; imagining readers of, 43–48; Iser's "implied reader" and, 28, 186n3; Jones vs. Partridge in context of small community vs. general public, 41–42; mock-epic style, use of, 49; narrator's role in, 35–37, 44, 187n23; new communal spaces in commercial venues in, 53; Paradise Hall environment vs. London lodging house in, 52; Partridge as example of "bad" reader, 29, 40–43, 47; Partridge's reaction to Garrick's *Hamlet,* 49–50, 188n42; as picaresque novel, 10; reader engagement in, 27–28, 43–45; shared meaning created in, 27–30, 43, 45, 48, 54; simultaneity in, 34–35, 187n19; Sophia's introduction in, 48, 50; stagecoach as communal space of narrative in, 6, 30–38, 53; stagecoach metaphor for reading in, 1–2, 9, 14, 16, 24, 27–28, 31, 54, 167; temporary communities of shared experiences formed in, 29–30, 50, 52–53; time and space as neutral media in, 35, 43, 186n2

transport: competing technologies (coach vs. railway), 5, 12, 25, 139, 149–50, 197n1; definition of, 15–16, 184–85n59; revolutions in, 12, 184n42. See also *specific types of transport*

transport metaphors, 9–15, 178; both literary and historical in nature, 11, 14; change of tenor and, 15; changing to reflect newer technologies of transport, 5; characteristics of transportation in, 3; communicative role of, 22; in conversation of Boswell and Johnson, 9; cultural and historical evolution of, 5; defined, 3; in Dickens's *The Pickwick Papers,* 132; discourse of sensibility and vehicle metaphor, 24; in eighteenth-century realist novels, 9, 24; Eliot's use of, 5, 25, 167, 169–71, 205n7; exclusion/inclusion of readers and, 3–7, 13; mediation and, 3, 6, 12–14, 22, 24, 55, 167; nineteenth-century realist novels continuing to use, 9–10; no distinction between movement of physical bodies or of information, 8; Postman's "media metaphor" and, 10;

transport metaphors (*continued*)
reader engagement and, 6, 24,
167–68; reading's relationship with,
6, 9, 14, 19, 167; in realist fiction,
3–10, 23–24, 167; Richards's subordination of vehicles to "symbolic
servitude," 14; Scott's use of, 1–2, 7,
81; in sentimental novels, 57; Smollett's use of, 24; spatial expansiveness
of, 9; temporal duration of, 9; texts
as vehicles, 73–78; Thackeray's use of,
139, 158; utilitarian view of transport,
6. *See also* mail coach as metaphor;
stagecoach as metaphor
transport technology. *See* technologies
of mobility
Trollope, Anthony, 178
Tucker, Abraham: bodily parts under
control of mediating instruments, 61,
63; compared to Sterne's *A Sentimental Journey,* 65, 78; *The Light of
Nature Pursued,* 58–63, 189–90n7;
placing spirit in vehicular state,
58–60, 68, 74, 190n7; postmortem
phenomenon of vehicular state,
62–63; Smith's approach to sympathy
and, 67; spiritual communication
without need for spoken word,
58–59, 64

Underwood, Ted, 183n34
unity. *See* localized knowledge and
history; shared meaning created by a
community

Vanity Fair (Thackeray), 139–66;
Amelia's miniature portrait of her
deceased husband as disruptive
memory in, 157–58; Becky as character who disrupts memory-based
community in, 155–56, 158; coachman Tony Weller from Dickens's
The Pickwick Papers in, 162; comparing stagecoaches with other

memory-provoking items in, 157;
competing technologies of transport
in, 25, 139; Dickens's *The Pickwick
Papers* referenced in, 148; difficulty
of assigning genre to, 140–41; generational transmission of memories
of stagecoach rides in, 154–55; as
historical novel, 153, 201n6; history
vs. personal memory in, 25, 139, 141,
143–47; home memories of displaced
characters in, 156; illusionism of,
161–62; lamenting that stagecoaches
will become romances for next generation, 152, 158, 162; literary-historical
continuity created by communicating and sharing memories in, 159–60;
on loss of stagecoaches and their
stories, 3, 25, 139–40, 148, 152–58,
162–64; "memory site," stagecoaches
serving as, 156–57; Napoleonic
Wars as era of, 153, 201n6; Osborne's
visit to Waterloo to create a shared
memory with deceased son, 158;
puppet show motif in, 140, 161, 164,
201n6; reader engagement in, 141,
159–62; readers' sharing access to
past novels, 159, 164–66; repeated
coach journeys to Queen's Crawley
in, 154–55; shared meaning and
narratives through memory, 153–64;
social relationships formed through
memory in, 159–60; technological
determinism and memories of stagecoach in, 139, 148–53; title's meaning
invoking three different worlds, 162;
verb "to remember" repeatedly used
in, 159–60; as Victorian realist novel,
140, 161–63, 165; youthful reading
habits depicted in, 165–66
Victorian era: detachment in, 205n17;
Dickens's *The Pickwick Papers* contrasting tension between Enlightenment and, 114, 130; drawing on
reasoning by precedent in, 196n38;

240 · INDEX

imaginary storytellers in, 143; information culture of, 114, 115, 126, 128, 132; inns and public houses' businesses negatively affected by nearby railway, 203n30; "knowledge texts" of, 126; portable memory's role in, 156; railways' growth during, 116, 152, 184n44, 198n17; serial publication in, 113, 120. *See also* industrial society; *specific authors*

Virgil, 172

virtual reality, 18, 19, 178. *See also* imagined communities

Walker, Helen (Jeanie Deans's original), 111, 197n71

Wallace, William, 146

Warner, William, 125, 187n23; *This Is Enlightenment* (with Siskin), 13, 189n4, 200n44

Waterloo, battle of (1815), 158, 161

Watt, Ian, 3–4, 56, 80, 189n3

Waverley (Scott): introduction explaining principles of historical narrative writing, 93; in search of picturesque landscape in post-chaise journey in, 1–2, 81; transport modes in, 182n20

Waverley Novels (Scott): Hazlitt praising, 194n7; popularity of, 105–7

Welsh, Alexander, 36–37

Williams, Raymond, 152, 178, 182–83n25, 203n37

women. *See* gender

Wordsworth, William, 87; "The Wanderer," 173, 177, 205n10

Yousef, Nancy, 189n4

Zimmerman, Everett, 195n22

CPSIA information can be obtained
at www.ICGtesting.com
Printed in the USA
LVHW051037221022
731314LV00002B/96

9 780813 947587